OTHER WOMEN

OTHER WOMEN

THE WRITING OF CLASS, RACE, AND GENDER, 1832–1898

ANITA LEVY

PRINCETON UNIVERSITY PRESS

PRINCETON, NEW JERSEY

Library of Congress Cataloging-in-Publication Data

Levy, Anita, 1955–
Other women : the writing of class, race, and gender,
1832–1898 / Anita Levy.
Includes bibliographical references and index.
ISBN 0-691-06865-8 (alk. paper) —
ISBN 0-691-01493-0 (pbk. : alk. paper)
1. English prose literature—19th century—History and
criticism. 2. Women and literature—Great Britain—History—
19th century. 3. Domestic fiction, English—History and
criticism. 4. Great Britain—Intellectual life—19th century.
5. Social classes in literature. 6. Sex role in literature.
7. Race in literature. I. Title.

PR778.W65L49 1991 828'.80809352042—dc20   90-42210

This book has been composed in Adobe Sabon

Printed in the United States of America by
Princeton University Press, Princeton, New Jersey

10 9 8 7 6 5 4 3 2 1

10 9 8 7 6 5 4 3 2 1
(pbk)

For J.T.

CONTENTS

ACKNOWLEDGMENTS

THIS BOOK was supported by many friends and colleagues on both coasts who deserve special thanks. A section of chapter 3 appeared under the title "Blood, Kinship, and Gender" (in *Genders* 5 [Summer 1989]: 70–85), and I would like to thank the University of Texas Press for permission to reprint. I also want to thank the editor, Ann Kibbey, for her attention to my work. An earlier version of material contained in chapter 4 was published as "The History of Desire in *Wuthering Heights*" (in *Genre* 19, no. 4 [1986]: 409–30). I am especially grateful to Robert Brown and Robin Ginsberg of Princeton University Press for their help in seeing this book through to publication.

I would also like to thank Page DuBois, Masao Miyoshi, and Katherine Shevelow for their personal encouragement and professional support. Special thanks must go to David A. Miller for his enthusiastic reading of the first draft, and to Chris Waters, who kindly agreed to read the Introduction in one of its final incarnations.

I am especially grateful to Nancy Armstrong and Leonard Tennenhouse for their friendship, as well as for their tough criticism, and for guiding this book through its various stages from beginning to end. They have my enduring gratitude and affection.

To my mother, father, and sister goes my thanks for their love and encouragement. Finally, many other friends and allies have helped me think about the political and social issues motivating this book. I am indebted to John Tharakan, Jane Zara, Ishwar Puri, Clotilde Puertolas, Antígona Martinez, and Anthony Hamins—old friends with whom I have talked and argued more times than I care to remember.

Williamstown, Massachusetts
November 1989

OTHER WOMEN

Chapter 1

INTRODUCTION: THE MAKING OF

DOMESTIC CULTURE

> The power of discourse is that it is at once the object of struggle
> and the tool by which the struggle is conducted.
> (*Edward Said, "Criticism between Culture and System"*)

> Indeed, . . . "the State" never stops talking.
> (*Philip Corrigan and Derek Sayer*, The Great Arch:
> English State Formation as Cultural Revolution)

IN THE COURSE of writing this book something strange began to happen. I found that I was haunted in the still of the night at my desk by what I came to call, for want of a better word, demons. Let me hasten to say that they weren't the kind many women write about and that drive them to thickly carpeted offices to sit in plush chairs and divulge long pent-up secrets to well-paid therapists. Mine were of a different order, belonging not to the psychological domain, but to that of culture. In short, I found that I was haunted by all the things I hadn't said in this book, and by all the traces of the women whose thoughts and desires were suppressed in nineteenth-century England with the rise to power of the new middle classes. If I could no longer hear their stories, told in factories where it was too noisy to hear, to babies too young to understand, men too drunk to listen, and mistresses too wealthy to care, it was not because I had no desire to listen. On the contrary, as a leftist intellectual, I knew that the politically "correct" work I most admired always spoke for those who apparently could not speak for themselves. Thus, in recent years, feminist scholars adopted the voices of women long excluded from history, as they understood it, to restore them to the world of the past, and so to rescue them from obscurity. Marxist scholars, especially those in Britain, recounted tales of working-class men and women from nineteenth-century Manchester and London, with the same end in mind. And, in so doing, they produced some very fine work that stands as a corrective to dominant versions of history. Such work, however, too often conceived of the historical data out of which it imagined the past— the Parliamentary reports, family records, and commissioned studies—as just so many mirrors through which to enter the real terrain of history, much as Alice enters Wonderland. Yet the question I asked was, did they actually succeed in breaking through to a more real past than that existent in the very language of their data? Or did their efforts to restore oppressed or marginalized groups to history, in the final analysis, contribute most to a very real and important politics of the present?

Like them, I knew that the women I could no longer hear in the texts of the human sciences and fiction had, indeed, existed. And I experienced a queasiness because I felt I should be writing about them, not about the discursive woman who emerged from the pages of the studies, reports, and novels that are the materials of this book. Because I live in a culture convinced that words are not real, that their power lies in their function as signs on the road to the other side of discourse in the "real world," I felt guilty for insisting, with Edward Said in the first epigraph to this chapter, upon the power of language to materialize new ways of seeing and being in the world, and so to make words real. Yet this was precisely how the thoughts, words, opinions, and beliefs of the real women of other classes and cultures were displaced by a newly constituted form of cultural knowledge about what it meant to be human. More important, as a result of this suppression all manner of positive cultural values and alternative sexualities were discredited, their outlines preserved now only as a faded memory in the political unconscious[1] of middle-class culture—that repository of cultural materials the political meaning of which we no longer understand because they have since been made the stuff of consciousness, a privatized domain that we imagine to be immune to class- and culture-specific determination.[2]

That this material is culturally rather than psychologically repressed information is crucial to understand. The point, I argue following Fredric Jameson, is to reassert "the specificity of the political content of everyday life and of the individual fantasy-experience and to reclaim it from that reduction to the merely subjective" (1981, 22). To do so is to reverse the priorities with which we usually think of the relationship between self and culture. It is to conceive of the self, and by extension the mind, as a cultural and historical construct the very character of which obliterates its own history as such. Psychological models legitimate this act of erasure when they attribute private motives to a mind apparently devoid of culture- and class-specific features. That traces of thoughts and desires of poor and dark-skinned women, the demons with which I began, reappear as material outside the bounds of my discourse, or even as negative features of the middle-class female self, is entirely consonant with the cultural phenomenon I am describing. It is but one consequence of the displacement of most women as "other" than normal, desirable, and English upon which this study focuses.[3]

As the political identity of these other women was subordinated to a class- and culture-specific norm, a new definition of what it meant to be human and female emerged. It was primarily a norm that placed those members of a different race, class, and sex in a negative relationship to the rational, middle-class, white Englishman. Out of this process of displacement was engendered a monolithic "other woman" who came to represent a whole range of sexual behaviors, class practices, and ethnic and racial groups. As she came to comprise myriad different social and sexual practices, the other woman displaced other women.[4] This book is about a woman with a discursive body, an imaginary construct that was produced in nineteenth-century representations of class, race, and gender. Thus, the title of this book deliberately plays upon the confusion between other women and representations of the other woman in the human sciences and fiction, to emphasize my focus on this very process of displacement. What I want to show is precisely that talking about other women, historically, has been the source of their displacement. Indeed, the human sciences and fiction, much like Corrigan and Sayer's "state" as described in the second epigraph to this chapter, "never stop talking." And in this lies the origin of their power.

As a result of this methodological and political choice, my study excludes other women of class and race—the factory workers, housekeepers, prostitutes, maids, or African women my title fleetingly and imperfectly remembers—and so reenacts their historical disenfranchisement. It does so to rematerialize forms of middle-class power that have since vanished into commonsense norms of self and identity still paramount to its daily enactment. This is no less essential a task than the retrieval of those other women whose place was usurped by the other woman in the history of writing in nineteenth-century England.

In tracing the construction of what I call the other woman, I am dealing almost entirely with the work of British authors and intellectuals. I do not wish to imply that this process occurred solely in England. On the contrary, writing about class, race, and gender is pervasive throughout the imperial nations of Europe, as Klaus Doerner, Sander Gilman, Michel Foucault, and others have demonstrated.[5] My point is to trace the relationship between the production of this female figure and a national identity in England during the period of great imperial expansion, roughly from 1840 to 1890.

To complete this preliminary explanation of my title, I must say a word about dates. This book is about the Victorian period. Yet it begins in 1832, five years before Victoria's accession to the throne, not, as one might expect, because this is the year of the first reform bill but because 1832 is the year of the devastating cholera epidemics that gave rise to sociological investigations of Manchester. Similarly, my study does not end with the death of Victoria in 1901, but with the publication of Havelock Ellis's landmark *Studies in the Psychology of Sex*. This historical moment witnessed the complete disappearance of the "other women" who appear in my title. They vanished from political memory as psychological writing made their thoughts, words, and sexualities features of a psychologically deviant female self.

In mounting my argument, I want to stress that I reject the idea of culture as a historical reflection or consequence of events in the so-called political or economic world.[6] It is in light of this assumption that I propose to follow the paper trail left by the army of researchers and writers who marched across the face of nineteenth-century England and whose work subsequently spawned the disciplines of the human sciences. Among them were the famous—Herbert Spencer, E. B. Tylor, Havelock Ellis—and the not-so-famous—writers and their work long forgotten, consigned to the dustbin of history that can no longer make sense to us across the disciplinary barricades subsequently erected. These predominantly middle-class professionals and intellectuals[7] invaded the terrain of the working classes, the "primitive," the criminals, and the insane—recording information, telling stories, and uttering pious truths about the lives, habits, and thoughts of the wretched and the not-so-wretched. Certainly those who conducted this research were well-meaning individuals. Yet as intellectually gratifying as this work was with its concerns for underdogs and others, it also served the interests of a particular class. As the researchers participated in the massive project that was the human sciences, the writing of "man" as a sociopolitical formation, they turned out a steady stream of studies, essays, catalogues, charts, and tables. This explosion of print was nothing more or less than a major historical event that appropriated and transformed the political and social information of everyday life into the materials of a standardized individual. This new individual was composed of an interior self enclosed within a gendered body and anchored to a family radically divided from the political world—an individual, I argue, fit to occupy the industrial world. For example, in his 1836 survey of the manufacturing population, *Artisans and Machinery*, the influential liberal social reformer Peter Gaskell described the individual as someone possessing "instincts and social affections, which can alone render him a respectable and praiseworthy member of society, both in his domestic relations, and in his capacity as a citizen" (6).

Before this moment in history there had been no such thing as a generic person. The individual had always been immersed in a sea of interests—regional, generational, religious, familial, occupational, to name but a few—whose competing terms carved out not one, but several identities for her in the world. Neither had the family been severed from the communal, political, and historical determinants—in the forms of rights, obligations, ties, and duties—that had authorized and defined it. As Leonore Davidoff and Catherine Hall have shown, the privatized family Gaskell imagined, a family enclosed within a house built in a "durable manner" with "better materials," divided into "distinct compartments" that "separated" the "sexes" (77), was utterly unfamiliar in the seventeenth and eighteenth centuries.[8] As the human sciences made the family solely her domain, it was the female who was the most susceptible to detachment from this rich world of relations. To her went the responsibility for the health, education, and welfare of this self-enclosed family.[9] Yet, as it was identified with the female body and understood to be an extension of her natural attributes, this mode of production was represented as secondary and derivative. In other words, it came to be understood as a mode of reproduction of daily life, the family, and the individual that bore little relation to the productive domain outside the household. No longer a structure providing the motive and organization for the production and exchange of goods, the family system seemed to be outside of time and of politics.

The project of the human sciences described and defined the reproductive realm of the individual, the home, and the family. In tracing the construction of this realm, I am really outlining a central moment in the creation of the gendered spheres of culture that are necessary for the unfolding of capitalism during the nineteenth century. This productive space, I suggest, actually played a vital role in shaping political economy, what we usually think of as the explanatory logic of nineteenth-century history. In displacing the artisan household, the reproductive realm enabled a gendered distribution of wealth. It also created gendered individuals who imagined social relations in gendered terms—the subordination of female to male.[10] Labor as defined by the reproductive sphere, then, is as much a part of the definition of "man" as a productive being as that provided by Marx in response to Ricardo and Smith. I know of few histories of the nineteenth century that take this form of production into account. Yet its importance in relation to what we usually consider the history of the nineteenth century is crucial; neither the productive sphere nor the reproductive sphere alone can explain this history.[11] While some have studied the project of the human sciences in bits and pieces, it is my contention that the division of these disciplines succeeds only in erasing their common history and their relation to the productive sphere. A crucial insight, namely, the importance of gender in the formation of modern culture, is obscured once the representation of the family is scattered into various disciplines.

When the human sciences are viewed as one entity, however, a simple question emerges: to what extent were the sciences of man first and foremost the sciences of woman? Early nineteenth-century social research presupposes a social role for working-class women as household supervisors; anthropology situates women within all kinship relations on the basis of their sexual desire; and psychology portrays women's consciousness as one that is simultaneously desirous and fearful of men. Fiction representing the nuances of heterosexual love helped to mystify as well as to disseminate the distinctively modern notion of the female formulated within the human sciences. Both the human sciences and fiction focused on the same object of representation, woman's body and mind. As these theories pursued their answers, they always found that answer in the female—within her role, mind, body, or mode of writing. It would appear that the human sciences depended on the notion of the gendered individual. As a feature suitable for application to a large group of people regardless of regional, generational, or genealogical ties, gender made the individual universal or generic. So general an answer is at best provisional; what I am most interested in demonstrating, however, is not the commonplace but the manifold and ingenious strategies by which the disciplines gathered knowledge and redefined nature to establish the hegemony of a gendered individual.

While the human sciences establish a series of boundaries between inside and outside, public and private, male and female, in fiction gender becomes the universalizing principle. It was fiction that both mediated between and popularized these domains by creating an imaginary realm for doing so. I do not mean to suggest that this occurrence in fiction is "imaginary" in the sense of being unreal; rather, fiction provides an "image" or site for the interaction of various languages used to talk about the self.[12] What is more, both the human sciences and fiction treated what were in fact new and unfamiliar divisions of the individual and the family as categories that had always existed. As they dehistoricized these areas, both kinds of writing moved history entirely into the domain of political economy, where it remains today.[13] One of my goals, then, is to dismantle an older, gendered model that narrativizes history according to predefined notions of sexual roles and spheres. Instead, I would like to articulate a model capable of historicizing the production of gendered spheres as such. In this way I hope to put these domains back into history and so to put women back into history. My purpose is to show how the history of discovering and universalizing women that is the project of the human sciences is part of the larger formation that we call middle-class culture.[14]

I realize it is unusual to include fiction in a discussion of the human sciences. If the connection seems questionable at this point, it is perhaps because the literary institution, following the lead of those disciplines, has taught us to isolate fiction from history. Yet there are precedents for the dissolution of generic differences understood as differences in the object of analysis and/or representation that are produced by the discourse itself. "Discourse," as elaborated by Michel Foucault, is one such concept that dissolves formal boundaries between text and text, and texts and practices, in order to catalog them according to a different logic. Thus, in *The Archeology of Knowledge* (1972) and the first volume of *The History of Sexuality* (1980), Foucault makes no generic distinctions when he speaks of *discourse* as a specialized language and practice constituting a form of power that both represents and constitutes that of which it speaks. Frederic Jameson's "master narrative" is another "dissolving" concept that collapses the distinction between text and culture[15]—all in a system where the master narrative is equivalent to a notion of political economy that does not acknowledge its power to constitute difference between productive and reproductive domains and that identifies power with production and puts it in the factory.

Having historicized the role of the human sciences in the formation of a reproductive domain detached from history, let me explain what I think history must be if fiction is to be historicized adequately. In order to talk about the relationship between representations of women and the formation of a modern institutional culture like our own, I will argue several points at once. First, I contend that the productive and the reproductive are one political formation that cannot have separate histories. To revise a feminist commonplace, the domestic is political, not just because sweeping floors and having babies is unpaid labor, but because it is represented as the normal and natural thing for women to do. My second point entertains the possibility that the classic unfolding of capitalism was at least to some degree predicated on writing by women or writing that appealed to the interests of women. To argue this is to call into question the subordination in Marxist terms of cultural activities like writing to economic affairs as another logic constitutive of differences between "reproductive" and "productive" spheres of culture. If the discourse of sexuality—of which writing by, for, and about women formed an essential part—is understood as productive of class-specific desires in the Foucauldian sense, then it is possible to understand how "reproduction" can become the "production" of social relations. Third, written representations of the self and the other, generated by a class of intellectuals and professionals that included women, enabled the new middle class to rise to hegemony. "Hegemony," as employed throughout this discussion, signifies that ubiquitous form of power to determine ruling definitions of "reality." Ruling reality, furthermore, is determined by those groups who get others to define themselves in relation to the ruling group. Because to dominate in modern culture means to determine the right and wrong ways of being human, the power of the established group is therefore assured. The hegemony of the dominant group depends heavily on the disappearance of these norms into naturalized and universalized forms of everyday life, the "common sense" with which we know the individual and the family today. And fourth, the history of fiction cannot be understood apart from the history of other forms of writing in the nineteenth century. Let me briefly outline a working theory of history that accommodates each of these points.

More than most of his successors, until rather recently at least, Marx was aware of the interconnection between the family, state, and economy.[16] Yet his theoretical work was not consistently informed by this awareness. He was, after all, primarily concerned with accounting for the rise to power of the new industrial classes and thus with representing a new political domain apart from the large landowning families who wielded power in early modern culture. One might look, for example, at his discussion of "production" in this passage from *The German Ideology*:

> The production of life, both of one's own labour and of fresh life in procreation now appears as a double relationship. By social we understand the co-operation of several individuals, no matter what conditions, in what manner and to what end. It follows from this that a certain mode of production, or *industrial stage*, is always combined with a certain mode of co-operation, or social stage, and this mode of co-operation is itself a "productive force." Further, that the multitude of productive forces accessible to men determines the nature of society, hence, that the "history of humanity" must always be studied and treated in relation to the *history of industry and exchange*. (1845–46, 157, emphasis added)

What is important to note is how reproduction becomes feminized when it is linked with biological reproduction ("procreation"). It is this move that determines its place in political and historical narratives to come. Moreover, to paraphrase Linda Nicholson's reading (1987), the meaning of "production" in the first sentence allows Marx to include the family under the "modes of co-operation" he catalogs. Notice that by the middle of the paragraph, its meaning has shifted to include only those "modes of co-operation" discovered within the "history of industry and exchange." In short, whereas *The German Ideology* is by no means entirely representative of his thought, it does indicate the manner in which Marx omits a theoretical consideration of the role of reproduction in history. My point is simply to suggest how political economy and its critique provided the theoretical justification for histories that reproduce this split. Over time, it has thus become increasingly difficult to understand the distinction between production and reproduction as an historical event in its own right.[17]

Understanding the differences between the productive and reproductive as a class- and culture-specific discourse or "ruling idea," one can consider in a radically materialist light the Foucauldian proposition that the modern state, as Nancy Armstrong writes, "was called into being in writing, exists mainly as a state of mind and perpetuates itself through the well-orchestrated collection, regulation and dissemination of information" (1987b, 12). In *Madness and Civilization* (1967) and *Discipline and Punish* (1979), Foucault attenuates the very distinction between the productive and the reproductive when he includes the prison, madhouse, school, factory, and by extension the household, as areas susceptible to organization and regulation in writing and practice, areas where the power of surveillance does its work. Indeed, as he argues in the first volume of *The History of Sexuality* (1980), even the forms of subjectivity we consider most essential to ourselves as individuals, such as sexuality, are culturally produced. There his most important strategies are to separate sex from the notion of sexuality and to consider sexuality as an entirely semiotic practice. In the Foucauldian formula, sexuality is inseparable from its representation, just as its representation is, in turn, inseparable from the rest of political history. Thus, sexuality can no longer remain in a domain of nature outside of and prior to representation. Since representations of sexuality are inevitably linked to the institutions and practices that produce them, it becomes possible "to consider sexual relations as the site for changing power relations between classes and cultures as well as between genders and generations" (Armstrong 1987a, 10). As a result, Foucault challenges the common belief that the middle class attained cultural and economic power by repressing sex—that is, by believing itself obliged, in Foucault's words, "to amputate from its body a sex that was useless, expensive, and dangerous as soon as it was no longer given over exclusively to reproduction. This class must be seen rather as being occupied, from the mid-eighteenth century on with creating its own sexuality and forming a specific body based on it, a 'class' body with its health, hygiene, descent, and race" (1980, 124). Sexuality, in this model, no longer remains an innocent fact of nature. Instead, Foucault shows us that when we understand sexuality as a natural phenomenon, we do so as a result of a complex cultural intervention designed to convince us of its universal and natural qualities. By returning sexuality to culture, Foucault demonstrates that to detach representations of sexuality from other social and political formations is to reproduce the split between nature and culture, reproductive and productive.

Having raised to the level of discursive phenomena the barrier between productive and reproductive domains, one can now situate writing in political history and, in this way, clear the way to seeing the intellectual labor of women as productive.[18] And so I move to the second point of the argument, which suggests that the success of capitalism in England was predicated upon written representations of the individual by, for, and about women. I am aware that to regard writing about the female self as fundamental to the formation of an economic order is to inject gender into methodologies, such as those of Marx, Althusser, and others, that theorize only the operations of class. Like Foucault, whose histories of sexuality, discipline, and madness are unconcerned with the history of gender, theoreticians of class generally ignore gender and ethnicity.[19] On the other hand, those that write about gender either neglect the role of class and race or subordinate one category to another. This book argues that class, race, and gender are inseparable. And when we accede to theoretical models that presuppose a distinction among the three, we reproduce unwittingly the logic of the three different terminologies of the human sciences, which collaborated to produce a single set of differences between self and other. I aim, in contrast, to show how different kinds of professional writing came to locate certain features within the body and mind of the woman that they also found inherent in poor and dark-skinned people. From this follows the necessity for integrating a feminist purpose into theories both of historical materialism and ethnicity. To do so is to extend to cultural studies the historical dimension it often lacks in order to talk about the female and about gender as a historical and fully politicized construct.

This book, arguing that gender is more than a cultural use of the body, leaves little room for the residual essentialism that clings to gender studies. Since the essentialist feminist critic regards the female as all but untouched by historical or cultural determinants, she unknowingly peoples cultural history with "women" who remain always already the same. Instead, my model understands gender as a strategy by which the modern middle classes legitimized a culture- and class-specific set of norms as nothing less than the stuff of human nature itself. In so disseminating gender-based behavioral norms, nineteenth-century British intellectuals did not so much subordinate women to men as establish one class of people whose women met certain standards of femininity that qualified them to care for other social and cultural groups whose women were improperly gendered.

While Foucauldian methodology cannot help us return gender to history, Gramsci's theory of hegemony, developed in his essays on the formation of intellectuals, does speak to this problem. Hegemony, or the ability to articulate ruling definitions of the "natural," according to the Italian theorist, involves two paradoxically related processes. A class becomes hegemonic once it has achieved self-conscious awareness of itself as a class, but a class must also create a basis of consensus among itself and subordinate groups (LaClau and Mouffe 1985). It must represent its specific interests as natural, necessary, and right, if not always desirable, for everyone. Gramsci's depiction of the hegemonic task is very important for my purposes because it opens the possibility of introducing intellectual labor—that labor necessary to bring a class to awareness of itself as such—into political history. This formulation, in turn, allows for the inclusion of the intellectual labor of women, such as that exemplified by mid-century domestic fiction, as well as socializing practices other than writing, in history. It allows one to imagine the middle-class revolution as a revolution at home as well as in the workplace, in representation as well as in practice.[20]

To illustrate Gramsci's first principle, consider that the middle class first had to distinguish itself from competing social groups—from the aristocracy with which it vied for social and economic power at the end of the eighteenth century, and later, in the first half of the nineteenth century, from the working classes. It did so by affirming in writing and in practice the unique character and importance of its body and sex, assigning to the female the care, maintenance, and maximization of the life of this body. While the cultivation of the sexed and gendered body differentiated the middle class from all other groups, it also provided the new truth that could remove individuals of competing classes from their place in history and culture and unite them according to a set of universals apparently common to them all. In this way the middle class could meet Gramsci's second requirement for hegemonic formation. Each individual could be assigned a unique pathology that distinguished him or her from every other individual, and certain groups from other groups. At the same time, and in apparent contradiction, desire was represented as firmly rooted in biology—namely, in sexual difference. This feature apparently united individuals across lines of race, class, culture, or generation and so authorized intellectuals and professionals of the dominant class to pronounce the "truth" about individuals, cultures, and historical moments with impunity.

To understand the role of professionals and intellectuals in the project of the human sciences, I have begun by subjecting the work of Marx and Gramsci to the question raised by the more recent work of Harold Perkin. In *Origins of Modern English Society* (1969), Perkin holds that theoreticians and conceptualists for the middle class constituted a separate "class," "sub-class," or "socio-economic group" separate from the class they served. It is Perkin's contention that this collection of lawyers, doctors, public officials, journalists, professors, and lecturers belonged to the professional middle class, "a class curiously neglected in the social theories of the age, but one which played a part out of all proportion to its numbers in both the theory and the practice of class conflict" (252). Although he recognizes that most theorists have treated this group as part of the middle class as a whole, Perkin maintains that their social ideal, based as it was on disinterested expertise and merit, differentiated professionals and intellectuals from the capitalist middle class. "It was in their interest," he writes, "to 'deliver the goods' which they purveyed: expert service and the objective solution of society's problems, whether disease, legislation, administration, material construction, the nature of matter, social misery, education, or social, economic and political theory" (260). Perkin argues that professionals and intellectuals, such as those swelling the ranks of health and welfare bureaucracies, constituted a subgroup within the middle class whose interests diverged, at times, from the class as a whole. I would argue that only later does their production identify intellectuals and professionals as a class within a class. A twentieth-century perspective makes it apparent that this class within a class acquired the power to define their own class per se, as well as others. We are also forced by the necessity of our own historical moment to see the history of this group that is now the dominant class. This class will come into its own only later in the formation of a "culture of experts," professionals, intellectuals, and supervisors responsible for the "packaging" of knowledge about everything from avante-garde art to daily nutrition. Yet their professional ethics, which Perkin feels guaranteed the neutrality of the nineteenth-century experts, did no such thing. In my view it operated on behalf of the new middle classes and materialized a very real form of middle-class power, both in writing and in practice. Thus, with Marx, I consider nineteenth-century intellectuals and professionals as adjuncts of the ruling class similar to factory managers and other institutional personnel, members of the professional managerial class. "Within this class," as he writes in the *The German Ideology*, "one part appears as the thinkers of the class (its active conceptualizing ideologists), who make it their chief livelihood to develop and perfect the illusions of class about itself" (1845–46, 41).

Gramsci departs from Marx primarily in that he conceives of the intellectual as a requisite member of any emergent social class. "Every social class," he writes, "coming into existence on the original basis of an essential function in the world of economic production, creates with itself, organically, one or more groups of intellectuals who give homogeneity and consciousness of its function not only in the economic field but in the social and political field as well" (1957, 118). Thus, "organic intellectuals" articulate the principles of the world view of the emergent class.[21] Their work enables that class to achieve the rhetorical and practical self-definition and cohesion so essential to hegemonic power. In a very real sense, without the agency of professionals and intellectuals—then as well as now—the dominant class would not have achieved or retained its hegemony. My argument that it did so primarily on cultural rather than economic grounds is based on a reading of materials by and about women, which shows that the formation of the modern political state in England was accomplished largely through cultural hegemony. I also view the power of modern culture in general, and written representation in particular, as historical forces possessing their own logic independent of, yet intertwined with, the economic sphere.[22] Edward Said argues that "the intellectual is not really analogous to the police force, nor is the artist merely propagandist for wealthy factory owners. Culture is a separately capitalized endeavor, which is really to say that its relationship to authority and power is far from nonexistent" (1983, 171). I would go so far as to suggest that in modern culture intellectuals virtually *take the place* of the police force. That is to say, representations and practices that construe the individual as a self-regulated and enclosed entity are more powerful than any police force in achieving and maintaining social control.[23]

Having argued for an expanded history that includes not only economic practices but domestic and sexual relations as well as information about the female domain produced by a newly authorized group of intellectuals and professionals, I must provide a brief example of the figurative strategies by which the human sciences collaborated to divide the cultural world into two distinct spheres. I will then conclude with a discussion of what fiction does to this cultural information to make it the basis of modern consciousness.

Domestic Fictions in the Disciplines

The cholera epidemics of the 1830s marked the rise of sociology. Influential philanthropists, reformers, factory commissioners, and doctors, such as Peter Gaskell, James Kay Shuttleworth, and Hector Gavin, went into the poorest recesses of the industrial city. Rather than see the problem of disease in the poor living conditions of the industrial poor, they located it in the morals and habits of the working-class individual. Kay Shuttleworth's 1832 study, *The Moral and Physical Condition of the Working Class Employed in the Cotton Manufacture in Manchester*, and Gaskell's 1836 study, *Artisans and Machinery: The Moral and Physical Condition of the Manufacturing Population*, to name but two, formulated the solution in terms of a language of morality and hygiene that enclosed the household from the world and that pictured women and children as dependent on a male who worked elsewhere. It was the improperly domesticated female, with her "entire want of instruction in learning of domestic economy," in Gaskell's words, who was most responsible for "the improvident habits" "forming the chief part of the curse upon the social condition" (64) of the new working class. He attributed the impoverishment of this class to the lack of a good woman within the home, rather than to the changed conditions under which the working class had to labor. Most important, in the final analysis, it is the woman who goes to work that he finds potentially disruptive.

Two decades later, anthropological treatises appeared during that scramble for land, resources, and bodies known as the expansion of the British Empire. Works by the "great white fathers" of anthropology, Edward Burnett Tylor and John McLennan, as well as those by lesser-knowns, imagined the "family of man," a concept structurally resembling the working-class family formulated by sociology, but one that authorized colonial domination. The very existence of the family of man was paradoxically jeopardized and guaranteed by female desire. Thus, in his 1865 study, *Primitive Marriage*, McLennan writes: "We shall be justified in believing that more or less of *promiscuity* in the connection of the sexes, and a system of *kinship through females* only have subsisted among the races of men among which no traces of them remain" (66, emphasis added). Only where women were "found faithful to their lords," in McLennan's words, could monogamous sexuality, and so the family as we know it, arise. In other words, as the desired object in a system of exchange, the female had the power to preserve the community as faithful wife and mother. As a desiring subject free to choose her mate, however, she disrupted that group. In this manner, anthropology imagined the female as the libidinous mother responsible for all kinship relations, and so it legitimated the sociological fiction of her as the promiscuous body and careless housekeeper.

Whereas sociology imagined the female at home and anthropology represented the female in culture, late nineteenth-century psychology developed the concept of the female in the self. Psychosexual studies by Richard von Krafft-Ebing, Havelock Ellis, and Italian criminologist Cesare Lombroso were among those that characterized the middle-class female as a hysteric who repressed the sexual desires supposedly acted upon by the working-class woman and the savage. A typical and very simple illustration of this principle is furnished by Ellis in his 1898 *Studies in the Psychology of Sex*:

> A young girl of seventeen had her first hysterical attack after a cat sprang on her shoulders as she was going downstairs. Careful investigation showed that this girl had been the object of somewhat ardent attentions from a young man whose advances she had resisted, although her own sexual emotions had been aroused. (221)

While this young woman simply repressed her sexual desire for the young man in question, the female criminals and prostitutes studied by Lombroso in his 1889 survey, *La Donna Deliquente*, resorted to more drastic action. They committed crimes of passion.

One should note how this analysis of the female makes specific norms of sexuality the basis for class identity—not only for the behavior of prosperous, profit-motivated people but also as a measure of all classes and cultures. Sociology presupposes a social role for the woman as household supervisor. Anthropology attributes to her both disruptive and restorative powers and bases all her kinship relations on her sexual desire. And psychology internalizes disruption when it portrays her consciousness as one that simultaneously desires and fears men. In addition to naturalizing the female, the disciplines disperse her history so that it exists only as a foil to the activities and achievements of the English*man*. In the end all these behaviors establish gendered sexuality as the motive force behind all human relations, giving it the totalizing explanatory power of common sense or mythology.

DISCIPLINARY STRATEGIES WITHIN FICTION

If the history of the female is thus dispersed, then it stands to reason that a historian of sexuality must dissolve the boundaries between those texts usually considered literary and those that are not. In this I am by no means inferring that analysis of the social sciences alone will yield sufficient understanding of a modern poetics of gender. In discussing a poetics of gender in the social sciences one must also come to terms with the historical force of fiction and the documentary value of cultural transformations recorded there. Particularly if one want to understand it as cause and not effect, the history of fiction cannot be understood apart from the history of other forms of writing in the nineteenth century. This is to say that the materials of what we now call sociology, anthropology, and psychology compose the field within which fiction must be read. This approach represents a marked departure from the traditional practices of "literature" or literary history that compare fiction with the poetic tradition.[24] This tradition necessarily excludes the history of social science paradigms precisely because such a tradition only reproduces the nineteenth-century division of knowledge into discrete bits of apparently unrelated information. In short, I regard all the texts considered here as part of one discourse and in dialogue with one another.[25]

In so doing, this book deliberately challenges established historicist models that presume a relationship between a "text" and a truer "context." Instead, it reverses the priorities with which literary histories usually consider this fundamental epistomological relationship, for two reasons. If fiction popularizes the suppositions about the individual, the family, gender, and desire that the social sciences "discover" in others of class and race, as I argue following Foucault and Said, then it follows that fiction is no less true than science. Each mode of writing simply contributes a different component to this cultural project. A second conclusion follows from the first. Unlike fiction, the social sciences claim to discover fundamental truths about the nature of human beings. Given this, writing in such a mode will automatically assume a different ontological status than fiction within a culture privileging scientific information. Yet in representing a human nature prior and external to itself, I suggest, fiction really refers to these other truth texts and not, as it would appear, to a truth or reality outside representation itself.

There is some justification, beyond my own immediate purposes, for doing this. Until late in the nineteenth century, fiction was not considered literature.[26] Rather, the novel was understood as a different body of knowledge that helped to train individuals, especially women, to take up their respective positions in the productive and reproductive spheres. "The novel's realistic bodying forth of a world," as Said observes, "is to provide representational or representative norms selected from among many possibilities. Thus the novel acts to include, state, affirm, normalize, and naturalize some things, values, and ideas, but not others"(1983, 176). The very power of fiction, furthermore, resides in its ability to disguise the selective process Said identifies. In this manner, its precise articulation of an ideological choice appears as a self-evident fact of nature, and not as the result of a sociocultural transaction. One can see why, in this light, Emily Brontë's *Wuthering Heights* devoted all its energy to locating social and political conflict within the individual and offering a resolution demanding changes only within the private domestic world governed by the female. What follows from such a definition of fiction, then, is the notion that to really understand a novel such as *Wuthering Heights*, one must read it as part of an ensemble of texts that includes the human sciences. No doubt this approach will annoy those who read Brontë as a descendant of the Romantic poets, seeking the "truth" of *Wuthering Heights* in the untamed imagination of a consumptive female Byron. To understand the historical role of fiction one must, I believe, figure out its relationship to other representations of gender and desire, with which fiction argued and which it confirmed.

The question for this study then becomes, what do novels do besides amuse their readers? I suggest simply that they provide modern readers with the materials for representing their desires to themselves, and in doing so they place limitations on how and what to desire.[27] By confining the limits of desire to the gendered body contained within the modern household, the novel teaches individuals to understand freedom in terms of adherence to or violation of these boundaries. These boundaries by no means remain fictional constructs. They become real when people en-vision their only sociosexual choices as marriage, living without gratifi-cation, or becoming mad. In this respect, too, fiction and history become one when they become part of both social and personal history.

If there is one thing I would like this book to do, it would be to help rematerialize the forms of ruling class power that have all but disap-peared into facts of nature, common sense, and the practices of everyday life. I would like this book to convey the power of middle-class represen-tations of sexuality to fashion individuals of the dominant class whose world has been reduced to the horizons of self and the walls of a home that social change can never enter. Middle-class hegemony depends not only upon institutions and practices of the state but upon the production and reproduction of people who "make it" because they want others to love and a house in which to love them. In Western middle-class culture love is not love, sexuality is not just sex; rather, these utterly familiar truths of daily life are powerful means that continue to depoliticize and dehistoricize the Western individual, making us forget our place in and obligation to the political and historical world.

Chapter 2

SOCIOLOGY: DISORDER IN THE HOUSE
OF THE POOR

> To be more accurate most men and women of property felt the
> necessity for putting the houses of the poor in order.
> (*E. P. Thompson*, The Making of the English Working Class)

> FATHER: You said *Why do things always get in a muddle?* Now
> we have made a step or two—and let's change the question
> to "Why do things get in a state which Cathy calls 'not
> tidy?' " Do you see why I make that change?

> DAUGHTER: Yes, I think so—because if I have a special meaning
> for "tidy" then some other people's "tidies" will
> look like muddles to me. . . .
> (*Gregory Bateson*, Steps to an Ecology of Mind)

IN THE EARLY nineteenth century in England certain individuals
made it their business to involve themselves in the health, living conditions, education, nutrition, and sexual practices of the poor. Philanthropists, reformers, factory commissioners, and doctors were among the
most prominent members of this diverse group of middle-class intellectuals and professionals, a class of individuals that is usually not factored
into modern history, who felt it necessary to put the houses of the industrial poor in order. To this end they braved the ill-paved, foul-smelling
streets and miasmic air of the slums to discover the poor. These poor were
known by many names—"the labouring classes," "the labouring poor,"
"the poorer classes," or "the labouring population." No matter the
name, representations of the working classes began to appear in countless
reports, articles, essays, treatises, bluebooks, charts, and tables. Taken
together, they represented a massive effort to categorize, measure, ana-
lyze, and classify every feature of the life of the laborer.

In shaping representations of the industrial poor out of the stuff of their
lives, social researchers did not appear to be assaulting the poor so much
as rescuing them from an evil economic system. To this end, they mar-
shalled idioms that spoke the vocabulary of numbers, morality, science,
cleanliness, and disease to evoke the injustice and inhumanity of working-class life. As they did so, however, a different picture began to emerge,

connecting the degradation of the working classes to the individuals themselves. When sociological writers united these languages within reports and studies, they unwittingly translated the materials of economic reality into those of a damaged or defective interior self, finally locating the worst offenses inside the female. It is this process I address in my readings of sociological tracts from the early nineteenth century. For as sociological writing produced and reproduced a new working-class self, it simultaneously changed the terms of cultural conflict, as well as the nature of the battle that would be won. Languages that initially described the incipient struggle between the working classes and a hostile economic environment became those which condemned working-class individuals for their own misery, identified the problem of and the solution to the condition of the working classes with the female, and so mitigated a potentially powerful political force. In saying this, I want to stress that sociological writing was not so much about this struggle as part of it. To speak of the qualities of texts identifying the problems of culture with those of the female, further, is to identify their role in a more extensive cultural process whereby certain areas of discourse were appropriated by middle-class professionals and intellectuals to construct the modern notion of gender.

In the pages of the official histories of sociology, the work of these social researchers, such as James Kay Shuttleworth, Peter Gaskell, Hector Gavin, and Henry Mayhew, are often ignored. "Histories of sociology," writes one historian of sociology, "[have] overlooked the attempts by individuals, whose primary concern was to collect facts about what they called 'the condition and progress of society'; to build up inductive generalities" (Kent 1981, 4). Instead these historians favor the more respectable intellectual genealogy afforded their discipline by such theoreticians as Auguste Comte, Karl Marx, Emile Durkheim, and Max Weber. Yet what sociologists discard, nineteenth-century historians often eagerly embrace. They love nothing better than to pillage data compiled by early social researchers for the facts and artifacts they yield, like archaeologists who have come upon an ancient, undiscovered tomb. The work of these social accountants, in other words, is often assumed to represent a true picture of reality, a bona fide record of the lives of the working classes, a compendium of facts and figures to authorize, support, and otherwise verify claims that historians would like to make. Social historian Gertrude Himmelfarb observes, to cite one example, that despite its many inaccuracies and ambiguities, historians and commentators continue to rely on Mayhew's *London Labour and the London Poor* as a reliable source about the poor and their labors (1973).[1]

There are reasons for this phenomenon, of course. Early sociological texts have all the attributes we have come to associate with scientific truth. If I may be overly reductive for a moment—they are usually long, abounding in "facts," charts, and tables. And like any self-respecting scientific document, they rely on statistics and figures to argue their case. Sociological accounts must provide an accurate picture of reality, we reason, for they have dutifully counted and laboriously recorded everything in the houses of poor people, from the number of windows in the building to the number of occupants to a bed. Numbers do not lie, or do they? This is the kind of exact, logical thinking we moderns are most comfortable with—the measuring and computing of our daily lives divided into discrete microseconds by digital watches.

Indeed, one might trace the modern cult of statistically confirmable information back to the English statistical societies whose researchers combed the back streets and alleyways of London and Manchester in search of facts. They believed that the royal road to knowledge lay in numbers[2]; as the fourth annual report to the council of the London Statistical Society noted in 1838:

> the spirit of the present age has an evident tendency to confront the figures of speech with the figures of arithmetic; it being impossible not to observe a growing *a priori* assumption that in the business of social science, the principles are valid for application only inasmuch as they are legitimate deduction from facts accurately observed and methodically classified. (Briggs 1973, 86)

Punch, that well-known arbiter of satire, had a slightly less enthusiastic view of the matter. "It is astonishing," it wrote in 1848:

> what statistics may be made to do by a judicious and artist-like grouping of the figures; for though they appear to begin with a limited application to one subject, there is no end to the mass of topics that may be dragged in collaterally on all sides. A few facts on mendicancy, introduced by one of the members [of the British Association for the Advancement of Science] became the cue for an elaborate calculation of how many meals had been given to Irish beggars in the last twenty years; and this was very near leading to a division of the meals into mouthfuls and taking out the canine, employed in the mastication of these twenty years' returns of meals. (Briggs 1973, 89)

The statistics grounding early sociology, both sources might agree, had their own logic. They were another language amounting to more than the sum total of the figures involved. More than telling a story with numbers, they spoke of a practice, a way of understanding topographical and textual space, as well as the distribution of bodies, that was fundamental not only to sociology itself but to the middle-class milieu in which it was devised. Statistics and the tables that contain them, I suggest, both presuppose and produce a reader that sees and imagines the problems of the social world in a distinct manner. To be comprehended, they call into being the ability to organize information categorically according to the principles of difference and separation of information into discrete units drained of class- and culture-specific complexity. Moreover, statistics imply numerical and semantic closure; in other words, the object of knowledge is automatically separated and differentiated from the knower. These principles were not unlike those governing the new discipline itself in the first decades of the nineteenth century. At the risk of reducing a practice at once socially simple and culturally powerful, it is safe to say that early sociological research was based on an implicit hierarchy. It is no accident that one class higher on the social and economic scale observed a lower, less fortunate class. Middle-class connections with the new discipline, furthermore, were far less innocent than those revealed in this formulation.

The social researchers whose writings I examine in this chapter were more that just disinterested yet sympathetic observers of the spectacle of urban poverty. Their medical, financial, and governmental affiliations prove them to be individuals whose interests were deeply expressive of and identified with those of the middle classes.[3] Many of them were members of the numerous statistical societies that had sprung up all over England in the first part of the century. Among the most prominent of these was the Statistical Society of London, founded in 1834, which counted among its members government officials, politicians, lawyers, doctors, and other "distinguished individuals." The society stated its goal as "the collection and classification of all facts illustrative of the present condition and prospects of society" (Kent 1981, 20). Statistical analysis was the chosen means to achieve this end; it was truly to become "state-istics"—a form of politically useful information required by the state. Statistics then were considered a neutral class of facts to "collect, arrange and compare," which would supply the state with correct information to facilitate its rule (JSSL 1839, 1:3). Ironically, the first venture of the Statistical Society was far from the neutral foray into numbers envisioned by its members. Instead, it was an eminently political project designed "to collect a statistical account of the various strikes and combinations [unions] which have existed in different parts of the UK for the purposes of altering the rate of wages and of introducing new regulations between masters and men" (JSSL 1839, 1:6). The committee responsible for this study drew up a list of some fifty-seven queries designed "to elicit the complete and impartial history of the strikes." It is significant that copies of this questionnaire were then distributed not to the workers themselves but "to many intelligent individuals connected with, or interested in the welfare of manufacturers and other industrial pursuits in which large bodies of operatives are employed" (*JSSL* 1838, 1:6). Note too that these "intelligent individuals" were the relevant authorities—the police, hospital and poor-law administrators, school managers, factory commissioners, and so on.

The statistical method and the ubiquitous questionnaire were so popular that they soon proved indispensable to government experts. Statistical societies were thus quickly preempted by Parliamentary committees, royal commissions, blue books, national census reports, and the like. "By the end of Queen Victoria's reign," Asa Briggs remarks, "very much in English life had been measured. . . . the collection of many of the relevant statistics ceased to be a major exercise in difficult and uncharted social investigation and became . . . an institutionalized routine with decennial returns and so on" (1973, 94).

In pointing to the class-based machinery surrounding these texts and authors, my concern is not simply to elucidate their history. Rather, it is to argue that such representations of urban misery cannot be treated as reflections of an a priori reality evident to anyone who walked the streets of English industrial towns and cities in the 1830s and 1840s; nor can they be attributed simply to the solitary actions or good intentions of a few isolated individuals apart from the class- and culture-specific matrix in which they were embedded. Early sociological writing, I contend in this departure from a more traditional politics of interpretation, must be seen as part of an ensemble of discourses enabling the new middle classes to consolidate their cultural hegemony, first in writing, then in practice. Writing about the working classes by members of the middle classes served a hegemonic function in two quite specific ways. First, it facilitated that process of distinction and separation so necessary, according to Gramsci, for an emergent class to differentiate itself as a self-conscious entity from other social groups (1957). Representations of the working classes, along with those of the "primitive," the insane, the criminal, and the "oriental," took their place in a dialectic described by Edward Said in his ground-breaking study of "orientalism" as one of "self-fortification and self-confirmation based on the constantly practiced differentiation of itself [culture] from what it believes to be not itself" (1979, 12). Such representations, in other words, establish boundaries between the self and the other, culture and nature, male and female, middle class and lower class. By representing *what it was not*, the middle class defined precisely *what it was* and so secured its corporate identity.[4]

Second, sociological representation of the working classes facilitated middle-class hegemony as it connected the working-class family and individual to a machinery of governance exterior to them. By mapping the social regions where political resistance originated, early sociology helped to control, regulate, and dissipate the profound threat that the lower classes represented to the middle classes. For if early sociological writing enabled middle-class self-definition, it also produced, by logical extension, a specific notion of the "the poor." This notion circulated and was exchanged as "truth" throughout the institutions of a middle-class culture increasingly responsible for the education, health, housing, employment, and discipline of those impoverished individuals.

The notion of the poor assembled by urban sociologists, in its most rudimentary and complex forms, was based above all on knowledge. Knowledge of every facet of working-class life was the aim of the first "tabular queries" distributed to investigators employed by the Statistical Society of London. Yet as these questionnaires demonstrate, what passed for "knowledge" was often nothing more than conjecture or opinion. An 1839 survey conducted by the society known as the *Report on the Working Classes in the Town of Kingston-Upon-Hull*, for instance, left the investigator at liberty to define a number of normative terms solely according to his own judgment. The agent was instructed only to record how he defined those terms. As one conscientious inspector described the dilemma:

> The word *comfortable* must always be a vague and varying epithet, to which it it impossible to attach any precise definition. In filling up this column, I was guided by observing the condition of the dwelling apart from any consideration of order, cleanliness, or furniture. If I considered it capable of being made comfortable by the tenant, I set it down accordingly; if it were damp, the flooring bad, and the walls ill-conditioned, I reported it uncomfortable. (Oberschall 1972b, 53)

Despite his scruples, this investigator settles for definition by default. What is important to note here is the degree of subjective interpretation built into this official model of inquiry. The inspectors provided with tabular queries by the board of health, moreover, were not expected to ask questions of the poor inhabitants whose houses they so boldly entered. Instead, they themselves answered questions ranging from "Is the house clean?" to "What is the state of the bed, closets, and furniture?" and filled in columns concerning "food, clothing and fuel" and the more subjective "habits of life."[5]

It is significant that many of the larger statistical societies employed this door-to-door approach only for a few years, after which time they began to rely on secondary analysis alone. Clearly, the statistical survey had established patterns of data collection and analysis no longer requiring original research. Of the numerous studies, reports, and surveys issued by the Manchester Statistical Society, "almost without exception the same information was collected and reported in the same format. One might say that the Society created a 'set piece' which served their purposes and with which they were unwilling to tamper" (Elesh 1972, 56). In studies of working-class life by unaffiliated authors who relied upon data gathered by their predecessors, one may find similar patterns. Frederick Engels, for example, borrowed much of his data for *The Condition of the Working Class in England in 1844* from James Kay Shuttleworth. Despite his more radical intentions, Engels's text unwittingly moralized the working-class much as Kay Shuttleworth's had.

It is fair to say that the one feature wedding depictions of the working classes to a monolithic notion of "the poor" was the language of morality common to them all. This language functioned in several interrelated ways. First, it allowed social and economic information to be represented in moral or hygienic terms,[6] since the language of morality enabled sociological writing to focus on the individual as the only relevant unit for social analysis. As a result, sociology was free to reject the compelling socioeconomic data on the increasing impoverishment of the laboring poor that threatened the complacency of the new industrialists and their professional peers because poverty might suggest that the system, not the individual, was responsible. Second, the language of morality linked the individual to sexuality in a new and more powerful way. As it focused on deviance and aberration, this language benefited from the vocabulary of perversions, disorders, conditions, and diseases supplied by the discourse on sexuality in legal, medical, and educational writing. In the language of sexuality, as Foucault tells it, each individual could be assigned a unique pathology distinguishing him or her from every other individual (1978). Together the cultural idioms of morality and sexuality combined to represent the condition of the working classes not so much as a consequence of their economic deprivation but as a symptom of their pathological depravity. Furthermore, both offered a model of the individual detached from social and economic circumstances, anchored instead to internal features of the self or of the body that were more amenable to educational, normalizing, or therapeutic interventions that involved little, if any, significant political or economic change.

In so representing the discipline of sociology as it emerged in the narratives of the early nineteenth-century social researchers, I regard it as one among a field of discourses that refigured the self and the family during the first half of the nineteenth century. This change, I suggest, occurred largely in writing that shifted the source of social disorder from "outside" causes—those linked to economic problems that would erode the authority of the middle-class intellectuals—to "inside" causes that authorized their control over the masses. Sociological writing performed a crucial role in this process by moving the individual and the family into a regulatory and therapeutic arena. There they might be observed, cataloged, analyzed, described, and made amenable to a form of social control based not in brutal coercion or overt displays of power but in self-regulation and discipline. Since this transformation was the result of a long process stretching out over two centuries, I would like to take a moment to explore it.

No one can say why the system of patriarchal relations that had organized social and political relations in England well into the seventeenth century began to weaken. However, as it did, the family gradually became the object of direct state management. This transition may best be described as one from a government of families in and through alliances to a government through the family. No longer a force of the same nature as that of the established powers, the family was subordinated to the state as it became an obligatory or voluntary relay and support for social imperatives (Donzelot 1979). It was a transformation, as Foucault tells it, in the "biopolitical dimension"—that domain of political technologies which, from the eighteenth century onward, defined the body, health, modes of subsistence and lodging, and indeed the entire space of existence in European countries (1980).

Slowly but surely the complex, undifferentiated space that had characterized the protoindustrial family—social and private, functional and festive, sexes and generations—underwent profound transformation. Through a set of internal divisions based on gender and generation the family came to support and authorize rather than resist the forms of power necessary for industrial expansion. However, the protoindustrial family did not always cooperate with capitalism as readily as many present-day critics and scholars believe. On the contrary, its conservative tendencies and traditional ties made it an agent of resistance, not change. "The family functioned *objectively* as an internal engine of growth in the process of proto-industrial expansion," Hans Medick writes, "precisely because *subjectively* it remained tied to the norms and rules of behavior of the traditional familial subsistence economy" (1976, 300). Medick refutes Weber, in other words, when he argues that it was not so much the "Protestant ethic" enmeshed with labor discipline that hastened early capitalist expansion, but the " 'infinitely tenacious resistance . . . of precapitalist labour,' anchored in the family economy" (1976, 300).[7] When nineteenth-century sociological observers measured the protoindustrial family and its members against a new set of categories defined according to the logic of division and separation, they made little cultural sense. Instead the same logic of spatialization, compartmentalization, and functionalization evident in the early statistical surveys created disorders where previously there were none. In this light, the family and its members seemed a dangerous site of illicit moral and physical mixture requiring, even demanding, intervention and control.

THE JOURNEY INWARD

In 1800 C. G. Stonestreet, a local enthusiast for the social and environmental improvement of London, offered the following solution to the problems besetting the capital. "The *perforation* of every such nest [slum]," he wrote in *Domestic Union, or London as it Should Be!*, "by carrying through the midst of it a free and open street with buildings suitable for the industrious and reputable orders of the people would let in that EYE and *observation* which would effectively break up their [the laboring classes'] combinations" (Dyos and Reeder 1973, 365, emphasis added).

Stonestreet's recommendation is remarkable for the way in which it illuminates both the presence of a very modern form of power constituted by sociological writing and several of its crucial discursive features. It is important to note that the figure of penetration, as embodied in the act of "perforation," links the physical and spatial arrangement of working-class neighborhoods to the human body in significant ways. Here a bit of etymology is helpful. In its nineteenth-century usage, "perforation" meant, as it does today, the act of boring or piercing; more important, it also signified an aperture that passed through or into anything, such as a passage, shaft, or tunnel. The term, then, implies the existence of an interior space communicating with an exterior space only by way of a connecting structure—the perforation itself. "Perforation" also signifies the accidental or pathological formation of a hole through a part of the body or the natural orifice of an organ.[8] Given this, it is possible to see how Stonestreet's language superimposes signifiers of architectural space over those of bodily space. The spatial and political instability he evokes in his representation of the urban environment become a function of physical and bodily disorder. Furthermore, both disorders are correlatives of the visual impenetrability of working-class neighborhoods that in the writer's logic can be made accessible to vision only by their perforation. It is vision—"that EYE and observation"—that makes order from disorder and so instantiates the sociological gaze as a form of power. Indeed, at the root of Stonestreet's words lie both the assumed right to submit the lower classes to observation and the implicit necessity to determine an action or formation to "effectively break up their combinations."[9]

To understand the politically charged significance of the notion of "combination," one must look to social practices of popular resistance at the beginning of the nineteenth century, for it was in this domain that many long-tolerated forms of popular resistance first acquired the designation *combinations*. According to British historian E. P. Thompson, such "riots," as these protests are mistakenly called, should not be seen as compulsive and spontaneous intrusions upon the social landscape. Rather, Thompson maintains that they represent social and ritual practice governed by what he calls the "moral economy of the poor," constituted out of "a consistent traditional view of social norms and obligations, of the proper economic functions of several parties within the community" (1971, 79). These riots were not "spontaneous disruptions of civil order" but forms of "symbolic behavior" in which everyone played specific and predictable roles marked by a heavy emphasis on order, restraint, and discipline. Thompson explains that the central act in the bread riots of 1740, 1756, 1766, 1795, and 1800, for instance, was not "the sack of granaries and the pilfering of grain or flour," as one might imagine, "but the action of 'setting the price' "—the negotiation of a fair price by the people and the seller or the authorities (1971, 112).

The increased violence that infused popular protest in the early decades of the nineteenth century marks the end of this tradition and the emergence of another. In the struggle of the Luddites over the machinery question, to cite one example, the traditional rhetoric of sedition is replaced by underground union organizations, the symbolic weapons are replaced by real ones, and the demand for higher wages supplants the demand for bread. During the years following the French Revolution, political activism in England was vigorously suppressed when a worried aristocracy joined hands with the new industrial classes to pass the first of the Combination Acts in 1799–1800, repressing trade unions, which were also known as "combinations." In the first decade of the new century, then, laborers and peasants were to suffer under the combined weight of severe economic exploitation and intense political repression.

As part of a cultural logic that rethought political and economic categories in terms of a moral and a sexual vocabulary, urban sociology metaphorically translated the "combination" problem into a problem of the mixture of dwellings and bodies, and ultimately into one of gender differences. As it did so, sociological writing defined these categories into powerful analytical tools. Returning to Stonestreet's diagnosis of the topographical troubles of London, it is easy to see the superimposition of a language of bodies and sexes over one of nascent class struggle. Just as the figure of penetration allowed the dwelling to be identified with the body, so the ill-defined and ominous choice of the term "combination" permitted political resistance to be rewritten as a disorder of buildings and bodies. Once created and authorized by this text and others like it, this rhetorical problem invariably called forth the same solution. Not surprisingly, authors and intellectuals like Stonestreet imagined that "combination," or the disorder of the working classes, could be disrupted effectively only through the enclosure, division, and separation of the working classes from the middle class, of the slum from the city, of disorder from order. What could be more effective for this purpose than a "free and open road" constructed through twisted streets and crowded alleys? And what would be better, moreover, to prevent the people from mounting viable political resistance?[10] Thus the author's enthusiastic urban planning became political planning when he imagined an enclosed space at once self-contained and accessible to surveillance.

I would like to move now from the features defining early sociological writing as a discourse to a closer analysis of the texts themselves. In so doing, it is possible to articulate the precise manner in which they offer a notion of the poor grounded not in economic categories but in those features predicated on the existence of an essential self. Represented as an essence because it was something apparently enclosed within a body, this self was to be discovered under the skin, almost like perfume confined within a bottle until its stopper is loosened.[11] The essential self, moreover, was not confined to simply any body, but to a body with a definitive gender, and one seemingly cut off from the social, economic, and historical world.

The strategies by which sociological writing identified this object were not always the same, although they did share certain commonalities. Perhaps it is best to begin with Arthur Young's argument for the enclosure of common land, *General View of Agriculture in Lincolnshire*. Written on the cusp of the century in 1799, Young's tract added a hitherto unknown angle to the widespread struggle for the enclosure of common land then being waged by landowners. Although the enclosure of commons had begun in the sixteenth century, the practice reached its peak between 1760 and 1820, a period that witnessed the wholesale loss of common rights (Thompson 1966). Enclosure of common land once in the domain of rural laborers affected the agrarian household in two fundamental ways: first, it was deprived of a crucial source of its subsistence economy; and second, a traditional, time-honored local prerogative was usurped. It is no secret that advocates for enclosure were moved by economic motives—the more land in private hands, the more prosperous the landholders. It is interesting to note, however, that Young's argument and others of its genre allowed for more than greed when they described unenclosed land as disordered spaces that encouraged, even produced, more disorder. More important, Young's enclosure propaganda portrayed those laborers who cultivated the land as "other," and as "other" in need of institutional control.

"Commonland," Young boldly announced, "is a breeding ground for *barbarians* nursing up a mischievous *race* of people" (Thompson 1966, 219, emphasis added). One should note first how Young's rhetoric confuses nature with culture when it reorganizes a specific group of people characterized by socioeconomic features into a "race." In the seventeenth and eighteenth centuries, a race was commonly regarded as a tribe or nation of people descended from common stock. Thus while the term conveyed a shared genealogy, it did not, until the late eighteenth century, signify a division of mankind having *physical* peculiarities in common.[12] Young's terms, then, incorporate both an older meaning of "race" determined by genealogical thinking and a new definition indebted to the emerging forces of biology and heredity. In either case, the laborers of Lincolnshire are rudely divested of their identities as individuals embedded within a complex network of regional, generational, and familial relations. Instead, they are metaphorically cast out of England as uncivilized "barbarians"—a prelude to their more literal and unceremonious banishment from land traditionally open to them. Even the nature of the land itself seems to justify this act as it metamorphoses, under the spell of Young's rhetoric, into a female parent breeding and nurturing deformed offspring—the "bad seed." Children neither of England nor of the economy, the rural laborers seem to belong to the earth alone. Autochthonous beings, they spring from nowhere and so exit Young's text and the land of their ancestors with nothing but deviance and otherness to their name.

One may observe the same deployment of biology and morality in Dr. Turner Thackrah's account of cotton operatives in *The Effects of Arts, Trade and Professions on Health and Longevity* (1832). "I saw, or thought I saw, a *degenerate race*," Thackrah recounts, "human beings stunted, enfeebled, *depraved*,—men and women that were not to be aged—children that were never to be healthy" (Thompson 1966, 329, emphasis added). What disfigures the workers' faces and saps vitality from their limbs is not poverty but moral weakness. Like Young's account, Thackrah's text casts the workers into a new category of aberrance entirely defined by and contained within the individual, one that erases economic, social, and political determinants entirely and relocates them within the essential self. Thackrah's factory workers are described as the genetic other, those who, like Young's laborers, exhibit negative features that originate in the domain of a newly defined individual.

It is fair to say that early sociologists like Young and Thackrah represented the working-class individual as a disordered space lacking appropriate boundaries. Following their lead, sociology shifted its analytical gaze from the filth of poor neighborhoods to the interior of working-class houses and tenements. There sociologists discovered that family life, rather than providing a haven in a heartless world, actually mirrored the disorder in the ill-paved streets and crumbling walls. It was an easy step for them to see the debased individuals as the cause for the debasing conditions in which they lived.

Peter Gaskell's *Artisans and Machinery: The Moral and Physical Condition of the Manufacturing Population* (1836) illustrates this move especially well. Gaskell begins with the best of intentions, blaming the factory system for the evils besetting the working-class family. "It is not poverty—for the family of the manufacturing labourer, earn what is amply sufficient to supply all their wants," he writes:

> it is not factory labour, considered per se; it is not the lack of education, in the common acceptance of the word:—no; it has arisen from the separation of families, the breaking up of households, the disruption of all those ties which link man's heart to the better portion of his nature,—viz. his instincts and social affections, and which can alone render him a respectable and praiseworthy member of society, both in his domestic relations, and in his capacity of a citizen; . . . (6)[13]

Gaskell invokes an older notion of the family only to reconstitute it according to a different model more suitable to forms of social control by the middle classes. Reading on, one discovers that it is not the dispensation of economic resources that disrupts the artisanal family, but the disposition of bodies and sexes. As Gaskell recounts the history of the early manufacturers, he concludes that the factory system in its earliest incarnations was responsible for the break-up of the family only in that it promiscuously herded male and female bodies together into a "hot-bed of lust"—the factory itself. Although male and female laborers had worked, eaten, celebrated, and slept side by side in the protoindustrial family for generations (Medick 1976), Gaskell can only imagine such congregation as illicit and immoral. Like Stonestreet, Young, and Thackrah, Gaskell creates a disorder of bodies and sexes where previously there was none. "Wherever men are congregated in large bodies," he proclaims in a "true proposition," "their morals must be deteriorated" (52). "The crowding together [of] numbers of the young of both sexes in factories," Gaskell's complaint continues, "is a prolific source of moral delinquency. The stimulus of a heated atmosphere, the contact of opposite sexes, the example of lasciviousness upon the animal passions—all have conspired to produce a very early development of sexual appetencies" (68). For Gaskell it is the body that is out of control, not the economic system. The female body, more specifically, suffers the most from an undisciplined and recalcitrant "nature." "The female population engaged in manufactures," Gaskell continues, "approximates very closely to that found in tropical climates;

puberty, or at least sexual propensities, being attained almost coeval with girlhood" (69). Like Young and Thackrah, Gaskell locates the worker in the domain of nature, outside of culture. However, Gaskell takes this process one step further when he makes sexuality the most fundamental manifestation of a "nature" unimpeded and uninfluenced by culture. He then focuses on the female and identifies female sexuality as that nature's most characteristic and problematic feature.

Gaskell insists the only solution to this rampant immorality is to introduce into the factory "strict discipline" and the division and separation of the sexes (66). Moreover, he claims, since the artisanal home as he has reimagined it already conforms to these specifications, it alone can serve as a proper model for such a reorganization. "No nostrums of political economy, no bare intellectual education, no extension of political rights," according to Gaskell, but only "the morals of the home" can make workers "a happy, respectable, or contented race of men" (66–67). In two important ways Gaskell's rhetoric opens up a separate epistemological and spatial category for factory workers. First, his language, like Young's thirty years earlier, mistakes a matter of economy for biology when it translates a group of workers who sell their labor power into a "race." Moreover, the new space to which Gaskell confines the working-class family bears a striking similarity to that of the factory—both are segregated according to sex.

Gaskell's study gradually progresses from the external condition surrounding the artisanal family to its internal features. The family itself eventually comes to enclose all the disorder causing the disruption of that household. Finally, it is the family members' "recklessness," "improvidence," "disobedience," "neglect of conjugal rights," and the "absence of maternal love" that are at the heart of the matter (Gaskell 1836, 219). Once the household has been identified as the problem, Gaskell imagines the solution in terms of a newly constituted household that cancels out the original artisanal family, whose lamentable passing prompted him to write the essay in the first place. The rehabilitated man observes moral and physical order when he builds a "durable house," divides it into "distinct compartments," and "separates the sexes; that his wife no longer be an instrument of labor, but depends upon him for support" (77). Gaskell's representation resurrects the household according to a model authorizing the same division of space and separation of the sexes that he advocated for the factory.[14] Most important, the home is to revolve around the figure of the domestic female, who becomes dependent upon the male for economic sustenance.

According to Gaskell, however, it is not the scantness or the unsteadiness of workers' wages but the absence of a good woman from the home that gives rise to the ills of the working-class. "Another misfortune," he writes,

> of a very prominent character, attends upon the female division of the manufacturing population. This is, the entire want of instruction or example in learning the plainest elements of domestic economy; and this single circumstance goes far to explain many of the improvident habits which form a chief part of the curse upon their social condition. . . . Of all these essentials to the head of a household the factory girl is utterly ignorant, and her arrangements, if arrangements they can be called, where every thing is left to chance, are characterized by sluttish waste, negligence, carelessness as to the quality of the food, and indifference as to the mode of cooking, and an absence of all that tidiness, cleanliness, and forethought which are requisite to a good housewife. (72)

Since bad habits and not the extremities of economic exploitation "curse" the working-class population, what better place to control those habits than in the home? Gaskell's answer is but one instance of a cultural logic that implicated both middle- and working-class women in the machinery of middle-class hegemony. Briefly, this logic was part of the process of self-definition that distinguished the middle classes more completely from the upper classes. In it the emergent middle classes represented the aristocratic body as dissolute, dissipating its resources in the never-ending pursuit of pleasure.[15] The healthy middle-class body, in contrast, ideally would come to mental and physical fruition under the guidance of doctors and teachers following rules established by a new canon of moral and hygienic instruction. As middle-class women formed privileged alliances with the medical and educational establishments, they too became responsible for the health of the middle-class body and its progeny. Doctors and mothers, to cite one instance, united to free the family's health care from the old wives' tales and traditional remedies previously dominating medical care (Trumbach 1978). Important here for my purposes is the way in which early nineteenth-century medicine authorized maternal know-how, thus empowering women within the domestic sphere, and by extension, in the social world; in turn, these newly empowered bourgeois women legitimized the medical institution (Donzelot 1979).

The laboring-class body with its contagions and diseases presented a problem requiring a solution of a different order. Such a mistreated, exploited body threatened to drain the resources of the state, and so it must be taught to care for itself with only minimal outside assistance. As Gaskell's dreadful portrayal of the home without a female illustrated, only a full-time homemaker could relieve this burden. The solution, however unwittingly formulated, was to propel the woman out of the factory and into a newly enclosed domestic space imagined first by middle-class intellectuals like Gaskell. Unpaid labor in the home not only reduced social expense but also alleviated competition between men and women in the market as it introduced hygienic principles into working-class life.

In both working-class and bourgeois families, these transformations could not have been successful without the active participation of women themselves. In slum and suburb alike, "women were the main point of support for all the actions that were directed toward a reformulation of family life" (Donzelot 1979, xxii). As painful as it may be for many contemporary feminists to recognize, women were often as much agents of hegemony as objects seized and defined by it.[16]

As fixtures of domestic life, women became responsible for ameliorating the worst behavior of family members.[17] Yet only if female desire were aligned with the family could this responsibility be fulfilled willingly. Gaskell's representation of sexual desire as a biological or hereditary phenomenon brings this cultural project one step nearer to fulfillment:

> The [sexual indulgence] does not end with the party first yielding to the temptation . . . , it descends from parent to child as an hereditary curse. Her [the mother's] family inherit the same lax feelings; her sons and daughters are both subjected to the same causes which prematurely evolved her own propensities . . . ; have the same failings; and become fathers and mothers in their turn. (1836, 105)

What began for Gaskell as a social condition has been translated into a moral and finally a biosexual problem. Gaskell's logic, in other words, follows the same trajectory as Young's. Both move from outside to inside, from collective to individual, from politics to biology, from culture to nature. Yet *Artisans and Machinery* differs from Young's work in that it ultimately identifies the problem of the working class as bad sexual desire and locates it within the female. Paradoxically, Gaskell also invests the female with a considerable degree of domestic authority as he makes it her duty to regulate and socialize the members of the family. In this move one may see in miniature a much larger cultural process that successfully defined the female as a point from which middle-class intellectuals and professionals could introduce cultural values into the family even while they sealed off the family and represented its internal organization as ideally independent of external circumstances.

INSIDE THE HAUNTS OF POVERTY AND VICE

In 1832, as cholera ravaged the slums of Manchester and threatened to infect the better neighborhoods, Dr. James Kay Shuttleworth took to prowling the streets of the stricken city. Hoping to find the cause of the epidemic, Kay Shuttleworth was led, much to his surprise but perhaps not to ours, deep into "the most loathsome haunts of poverty and vice" (1832, 4). Like so many of his colleagues, Kay Shuttleworth was no ordinary observer of the spectacle of early industrial poverty. It had long been his "custom," he writes, "to frequent the precincts of vice and disease in the exercise of public professional duties and for the purposes of local observation and inquiry" (1832, 4). On this occasion, as a member of the hastily formed Manchester Board of Health, Kay Shuttleworth again made the journey into the heart of the industrial city in an official capacity. In his *The Moral and Physical Condition of the Working Class Employed in the Cotton Manufacture in Manchester* (1832), the record of that expedition, one can again see the rhetorical strategies of sociological representation translating the features of the exterior into those of the interior self, then discovering the solution in terms of the female.

Not surprisingly, Kay Shuttleworth's portrait of the industrial poor resembles Gaskell's in *Artisans and Machinery* in several crucial respects. Like Gaskell, Kay Shuttleworth was a liberal motivated by genuine humanitarian concern for the human victims of industrialization. He also shared Gaskell's unshakeable belief in the irresistible power of "facts" to galvanize public opinion. Most important for my purposes, both *The Moral and Physical Condition of the Working Class* and *Artisans and Machinery* represent the working-class as an illicit mixture of bodies and sexes, a disordered space lacking appropriate boundaries. Yet here the resemblance ends. Kay Shuttleworth's study significantly expands the vocabulary available to sociology by adding the language of disease; in so doing, it articulates another moment in the discursive and practical partnership between sociological writing and state power.

The language of disease was ideally suited to join forces with that of morality because both emphasized contaminants, contagion, and the internal state of the body. While the language of morality foretold the dangers of the illicit mixture of bodies and sexes, the language of disease effectively opened up the working-class individual to new forms of scrutiny as it translated a political scandal into a sexual one. With cholera as its messenger, the language of disease confirmed the prophetic voice of morality. The body as well as the moral and therefore sexual "nature" of the working-class individual was deformed by intemperance and sensuality. Weakened by drink, laid low by debauchery, heaped together indiscriminately in crowded dwellings, the working-class body invited, even encouraged, the invasion of disease. This notion of the working class as represented in sociological writing solicited and authorized the intervention of the medical establishment. With it came an entire apparatus of procedures, regulations, and measures tying the working classes more firmly to middle-class governance. Kay Shuttleworth's *The Moral and*

Physical Condition of the Working Class is an official document of one such intervention. As such, it is distinguishable from Gaskell's *Artisans and Machinery* by the degree to which it implicates sociological writing in a particular instance of middle-class power—the board of health.

The hurried formation of this official body during the crisis of 1832 is significant for the way in which it highlights the convergence of the tools of sociological analysis with the disciplinary mechanisms of the state. Members of the board of health were sanctioned by local authorities to carry out a series of observations and inspections of the population as a whole, but especially of the working classes. The threat of cholera, Kay Shuttleworth informs us, convinced dubious manufacturers that "the minute personal interference of the higher ranks is necessary to the physical and moral elevation of the poor" (1832, 11). With this spirit and "in anticipation of the invasion of Cholera, the inspection of streets and houses of the large towns were performed with a zeal and energy" hitherto unknown (1832, 11).

In later incarnations, the board of health commanded tremendous power and resources, the bulk of which rested in the hands of medical officers of health who were appointed unofficially during the cholera epidemic, their position sanctioned by law in 1847 (Wohl 1973, 604). The duties of medical officers increased tremendously throughout the century, until eventually the officers supervised the water supply, the cleanliness of houses, overcrowding, the registration of diseases, births and deaths, the control of epidemics, cemeteries and mortuaries, and last but not least, street cleaning. "The medical officer had one or more sanitary inspectors—called by contemporaries 'medical police'—under him, and it was their duty to make house-to-house visitations" (Wohl 1973, 606). In short, medical officials, in conjunction with local authorities, ultimately formed a type of inspectorate, with all its connotations of authority, control, supervision, and surveillance.[18]

In *The Moral and Physical Condition of the Working Class*, the figure of "cholera" allows Kay Shuttleworth to turn the analytic gaze of the sociologist and the doctor on the bodies of the poor. Not surprisingly, he discovered, much in the same way Gaskell did, that it was not poor sanitary conditions or overcrowded rooms that spread disease, but the negligence and sexual misconduct of the victims themselves. Cholera, he warned, would remain endemic among the poor as "the strongest admonition of the consequences of insobriety, uncleanliness, and that improvidence and idleness which waste the comforts of life, induce weakness and invite disease" (1832, 6). Kay Shuttleworth's laborers become more than victims of disease; they become the incarnation of disease itself. The poor, that is to say, are rhetorically identified with the contagion, their political struggles with the epidemic threatening the very life of the middle-class body. Thus, what was originally an exterior feature is translated through the language of disease into an aspect of the interior, essential self. When the language of disease diagnosed a disorder of bodies and sexes, it proposed, as the language of morality had done, to remedy the problem not by altering the economic conditions under which the poor labored but by rearranging the bodies themselves. Note, then, what happens to the language of disease as Kay Shuttleworth uses it to continue sociology's journey into the interior.

One might begin by focusing on Kay Shuttleworth's account of the conditions he found at the center of the industrial city. "He whose duty it is to follow the steps of the messenger of death," he recounts in horror:

> must *descend* to the abodes of poverty, must frequent the close alleys, the crowded courts, the overpeopled habitations of wretchedness, where pauperism and disease *congregate* round the source of social discontent and political *disorder* in the centre of our large towns, and behold with alarm, in the hot-bed of *pestilence*, ills that fester in secret, at the very heart of society. (1832, 8 emphasis added)

In Kay Shuttleworth's alarmist rhetoric the social body is translated into a physical body, and society's most underprivileged members are translated into the "pestilence" threatening its health and well-being. The task of the medical professional, Kay Shuttleworth implies, is to reach the very heart of this body in order to diagnose the contagion endangering its life. To do this, the professional undertakes a ritual passage from outside the slum to inside it, from the exterior of the body to the interior. Kay Shuttleworth does not simply walk to the working class neighborhood, he *descends into* it.[19] In this manner working-class space is again represented as an enclosed, bounded interior, akin to the inside of the body, that must be perforated—made accessible to vision. At the center, the middle-class intellectual finds a mess; or perhaps more accurately, he makes a mess. The people are too many, and disease "congregates" indistinguishably with "political disorder." I would like to note how once the language of disease arises, it is a simple step to link political resistance ("disorder") to moral and physical "disorder." This logic conveys Kay Shuttleworth's analysis, like Gaskell's, from outside to inside, from culture to nature, from social to individual, from economy to sexuality. Furthermore, as it creates disorders where previously there were none, *The Moral and Physical Condition of the Working Class* focuses on the female as both the source for and answer to working-class failures.

As Kay Shuttleworth maps the path of cholera through the slums, his topography reproduces in miniature the logic of the sociomedical gaze. Noting first that the disease usually occurs in the "most narrow, ill-ventilated, unpaved streets," he rapidly pursues its course into houses that are "uncleanly, ill provided with furniture," "dilapidated," "badly drained," "damp," and "pervaded with an air of discomfort if not squalid and loathsome wretchedness." He does not stop there, however; he finds the tenants similarly wanting. Not only are they "ill-fed" and "ill-clothed"— outward signs of their reduced economic circumstances—but their extravagance, making them "at once spendthrifts and destitute," leads them to deny themselves "the comforts of life, in order that they may wallow in the unrestrained license of animal appetite" (1832, 28–29).[20] If the link between the economic condition of the working classes and bad sexual desire is not amply clear by this point, Kay Shuttleworth makes it even more explicit. "Uneconomical habits and dissipation are inseparably allied," he writes; both are "fertile sources alike of disease and demoralization." "Both factors," he concludes ominously, authorize the presence of "police regulations or general enactment" (1832, 29).

Finally, Kay Shuttleworth reaches the center of the household—the bedroom—where he finds to his great disgust a whole family "accommodated on a single bed, and sometimes a heap of filthy straw and a covering of old sack hiding them in one indistinguishable *heap*" (1832, 32, emphasis added). Here the logic of "combination" converts politically potent material into sexual scandal and the working-class family into a "heap"—an indistinguishable mass of bodies and sexes. "Dissolution then radiates outward from the center," Nancy Armstrong observes of Kay Shuttleworth's discovery, "where sociology has staged the primal scene as Shuttleworth voyeuristically peers into the basement rooms that pigs cohabit with their masters, into lodging houses where people sleep in shifts 'without distinction of age or sex', and from there into open privies that may serve as many as two hundred people" (1987a, 171).

Once the language of disease, legitimized by the new notions of biology and heredity, confirms the disorder of the household and the culpability of the working-class individual, it is an easy step to define the working class as "other" in need of institutional control. Where Kay Shuttleworth begins by following cholera home from the tavern with the working man, who "conveyed in his own bosom . . . the fatal element of contagion to poison his offspring" and "desolate his home" when least aware, he concludes by primitivizing the working classes and identifying them as a race whose contagions must not be allowed to spread. The lower-class body, then, is no longer the carrier of the disease but the source. Thus Kay Shuttleworth condemns marriages among the poor since such unions only increase a "squalid and debilitated race, who inherit from their parents diseases, sometimes deformity, often vice, and always beggary" (1832, 47).[21]

Once the problem has been situated entirely in the household and the individual within, Kay Shuttleworth, like Gaskell, imagines the solution in terms of a newly defined domestic configuration centered around the female. "The early age at which girls are admitted into the factories," he complains, "prevents their acquiring much knowledge of domestic economy, and even supposing them to have had accidental opportunities of making this acquisition, the extent to which women are employed in the mills, does not, even after marriage, permit the general application of its principles" (1832, 69). Simply returning the working-class female to the home will not alleviate the problem completely. It is the "educational system," according to Kay Shuttleworth, that must fill in the gap by instructing "young females of the poor" in "Domestic Economy." Such an education, Kay Shuttleworth hopes, would eliminate "those pernicious traditional prejudices" in favor of "wholesome advice concerning their duties as wives and mothers" (1832, 72). Thus only if the female inside the home is connected to professionals outside the household will the problem be solved.

Sociological writing followed the pattern I have mapped in both Gaskell's and Kay Shuttleworth's work well into the middle of the nineteenth century. One should remember that sociologists often resorted to data collected by their colleagues to tell their stories. As a result, many sociological representations of the poor were little more than compilations from other sources interspersed with bits of authorial wisdom and commentary. Yet, even in such cases, the logic translating political into moral and sexual material was so firmly embedded in sociological analysis that it shaped even the most disparate sources into the same narrative pattern. Hector Gavin's *The Habitations of the Industrial Classes* (1851) is one such text that illustrates well the immense power of socio-logic as I have defined it.

By now there should be little need to linger over the precise manner by which Gavin's narrative travels from the exterior to the interior. What is most interesting is that by 1851, the year of its publication, Gavin felt no need, unlike Gaskell and Kay Shuttleworth earlier in the century, to pay even the most cursory attention to the larger political or economic factors responsible for the appalling state of the poor. "It is undesirable," he writes, "to attempt to enter into the vast and comprehensive subject of the causes which render town and population unhealthy, and necessary to confine attention to the actual condition of the dwellings and their influence on the physical, social and moral condition of the industrial classes" (1851, 20). The problem, according to this logic, is one that may be neatly divided and enclosed by streets, houses, and bedrooms.[22]

Predictably, Gavin's source enters the working-class house, where he steadily makes his way into its most secret recess, the bedroom. To his utter horror, he finds sleeping there "as many as ten or fifteen persons of both sexes, in addition to the man, his wife and five children." To make matters worse, another source discovers a donkey stabled in the kitchen while all around a family of ten slept—"persons herding together without separation of age or sex" (1851, 73)—unperturbed by the presence of the loathsome creature. One informer would have us believe, moreover, that the poor prefer such arrangements to more commodious ones. According to his logic, they simply choose to disregard the ventilation of dwellings, their crowded state, and the want of cleanliness. So that, when the occupants retire at night fatigued, "they congregate *en masse*, in filthy beds, in the rooms in which they eat their food" (1851, 73).

It cannot be stressed enough that, in addition to disclosing the household mess, the text also establishes the conditions for returning the working-class woman to the domestic arena. As observed in *Artisans and Machinery*, it was the female body that was figured as disorderly and out of control. Its recalcitrant nature, further, was severely tested by close contact with members of the opposite sex in the immoral confines of the factory. So too, in the fetid darkness of overcrowded rooms, despite the fatigue that hard labor brings, the logic of "combination" can only imagine illicit sex. Thus the chief danger in the "absence of decent separation of sex" in the household, Gavin decries, is "unrestrained passion" and "easy gratification." Both are unconducive to the "moral restraint, prudential consideration, and self-government" he imagines for a female "early surrounded by families of children" (1851, 74). Furthermore, Gavin warns, "the absence from the home of the husband and drunkenness are inevitable" if the men's wives are "ignorant of, and indifferent to, the obligations of their position, unacquainted with domestic economy, and wasteful, careless of their homes and of their persons, incapable of conducting the ordinary household affairs, or producing cheerfulness and comfort by the fireside" (1851, 74).

I want to highlight two important points here. First, Gavin advocates internal rule ("self-government") as the surest route to the control of unruly female desire. Second, as the working-class female is given domestic authority by middle-class professionals, she is also asked to render services in return. That is, it becomes her responsibility to monitor her husband's movements, to make sure he is sober, at home, and in bed early for the work day on the morrow. The political ramifications of this task are obvious, perhaps, but nonetheless crucial—good homelife reduces the possibilities for political unrest. One of Gavin's experts, Dr. Southwood Smith, admits as much. "We all know," he exclaims, "how greatly a clean, fresh, and well-ordered house tends to make the members of the family sober, *peaceable, and considerate of the feelings and happiness of each other*" (1871, 70, emphasis added).

STREETS UNSAFE FOR WOMEN

In the figure of the prostitute social researchers discovered everything the domestic woman was not and perhaps a bit more. Once sociological representation naturalized female sexual desire, condemning its overly licentious and easily gratifiable character, it was easy to demand its curtailment and to proscribe its limits within the walls of the house, the confines of the family. When sociological writing represented the factory as a space of sexual combination posing a danger to the female, it counterposed the domestic interior as a safe haven for the female. Only there could she protect herself against the consequences of illicit sexual traffic. As a result, those females remaining outside domestic boundaries were isolated and easily targeted as a primary threat to the sanctity of the home. The representation of the prostitute in Henry Mayhew's classification study of the poor, *London Labour and the London Poor*, elaborates and extends this process initiated by early nineteenth-century sociological writing. By making all forms of sexual conduct illicit, except those sanctioned by middle-class norms, I argue, Mayhew effectively outlaws the single woman. In so doing, Mayhew's work represents an economic problem in terms of deviant female sexuality and thus reproduces the logic of sociological writing.

Mayhew's multivolume study originated in a series of articles focused on the poor published in the *Morning Chronicle* from 1850 to 1852. Those articles along with the resulting study have occasioned much praise from historians and cultural critics. Eileen Yeo, for instance, insists that the material from the *Morning Chronicle* series "entitle Mayhew to an important place in the history of social investigation" (Yeo and Thompson 1971, 312). Calling him the "the discoverer of the poor," Gertrude Himmelfarb argues that Mayhew's work "did more to focus attention upon poverty in London than any other single work" (1985, 312). By now, however, one should be well aware that by mid-century the plight of the poor had been the subject of an overwhelming number of middle-class writers—scribblers and diligent alike—so many, in fact, that the poor hardly needed "discovery." As Barbara Ehrenreich writes in another context, "why did the working class, or the poor, have to be 'discovered' in the first place? From whose vantage point were they missing?" (1989, 23) Indeed, I would argue that *London Labour and the London Poor* represents the most blatant attempt on the part of middle-class intellectuals to locate the problem of the working class in the working-class female and to defuse the explosive question of the condition of the class by sexing and psychologizing it.

Mayhew begins by classifying the working population of London according to three major categories—"Those Who Will Work," "Those Who Cannot Work," and "Those Who Will Not Work"—categories that measure the will to work as if it were a biophysical or characterological trait. Absent is the role economic necessity plays in labor patterns. Prostitutes, in Mayhew's scheme, along with vagrants, beggars, cheats, and thieves are among those who will not work. The prostitute does not labor, that is, because she chooses her profession out of sexual desire rather than economic need. "In cold climates, as in hot climates," he writes, "the passions are the main agents in producing the class of women that we have under consideration" (1861, 212).

The table of contents of the volume devoted to "Those Who Will Not Work" makes it easy to see the way in which sexual categories negate or subsume economic or social ones, much in the way Mayhew dismisses the economic dimension of prostitution. Since prostitution for Mayhew is but one more form of the illicit traffic of the sexes, he lumps together prostitutes and women he calls "Kept Mistresses," "Soldiers' and Sailors' Women," and "Those who live in low lodging-houses" in a new category labeled "Prostitutes and Their Dependents." The category of "prostitution" not only cancels out indigenous working-class living arrangements, it also expands to include forms of female labor outside the home that were previously socially legitimate. Thus, under "Clandestine Prostitutes," for instance, Mayhew inexplicably includes "Maid Servants" and so sexualizes any female labor performed any place but in one's own household. Finally, Mayhew does to female domestic labor outside the home what Gaskell and Kay Shuttleworth do to female factory labor. Both kinds of female labor become species of sexual misconduct rather than legitimate expressions of economic need.

When Mayhew defines the prostitute as the figure for all criminality, the category of prostitution takes on enormous proportions. "Literally construed," the journalist writes:

> prostitution is the putting of anything to a vile use; in this sense perjury is a species of prostitution, being an unworthy use of the faculty of speech; so again, bribery is a prostitution of the right of voting; while prostitution, specially so called, is the using of her charms by a woman for immoral purposes. ... *be the cause*, however, *whatever it may*, the act remains the same, and consists in the base *perversion* of a woman's charms—the *surrendering* of her virtue to criminal *indulgence*. (1861, 4:35, emphasis added)

In Mayhew's terms, prostitution is a moral and sexual pathology ("perversion," "indulgence") that is the source of all crime. It is intriguing to note the impulse that internalizes the crime, making the prostitute responsible for her own exploitation; it is in the "use" of her "charms" and the "surrender" of her "virtue" that the essence of the crime lies. What begins as just one type of crime among many expands, as Mayhew continues, into the crime by which all others are measured. Not only does he use the prostitute as the index for criminality among working-class Londoners, but he sees her as the figure uniting the civilizations and cultures he blithely surveys in good anthropological fashion in the course of the volume. As he pursues the prostitute through history, culture, and geography, from ancient Greece to Africa, from Babylon to New Zealand, Mayhew implicitly makes sexuality the defining feature of both cultures and individuals.

It would be unfair to claim that Mayhew does not acknowledge economic necessity in the making of a prostitute. Noting "the low rate of wages that the female industrial classes receive, in return for the most arduous and wearisome labour," he admits, "innumerable cases of prostitution through want, solely and absolutely, are constantly occurring" (1861, 4:213). If factory work is not a viable choice for the working-class woman, then marriage must be the other means of evading a life of prostitution. Unfortunately for the single female, however, her choices are regulated by the demographic law of supply and demand; as Mayhew warns, "one hundred and five women in England and Wales are born to every one hundred males" (1861, 4:213). To confirm visually what the numbers foretell, Mayhew includes two maps of England among the many at the end of the volume. While the first map assures the young man that he will marry early, the second conveys a bleaker message to the young lady whose search for a husband will be impeded by the shortage of eligible English bachelors.[23]

What is one to make of Mayhew's emphasis on the shortage of men? What vision of social reality does the language of numbers create and verify? More important, how is his focus on the dearth of men and the abundance of women linked to his representation of the figure of the prostitute? To answer these questions, compare for a moment Mayhew's characterization of the working-class female with that of his sociological predecessors. For both Gaskell and Kay Shuttleworth, the working-class woman who abjured the factory for the home had the greatest chances for domestic bliss, healthy, moral children, and an admiring husband. Only in the domestic environment would a woman be free of the constant sexual temptations posed by the factory, the street, and her own errant desire. For Mayhew, what happens to the single working-class woman who does not or cannot adhere to these middle-class guidelines is not a pretty picture. First, Mayhew condemns and dismisses most working class sociosexual arrangements as mere species of prostitution. Second, in emphasizing the scarcity of marriageable men, Mayhew regards marriage itself as a rarer and therefore a more desirable commodity. Both these stances advocate, even necessitate, marriage as the only viable alternative to prostitution—not just any form of cohabitation, but a middle-class marriage. In essence, I suggest, *London Labour and the London Poor* is the culmination of early nineteenth-century sociology's preoccupation with the female, and it does no more and no less than outlaw the single woman.[24]

The publication of Mayhew's extensive study of the prostitute in 1861 coincided with a movement in medico-judicial spheres to contain prostitution by a system of police and medical supervision (Walkowitz 1980). In effect, this predominantly middle-class movement rendered the situation of the single woman as tenuous in practice as *London Labour* did in theory. I argue that one cannot comprehend this deployment of social force against the prostitute unless one looks to discourses like Mayhew's, and more specifically to the logic of social research that singled out the female as the solution to the condition of the working classes. By shifting the blame for that condition from the exterior to the interior of the working-class individual, from economic to sexual factors, from cultural to natural explanations, and finally by locating the solution in the suitably domesticated woman, early sociology made new medico-judicial interpretations of and practices toward prostitution possible, if not necessary.

The most infamous of these practices were the Contagious Diseases Acts of 1864, 1866, and 1869 that were enacted to control the spread of venereal disease among enlisted men in garrison towns and ports. These laws enacted the logic of sociological discourse by shifting the perceived source of pollution and criminality from male to female, from exterior to interior features, from the middle class to the working class.

Under the Contagious Diseases Acts, a woman only had to be identified as a "common prostitute" by special plainclothed police to be forced to undergo bimonthly internal examination and to be registered as a prostitute. While the definition of "common prostitute" was extremely vague, allowing local police extraordinary power, the message behind the legislation was not. The streets were unsafe for women, it implied, especially working-class woman, who could be accosted at any moment by the gaze and instruments of authority empowered to scrutinize them for visible and hidden signs of sexual deviance and criminality. Since the legislation identified the female body as the source of contagion, registered women were forced to undergo invasive vaginal exams, which they regarded as a form of "instrumental rape" (Walkowitz 1980, 202). The very public nature of the examination and the permanent visibility of the examination house (Walkowitz 1980) penetrated working-class space—both architecturally and bodily—in the manner advocated earlier in the century by Stonestreet in his diagnosis of London's ills. Both forms of surveillance were a constant reminder of a type of state power that is permanent in its effects, even if it is discontinuous in its actions (Foucault 1979). In other words, just the mere suggestion of the examination and the presence of medical and legal authorities in working-class communities constituted a threat, which reduced the need for the actual exercise of that power. Nevertheless, middle-class power was brought to bear on the body of the working-class female with all its might when this national legislation mobilized the entire medico-judicial apparatus from the Admiralty to the War Office, who in turn relied on provincial magistrates, doctors, and hospital authorities to enforce both sanitary and penal measures (Walkowitz 1980).

Prostitutes, as Judith Walkowitz so eloquently explains in *Prostitutes and Victorian Society*, were virtually indistinguishable from working-class women in general. They were usually integrated into the social life of the working-class community, which recognized the economic necessity of their sexual choices, and sometimes they formed enduring relationships with working-class men. What middle-class researchers interpreted as illicit sexual conduct, working-class women and men understood as survival; and they often tolerated prostitution along with cohabitation, concubinage, and autodivorce. The intensification of medical and police supervision, however, created a new outcast class of sexually deviant females. In this way, the prostitute's relationship to the working class as a whole was severely attenuated, if not destroyed beyond recognition (Walkowitz 1980, 5). This point returns us to the discourse of sociology itself and to Mayhew's representation of the prostitute. Both the discourse and the practice prohibited or outlawed the single woman by closing down previously available avenues for her economic survival. The logic behind the social and legal practice of the acts appears remarkably similar to that of sociological writing itself. By making possible a new interpretation of the working-class female, I suggest, sociology also provided the government with a model for making a recalcitrant and dangerous group more tractable and amenable to middle-class hegemony. "As single women residing outside their families," Walkowitz observes, "registered women were perhaps the most vulnerable members of their community; consequently, official intervention into their lives offered police an easy opportunity for general surveillance of the poor neighborhoods in which they resided" (1980, 192). The containment of criminality within the confines of female sexuality served another important function as well. When sociological writing and practice sexualized political resistance and so classified it as deviance, it neutralized a potentially dangerous threat to the middle classes.

It is fair to say that as sociological writing represented the working-class individual as innocent of cultural determination, a new representation of the self emerged, defined according to its biological, sexual, or racial features alone. Although early nineteenth-century professionals and intellectuals portrayed these characteristics as indigenous to the working class, those individuals were, nonetheless, subject to reform and modification with proper tutelage and good self-government. In so representing the industrial classes, middle-class intellectuals and professionals created new inroads for themselves and their class into the lives of working-class people. Sociology, I have argued, reduced a problem of national proportions to one of streets, houses, and bedrooms; its solution, I would add, took on similar dimensions. If the problem resided in the individual, its solution lay in a household similarly closed off from the economic world. With this logic, sociologists imagined a new domestic space, sealed off from harmful outside influences yet connected strategically to forms of governance defined and controlled by middle-class professionals and intellectuals. They imagined the working-class female in that domestic scene. Removed from the sexually stimulating atmosphere of the factory, separated from contact with all but the nuclear family, unruly female desire could be properly channeled, its duties and responsibilities ideally aligned with the goals and needs of capitalism. To complement the good woman in the home, sociology imagined the bad woman in the street. Both representations became possible precisely because sociology imagined sexual desire in biological or genetic terms as a drive both uncontrolled and controllable, yet very much "female" in essence. It would then be up to the discourse of anthropology to create the science of race and the rules of gender.

Chapter 3

ANTHROPOLOGY: THE FAMILY OF MAN

> The first cry of a newborn baby in Chicago or Zamboango, in
> Amsterdam or Rangoon, has the same pitch and key,
> each saying, "I am! I have come through! I belong!
> I am a member of the Family."
> (*Edward Steichen and Carl Sandburg*, The Family of Man)

> We need to anthropologize the West: show how exotic its con-
> stitution of reality has been; emphasize those domains
> most taken for granted . . . ; make them seem as
> historically peculiar as possible. . . .
> (*Paul Rabinow, "Representations are Social Facts"*)

WHEN HENRY MAYHEW counted thieves and costermongers in *London Labour and the London Poor*, he entered into a well-established trade. While his may not have been the first study to inventory the urban working classes of London, it was, by and large, the most exhaustive and perhaps the most ingenious.[1] With roving eye and eager mind, Mayhew traveled from the heart of London's East End to the farthest corners of the globe and back to the beginning of recorded history in an effort to catalog "Those Who Will Work," "Those Who Cannot Work," and "Those Who Will Not Work." As the final volume settled down to enumerate the last obstinate types, it focused almost exclusively on the figure of the prostitute, construing that figure as the model for all criminal types and prostitution as the metaphor for all crime. Such a move transferred a notion of female sexual deviance to the urban working classes as a whole. Within this taxonomy of deviance, furthermore, Mayhew nested what amounted to a cross-cultural analysis of ancient and modern marriage customs. This curious slippage is illustrated as he shifts from describing "the extent and character of the prostitute class of women" to "those countries where marriage was an institution, and those . . . savage communities where the intercourse of men with women is looser than that of beasts" (1861, 4:37). By including all marriage customs within a taxonomy of female sexual deviance, *London Labour and the London Poor* provides a model for all anthropological procedures, which, this chapter argues, universalized a class- and culture-specific notion of the family on the basis of deviant sexuality.

To begin a discussion of nineteenth-century "anthropology"[2] with a mid-century sociologist is unorthodox to say the least.[3] By considering anthropology and sociology as part of the same determined moment in history, rather than as discrete disciplines constituted by a succession of separate moments, I am asking my readers to dispense with the expectations of intellectual history. Like the nineteenth-century practices of philology and ethnology, intellectual history characteristically pursues an origin in language, race, an "idea," or "intellectual trend." Following this tradition, I could point out that when Mayhew presumed he knew what human nature was, he simply joined a long line of seventeenth- and eighteenth-century "thinkers"—Vico, Montesquieu, Condorcet, to name a few.[4] However, as histories of ideas identify thought with other thought, piecing together intellectual genealogies like so many fabrics in a patchwork quilt, they transcend the vicissitudes of history, culture, and class. In this manner, moreover, nineteenth-century intellectual history appropriated huge chunks of historical time for its own by forging a chain of "pure" ideas thought to originate in imaginations unmarked by culture or history. As it erased all traces of difference, intellectual history disguised, even obliterated, the historical character of the new middle class itself. Without reference to the materiality of social and economic history, the middle class as an ideological entity disappeared into a fact of nature.[5] The history of ideas, I suggest, naturalized ruling-class power, and to this day it remains a powerful instrument of middle-class hegemony. When contemporary middle-class intellectuals indulge in its rituals, they too contribute to the maintenance of ruling-class power.

I begin with *London Labour and the London Poor*, more often hailed as a sociological masterpiece, to articulate the historical and discursive moment constituted by the intersection of "anthropology" and "sociology"[6] and to underscore the rhetorical and ideological unity of those would-be disciplines. At the same time, I want to stress the different ways in which they gendered cultural information. I do not claim that the human sciences spoke in one voice, nor do I suppose "a mental continuum over which a range of *resemblances* is spread" (de Certeau 1986b, 175). That would imply an orthodoxy anthropology and sociology did not possess. Rather, I intend to show how meaning is constituted within the human sciences only as a set of differential relations. "For propositions, texts, or institutions, as for the words of a language," Michel de Certeau has written, "the value accorded each element is determined and can be explained only by the relations into which it enters. What must be rediscovered is the overall *organization* of meaning which has determined specific meanings, and to which the elements of those meanings refer in referring to each other" (1986b, 175). In this light, I suggest, the discourse of anthropology performed a different but no less crucial function in the formation of the gendered self. Sociological discourse permeated the middle and working classes, vertically uniting them by means of a common notion of the natural origin of the gendered self. As anthropological discourse formulated oppositions between nature and culture, primitive and modern, kin and family, other and self, black and white, female and male, it horizontally united cultures and races without respect to history or to difference. Anthropology represented the self and the racial or ethnic other as part of one formation—"humanity," or the "family of man." It is with this spirit that nineteenth-century anthropologist E. B. Tylor could declare so confidently and expansively that

> surveyed in a broad view, the character and habit of mankind at once display that similarity and consistency of phenomena which led the Italian proverb-maker to declare that "all the world is one country, *tutto il mondo e paese.*" To general likeness in human nature on the one hand, and general likeness in the circumstances of life on the other, this similarity and consistency may no doubt be traced. (1874, 6)

I am convinced that many still subscribe to Tylor's view of "human nature." Since we know what is a "man," we recognize "him" everywhere. He is the Peruvian Indian photographed high in the Andes. She is the hatted and gloved matron captured in the act of sipping tea in London. These disparate images reach out from the pages of such coffee table volumes as the ubiquitous *Family of Man*, proclaiming their membership in the sea of humanity stretching from India to California. No matter that one eats from the earthen dish of poverty, the other from Wedgewood. Deep down we are all the same, this model proclaims. Do away with the troublesome fetters of class, ethnicity, race, or gender. Scratch that surface, and you find a human being. *We are all the same*, and even if there exist inequality, oppression, and injustice, the "haves" and the "have nots" ultimately bathe in the same golden light of humanity. The dream is a potent one; to this day it enthralls us, offering hope that if we could but galvanize man's humanity to man all would be well. Yet the family of man as anthropology imagined it had its poorer relations. In the grandiose embrace of the science of man, hierarchical distinctions between cultures and peoples were not abolished. Instead the "other" was simply assigned a different place in the order of things, as anthropology re-hierarchized "him" according to a new set of standards. That is, once it destroyed the "other" political order, nineteenth-century anthropology constituted the other within a disciplinary structure based on modern middle-class norms of heterosexual monogamy. Later I show how sexualizing the other made this possible. Suffice it to point out here, however, that anthropology, in consort with sociology and domestic fiction, contributed more to the definition of the middle-class family than to that of the family of man.

It is the self-referential function of anthropological discourse within middle-class culture that I would like to address in this chapter. This dimension has seldom, if ever, been discussed in histories or critiques of anthropology. Contemporary anthropologists and historians of anthropology are quick to excoriate their discipline for its collaboration with imperialism and colonialism. However, they are generally silent as to its role closer to home; yet the reasons for this omission are crucial. That is why before turning to a more complete analysis of the function of anthropology, I would like to rehearse briefly the arguments condemning the discipline and its dubious origins amid racism and imperialist expansion.

The social and political upheaval of the 1960s caused many progressive anthropologists to turn a sceptical eye on the profession that had accompanied missionaries into South Africa and troops into Algeria. It was no accident, they concluded, that some of the most important anthropological treatises appeared at the same time that Africa, Asia, and much of the rest of the world experienced the burden of British imperialism. These texts, among them works by the "great white fathers" Edward Burnett Tylor and John McLennan, as well as a host of lesser-knowns, both authorized and legitimated colonial practice through their relentless production of the discourse of the racial and cultural other. Examples of this well-mannered malignity abound. Lest anyone mourn the death of the family of man, it would be useful at this point to cite a few of its more scurrilous instances.

In *Anthropology* (1896), Tylor begins his epic study of "primitive" cultures by asking his readers to suppose themselves "standing at the docks in Liverpool or London, *looking* at groups of men of races most different from our own" (2, emphasis added). In this rather innocuous fashion, he situates the reader in the position of the observer and therefore, according to the Foucauldian formula, in the site of knowledge and power. "There is the familiar figure of the African negro," he continues, expanding the imaginary scene,

> with skin so dark-brown as to be popularly called Black, and black hair so naturally frizzed as to be called wooly. . . . A hatter would at once notice that the negro's head is narrower in proportion than the usual oval of the hats made for Englishmen. It would be possible to tell a negro from a white man even in the dark by the peculiar satiny feel of his skin, and yet more peculiar smell which no one who has noticed it is ever likely to mistake. (2)

The features distinguishing the African from the English, according to Tylor, are entirely physical, even sensual. There is no mistaking the sight, smell, or feel of an African. At this very fundamental level, then, the other is confined to a physical body that is certainly human, but so unmistakably other as to confuse no one, not even a blind person or a London hatter. Difference is literally a matter of common *sense*.

"Account of the Dissection of a Bushwoman" (1867), a shocking report by W. H. Flower and James Murie, also focuses on the physical body of the other to demarcate first "human" similarity but ultimately difference among peoples. As they measure the African female body before them, the anatomists "are struck with the remarkable agreement between them ['Negro' proportions] and those of the European child between four and six years old. It would indeed appear as if the proportions of a child of that age had been permanently retained" (194). Flower and Murie, of course, are fluent in the familiar nineteenth-century idiom of paternalism. Yet one should not be fooled; there is more at stake in their proceedings than such clichés might first suggest. Specifically, here one finds a perfect model for anthropological thinking that abolishes differences between the self and the other in order to reinstate them according to a new set of rules. When anthropological writing privileged anatomy over culture or history, as in this instance, it also produced and reproduced a notion of universal "man" to which African and European bodies could be compared. Hierarchical distinctions between human beings were apparently cancelled out in favor of this all-pervasive biological humanism. However, from the ashes of the old hierarchical order rose a new one. As Flower and Murie tell it, the African can be compared to the European (in "remarkable agreement") only inasmuch as the child resembles the adult. In other words, universality is a convenient fiction, even an illusion, behind which lurks a new supremacist logic for subordinating the racial other within a new hierarchy.

There are, of course, many such outrageous examples in the annals of nineteenth-century British anthropology. Yet even this brief sampler suggests that anthropological writing constituted one of the official knowledges of colonialism—pseudoscientific, typological, legal-administrative, and eugenicist (Bhabha 1986). Racism was not only institutionally sanctioned and discursively produced by imperialist practice, it was also produced by, and itself produced, the frantic search for the origin of "man" preoccupying anthropology at mid-century. It is to this controversy that I now turn to continue this brief excursion into the history of twentieth-century anthropology.

The two major strains of pre-Darwinian anthropology were divided primarily by the question "is 'mankind' one or many?" Monogenists or "ethnologicals" concluded that the human race was originally one, their belief based on ethnological data gathered from "the study of the linguistic, physical, and cultural characteristics of dark-skinned, non-European, 'uncivilized' peoples" (Stocking 1987, 47).[7] Polygenists or "anthropologicals" vehemently rejected such findings, relying instead on the equally biased data of physical anthropology to demonstrate that humans had descended from separate ancestors (Gould 1981, Stocking 1987). Today pre-Darwinian anthropology seems quite messy, characterized by intense disagreement and contradiction. Monogenists and polygenists, however, essentially agreed to disagree when their discourses drew on different sources of data; their common object of knowledge remained the dark-skinned "primitive." On this occasion and others like it, anthropological discourse simply constituted both sides of the argument. Thus "the differences cancel one another out insofar as they were used to express something identical underlying them all" (Laclau and Mouffe 1985). While it apparently represented both sides, liberal discourse remained true to only one.

So critical were the ramifications of the monogeny/polygeny dispute that it galvanized the young profession. The two most important professional societies, the Ethnological Society of London and the Anthropological Society of London, were formed as a result of it, and so anthropology reached institutional status as sociology had done, vis-à-vis statistical societies. Like the debaters themselves, the societies appeared to reflect the contradictory field and embrace a wide range of political and anthropological tendencies. In reality, there were few differences between them. In 1842 the humanitarians of the Aborigine Protection Society abandoned charity for science, metamorphosing into the Ethnological Society. "Rather than 'protecting the defenceless,' it would 'record the[ir] history,'" and a resolution was passed to the effect that the best way to help aboriginals was to study them" (Stocking 1987, 244). Devoted polygenists who could not or would not disguise their racism with paternalism, such as James Hunt, found the atmosphere increasingly uncongenial; in 1863 they organized the rival Anthropological Society.[8]

In the years following the publication of Darwin's revolutionary *Origin of Species* in 1859, traditional ethnology and the newer physical anthropology were both accommodated within an evolutionary, developmental framework. Both humanitarianism and racism were ostensibly rejected in favor of a "science" separated from politics (Rainger 1978, Stocking 1987). However, the underlying structure of anthropological knowledge before and after Darwin, etymology notwithstanding, remained very much the same. Indeed, the basic lineaments of that body of knowledge resembled those of sociology; both produced a dichotomy between the intellectual or professional observer and the culturally distant, lower-class, primitive, or dark-skinned object of knowledge and power.

With such a genealogy, it is easy to see why colonizer and colonized might seek to disown or at least revise their collective past.[9] In the past twenty years a plethora of articles have appeared within the American and European anthropological establishments reassessing the interrelationship between anthropological knowledge and power.[10] A brief review of the argument waged against anthropology will outline the shape of the conflict. A reassessment of the discipline was forced upon French intellectuals in the 1950s by the struggles of the Vietnamese and the Algerians against French colonialist oppression. Spurred on both by these conflicts and by the writings of African intellectuals and poets in the negritude movement, French anthropologists could no longer ignore imperial relations, formal and informal, or harbor any hope of piecemeal reform (Clifford 1986). For American anthropologists it was the turbulent 1960s that strained a set of ethnological practices to the breaking point. In 1969 the Radical Caucus of the American Anthropological Society issued the following proclamation at their annual meeting in 1969: "Anthropology since its inception is a discipline developed alongside and within the growth of colonial and imperial powers. By what they have studied (and what they have not studied) anthropologists have assisted in, or at least acquiesced to, the goals of imperialist policy" (Hymes 1974b, 50–51). Since that time, the voices critical of anthropological practice and theory in the United States and Europe have risen dramatically to resound in the halls of academe and the fields of Samoa.

Common to most if not all, significantly, is the notion that "imperialist policy" is formulated ideationally—that is, independently of its representation in discourse. This dichotomy is quite clear, for instance, in William S. Willis's "Skeletons in the Anthropological Closet." "White rule with its color inequality," Willis writes,

> is the context in which anthropology originated and flourished, and this context has shaped the development of anthropology. The formalization of anthropology in the nineteenth century coincided with the shift from "booty" colonialism to imperialism, which stressed profit from the control, exploitation, and preservation of cheap colored workers and consumers. (1974, 122)

Willis's model emphasizes economic determinism ("the shift from 'booty' colonialism to imperialism"), as well as an indeterminate "context" ("white rule" and "color inequality"), in order to account for "the development of anthropology." What this model cannot account for, however, is the internal coherence of anthropology as a discursive phenomenon that is not simply reproductive of economic conditions, but productive of its own cultural logic.[11]

Those commentators and critics who come closest to home still shy away from investigating the connections between anthropology and middle-class hegemony in nineteenth-century England. In "Culture and Imperialism: Proposing a New Dialectic," Mina Davis Caulfield eschews economic determinism to focus instead on anthropology as one discourse among many constitutive of the self-definition of Europeans and North

Americans at large. "The ideologies of white supremacy and cultural superiority," writes Caulfield,

> have been generally regarded in the literature as rationalizations for economic and political domination and as mechanisms by which such domination is exercised. . . . they must be regarded as something more: they are cultural expressions, part of a cultural value system and important items in the cultural self-definition of West Europeans and North Americans. (1974, 198)[12]

By making anthropology a function of a "cultural value system," Caulfield renders the discipline more autonomous and less a by-product of the economic domain. She recognizes, with Edward Said, a dialectic between Western notions of the self and Western representations of the Eastern other as mediated by anthropological discourse. She fails, however, even to consider that anthropology might have been a means to establish the ideological hegemony of the middle class over the working class within England. In so denying the agency of middle-class hegemony *within* the West, Caulfield weakens her otherwise strong position.

If critiques of Victorian anthropology as a foot soldier in the wars of imperialism or orientalism are less than satisfying, the same may be said for those of feminism that are blind to all but gender as a meaningful category of history. In the 1970s, with the heady winds of feminism blowing, writers and critics brought what they considered to be a subversive logic to Victorian anthropology. Early feminist work in the history of anthropology concentrated almost exclusively on a group of texts concerned with the origin of the Victorian family, often referred to as the mother-right debate. Mother-right texts such as Maine's *Ancient Law* (1861) and Bachofen's *Das Mutterrecht* (1861) defined civilization not in political terms, as had their seventeenth- and eighteenth-century predecessors (Coward 1983, 19), but in sexual terms. Instead of inquiring into the nature of sovereign power, these texts construed the prehistory of civilization in already gendered terms: they represented power as the distribution of prerogatives and limitations between male and female or, in their terms, between patriarchy and matriarchy. In so doing, mother-right anthropology constructed a distant past in which to anchor peculiarly middle-class truths about gendered power relations within the family.

To argue against Victorian anthropology, feminist commentators relied solely on the binary logic of gender difference, itself a product of nineteenth-century anthropological thinking.[13] As a result, they began with the presupposition that the category "woman" always already bore its contemporary connotations. From this beginning feminist writers ended by reaffirming, even reauthorizing, the categorical difference between male and female produced in nineteenth-century writing, the very difference we are now striving to historicize (Conway 1972, Duffin 1978). In Elizabeth Fee's estimation, to cite one instance, anthropology's massive reassessment of the past implicit within the mother-right debate was the response of a male-dominated discipline to the threat posed by nineteenth-century feminism (1976). Fee's particular feminist model obscures, however, the crucial role of class that made both Victorian feminism and anthropology part of a single phenomenon that essentialized sex (Walkowitz 1986). Fee's position is characteristic of early feminist work in its understanding of power solely as a function of gender rather than one of class or race; early feminism itself secured the interests of class by representing itself as a matter of gender.[14]

If, however, as I argued in the previous chapter, the middle class attained cultural hegemony first and foremost through self-affirmation, then it becomes possible to articulate not only the relationship between anthropology and representations of the other, but also that between the middle-class individual (including, of course, the intellectual) and the science of man. I want to shift critical attention away from the current focus on the anthropological construction of the other, in order to determine how nineteenth-century anthropology developed the vocabulary by which middle-class culture came to know *itself* and others according to the norms of sexuality, gender, and the nucleated family.

To fully appreciate the extent to which anthropology collaborated with sociology, fiction, and psychology, it must be reconstituted in terms of a logic different than that conceived by historians of anthropology. There is little point in attempting to reconcile those who thought Adam and Eve came in a variety of colors and styles with those who did not think so, or adherents of patriarchy with matriarchalists. To enter into this debate is to assume that anthropology's contradictions indeed represent all sides of the argument; instead, I believe that they reveal a strategy whereby intellectuals agree to disagree on issues within a framework, so that the framework itself remains the more firmly in place and far-reaching in scope.[15] I view anthropology as "part of a multiplicity of discursive elements that can come into play in various strategies" in order to reveal, conceal, or enunciate the required or the forbidden—according to "who is speaking, his position of power, the institutional context in which he happens to be situated" (Foucault 1979, 100). With Foucault, I consider discourse not just a group of signs but "practices that systematically form the objects of which they speak" (1979, 49). If contemporary anthropologists have been reluctant to question their own practices closely, perhaps it is because the contradictions within nineteenth- and twentieth-century anthropology that conceal the ways in which the discourse operates also conceal its political logic from those in the profession whose subject positions have been constituted by it. Intellectuals and professionals, as

Gramsci observes, may willfully divorce their interests from those of the dominant class, preferring to see themselves with utopian vision "as autonomous and independent of the ruling social group," "clothed in their own character" (1957, 120). However much one attributes to conscious agency, the fact remains that anthropologists consistently ignore the links between their own discipline and existing hegemonies within the West, preferring to recapitulate anthropological fascination with "the rest."

THE ORIGIN OF THE FAMILY

I am convinced that when anthropological writing is understood as a discourse endowed with a political logic of its own, one feature becomes utterly clear. The language of kinship weds almost all anthropological representations of dark-skinned "savages," be they African or Guinean, ancient or modern.[16] This language functions in two interrelated ways. First, as a distinctive idiom for talking about everyone but "ourselves," kinship represents the genealogy of others not "us" and so universalizes the dehistoricized and depoliticized—hence, the "natural" "family of man." Second, the other's empirical presence, verified by ethnographic data, missionary reports, and other tales, turns into his theoretical absence (Fabian 1983) as the language of kinship construes a particularized representation of the middle-class English family.

We know the language of kinship in early modern culture was a political language connoting position, place, and power within the aristocratic community. Membership within that community rested, more than anything, upon the purity of one's blood. "Blood" was a highly metaphysical notion. The special character of the ruling-class body lay in its unsullied blood, which, most important, retained its mystical power "no matter the sex in which blood might be embodied" (Tennenhouse 1986, 20). According to its logic, the aristocratic body, above all, must remain pure. Its marriage rules and related sexual practices were governed by the twin principles of unity and identity that ensured an elite body, enclosed and pure. Practical and textual instances of these principles occur in Elizabethan and Jacobean depictions of aristocratic culture. In 1570, when Elizabeth sharply limited the number of peers in the realm, for example, she guaranteed that membership in the aristocratic community would be both highly desirable and extremely restricted. Shakespearean comedies, such as *Twelfth Night*, allow for the production of a pure political body as the characters' marriages eliminate potential threats to the aristocratic oligarchy. Shakespeare's chronicle history plays, as well as chronicle history itself, suggest kinship and kingship were one and the same. Kinship and the sexual practices associated with it were a form of power that determined political alliances as well as enmities. The stability and longevity of aristocratic rule, moreover, was predicated upon the antiquity of its ancestry and the unique character of its marriage alliances. Most important, as all these instances show, the sexual and the political were unified within the aristocratic social order. Based in the principles of unity and identity, kinship paid less heed to the logic of gender difference than it did to the metaphysical purity of the individual and the cultural body.

No one can say exactly what happened to the kinship system or why it went into decline some time in the seventeenth century. While I cannot provide a total picture of the whole process, I can speculate about how the hegemony of patrimony based on the metaphysics of blood came to its demise, suggesting something of the complex forces that eroded the aristocratic notion of sexuality even though landowning classes maintained political and economic dominance well into the eighteenth century. There is evidence that when the kinship system could no longer adequately support economic processes or political institutions, it gradually lost some of its importance. "Particularly from the eighteenth century onward," Foucault observes, "Western societies created and deployed a new apparatus which was superimposed on the previous one, and which, without completely supplanting the latter, helped to reduce its importance. . . . the deployment of sexuality" (1980, 106). Unlike alliance, sexuality looked forward to the progeny whose strength and endurance mirrored those of the class as a whole. Middle-class hegemony was not just a matter of economic dominance or ideological self-definition. It was a "physical" matter as well, attested to by the large number of works published at the end of the eighteenth century on "body hygiene, the art of longevity, ways of having healthy children and of keeping them alive as long as possible, and methods for improving the human lineage" (Foucault 1980, 125). With notions of sexuality and the healthy body, the emerging middle classes laid claim to a distinctive class "body" differentiating them both from the aristocracy and the laboring classes.

As gender replaced blood as the most revealing feature of the individual, the rules determining permissible and impermissible unions changed. As a result, the organization of the family also changed. The family became the privileged locus of affects, sentiment, and love, as well as the privileged point of development of sexuality.[17] Middle-class marriage and the family it begat ostensibly had no rules other than the dictates of the heart.[18] They were, in fact, based on separation and difference—of domestic space from political space, domestic labor from labor, leisure from work, female from male. Within early modern English culture, then, the vocabulary of kinship established boundaries and differentiated between aristocrat and nonaristocrat, pure and impure, social interior and exterior, powerful and powerless. With the gradual accession of the middle classes to cultural and economic hegemony in England, the language of kinship was contested by a new language of sexuality. Gender in this idiom became absolutely incompatible with kinship, where it had once been a subordinated factor determining human identity.

The notion of alliance did not disappear with the advent of the gender system. To cite one instance, the "social season" among the upper classes (so depicted by Jane Austen and Fanny Burney) ensured that endogamy could proceed undisturbed among successive generations. Thus kinship as well as commerce were necessary ingredients for preserving class unity. Despite the survival of such marriage practices, the notion of kinship came to serve a new purpose when it was subordinated to the demands of the gender system. This transvaluation may be clarified if we shift from marriage practices as represented in early nineteenth-century fiction to representation itself—that is, to realism. While new notions of political economy developed that located the source of class power in various places within the economic sphere, the social sciences and especially anthropology devoted their efforts to formulating a new model of kinship. It was a class- and culture-specific model to be sure, but one that appeared universal and natural. Within this new mode of class identity, kinship became a residual element that played a powerful, legitimizing role. The formation of this new family model out of older historical materials lent the emergent middle classes an *appearance* of legitimacy and permanency it would not otherwise enjoy. This feature of the hegemonic process is similar to that described by Antonio Gramsci, who writes, "every 'essential' social class emerging into history has found . . . intellectual categories which were pre-existing and which, moreover, *appeared* as representative of an historical continuity uninterrupted even by the most complicated and radical changes in social and political forms" (1957, 119, emphasis added). It is fair to say that such a legitimizing strategy is at work whenever there is the illusion of a smooth historical continuum in any cultural discourse.

Anthropology, I suggest, was one hegemonic discourse among many that gave the new ruling class the powerful right to say what was "natural" about human nature and "human" about human beings. As such, it made a voracious claim to the past and the future, to other peoples and other races. To harness this tremendous power in service of the middle class, anthropological writing had to appropriate and transform the archaic materials of the family. Only in this way could the crucial links between the new class and older and other social formations be established. Paradoxically, the language of kinship combined with the new idiom of gender to distinguish the emergent class from all other social groups by specifying its unique qualities. More specifically, anthropological writing allows one to observe the displacement of one set of signifieds by another, distinctively modern, set designating human identity. Anthropological writing transformed the language of kinship into the language of gender. This process of cultural change, as I see it, resembles that described by Michel de Certeau, in which "the same words and the same ideas are reused, but they no longer have the same meaning, they are no longer thought and organized in the same way" (1986b, 178). As sexuality displaced alliance, kinship no longer exclusively reinforced a notion of class identity based on similarity, blood, and ancestry, but supported one based on gender.

When anthropological writing embedded the language of an older English social formation within the representation of the culture of the other—the "primitive," the African, or the "Oriental"—it actually appropriated the culture of the other.[19] The language of kinship identified the history of the other with the history of the self.[20] Much the same thing happens when people read *National Geographic* and recognize themselves and their families in an account of Trobriand islanders. In such cases, anthropological language conveys a sense of human commonality, despite the obvious differences between an American family and Trobriand islanders.

The language of kinship collapses differences so that new differences may be produced. Thus, as it reemerged in the anthropological domain, kinship established the other as historically prior to the self. Because they seemed to precede the modern family, "primitive" kinship rules themselves appeared to give rise to the new field of anthropology, much as the discourse of archeology dug up the past to discover the present.[21] If the condition of the working class continually prompted social researchers into action, then the "primitive" or uncivilized character of the "native" similarly demanded investigation. In truth, it was just the other way around: anthropology controlled the other in and through representation.

PRIMITIVIZING THE PAST

To illustrate the process by which the language of sexuality displaced the language of kinship, I use two influential texts of "cultural anthropology"—John McLennan's *Primitive Marriage* (1865) and Herbert Spencer's *Principles of Sociology* (1876–96). Any number of texts would do as well—John Lubbock's *The Origin of Civilisation and the Primitive Condition of Man* (1870) or Edward Burnett Tylor's "The Matriarchal Family System" (1896) to name but two. The point, however, is not to make an exhaustive survey of the thematics of the family in anthropological writing but to isolate specific instances of a more general middle-class preoccupation with the new notion of the household, the family, and the domestic woman that divorced the category of gender from the political world and situated it in the domain of nature. Since anthropological texts, like those of the social researchers, are by and large products of middle-class intellectuals despite individual ties and localized interests, it is fair to say that their languages behave in an identical fashion.

To insist that both *Primitive Marriage* and *Principles of Sociology* revise an earlier understanding of kinship in the service of gender difference is to unite two voices that are often considered antagonistic in the larger enterprise of middle-class hegemony. In the annals of anthropological history, McLennan is considered a "founding father" of the discipline,[22] while Spencer occupies a relatively "marginal" position. Historian of anthropology George Stocking insists that despite his tremendous influence on British intellectual life in general, Herbert Spencer was marginal both to his contemporary community of British anthropology and to the tradition that developed from it (1987). Stocking leads one to expect that *Primitive Marriage* and *Principles of Sociology* have little in common because they originate in domains of knowledge since divided into separate disciplines. Thus their analysis is incompatible with the demands of intellectual history, or the history of ideas, which require the historian to identify thought with other thought within a disciplinary continuum that disregards the vicissitudes of history, culture, and class. Because intellectual history transcends history in a very literal way, it is impossible for Stocking to understand these textual artifacts as parts of the same determined moment in history. Yet only by dissolving the formal boundaries between text and text and between texts and contexts can one ever hope to discover the way gender is an instrument of class.

Primitive Marriage and *Principles of Sociology* return repeatedly to a set of four interrelated notions—exogamy/endogamy, polyandry, primitive promiscuity, incest—that illustrate the displacement of kinship by the idea of gender.[23] What the various notions share, I argue, is the sudden disassociation of sexual from political content; thus occurs the equally abrupt denial of political authority for the social fact of gender. While each notion attests to the redefinition of kinship by gender, each is also a testament to older preoccupations with the purity of the physical or social body. I believe that the four notions constitute sites where the political language of kinship is turned into the stuff of nature and primitivized.

In *Primitive Marriage* (1865), John McLennan recounts the obstacles he confronted investigating the topic most fascinating to him. Not only "is the record from which our facts have to be drawn" "imperfect and unconnected," he complains, but those facts are so "sparsely scattered" over a "wide field" as to make their compilation next to impossible. So he laments:

> while on matters of no moment they enlarge *ad nauseam*. But, too often they have nothing to tell. Skirting a coastline the traveller sees natives at points here and there, and can describe their dress and personal appearance, of their habits he is as ignorant as a child of the free life of the beasts he sees in a caravan. Where the opportunities of observation are better, the observer often does not know what to look for. (40)[24]

It is significant that an eighteenth-century traveler could not "see" what the nineteenth-century observer sees. To McLennan and his contemporaries, neither the truth of primitive cultures nor the prehistory of his own is to be found on the ornately decorated surface of the body. It "remains unwritten" in a history of other races (1865, 65).[25]

Before the word, McLennan implies, there were males and females, and there was sex. Yet to talk about sexual relations in primitive cultures, he must find the right words. He does so by coining two new terms—exogamy and endogamy.[26] Simply put, to be "exogamous" meant to have sexual relations with someone unlike the self and to be "endogamous" meant to have them with someone like the self. McLennan's vocabulary sets up a new principle of othering based upon the innate "truth" of the sexual self. Bolstered by middle-class incursions into the streets of Manchester and the far corners of the empire, this principle gained strength and gradually supplanted an older notion of otherness defined by one's relative position inside or outside the aristocratic community.

It is crucial to understand that the notion of exogamy/endogamy allows McLennan, and those colleagues who subsequently adopted his formulation, to talk about the disposition of always already gendered bodies throughout history and around the world by making sexual attraction the underlying principle of all social formations. Thus, it established the hegemony of middle-class sexuality in three interrelated ways. First, exogamy/endogamy produces only one kind of social division—male and female—within the family and the community. Second, according to this logic familial relationships are identified as the model for and incitement to sexual desire, making the nucleated family the locus of sexuality. Finally, and most important for my purposes, the concept radically disrupts, if not entirely destroys, the coherence of sexual and political relations that justified the early modern system of alliance. Let us consider more closely the manner in which this notion functions.

Both *Primitive Marriage* and *Principles of Sociology* assert that the modern family originated in an inarticulate, disordered mass. "In the earliest groups of men," Spencer explains:

there cannot have been any established rules about marriage. *Unions of sexes must have preceded all social laws.* The rise of a social law implies a certain preceding continuity of social existence; and this preceding continuity of social existence implies the reproduction of successive generations. Hence, reproduction entirely unregulated by interdicts, must be taken as initial. (1898, 628, emphasis added)

If one compares Spencer's vision of what is essentially the pre-Fallen world with Milton's in *Paradise Lost*, it is possible to see the logic of gender overtaking that of alliance. To Milton the intermingling of undifferentiated bodies occurs in heaven. When Adam questions the Angel about the sexual relations of angels in heaven,[27] the Angel replies:

> Whatever pure thou in the body enjoy'st
> (And pure thou wert created) we enjoy
> In eminence, and obstacles find none
> Of membrane, joint, or limb, exclusive bars;
> Easier than Air with Air, if Spirits embrace,
> Total they mix, *Union of Pure with Pure*
> Desiring; nor restrain'd conveyance need
> As Flesh to mix with Flesh, or Soul with Soul.
>
> (7.1.622–29, emphasis added)

The ideal intermingling of essences that is Milton's heaven is a figure for the ideal union within the aristocratic community—the "Union of Pure with Pure." This goal of alliance to retain the homogeneity of the group is transformed into anarchic, presocial disorder in Spencer's depiction.[28]

In this earliest "stage," according to McLennan, a notion of "blood ties" gives way to a "system of kinship" among the members of the group. "Previously individuals had been affiliated not to persons, but to some group," he states:

> The new idea of blood-relationship would more readily demonstrate the group to be composed of kindred that it would evolve a special system of blood-ties between certain of the individuals in the group. The members of a group would now have become brethren. . . . The development of the idea of *blood relationship* into a *system of kinship*, must have been a work of time . . . (1865, 64–65, emphasis added)

"Blood" and "kinship" are disassociated precisely as they take on new meanings in this figuration. The idea of "blood" informed the aristocratic body with a purity and uniqueness mystically connecting it to an ancient genealogy. As a consequence, kinship defined and was determined by one's relative position within the pure community. In profound contrast, here the signifier "blood" comes to stand for a notion of *individuated, biological* similarity. In other words, "blood-ties" are said to exist "between certain of the individuals in the group." At the same time, the archaic meaning of "blood," once synonymous with "kinship," is transposed into the definition of "kinship." Notice, moreover, that this semantic transference is matched by a diminution in the social significance of kinship organizations. While "kinship" itself evokes an earlier England, in McLennan's new formulation it signifies merely a vague "affiliation" to "some group." I stress here that this massive redefinition of the family must be understood as equivalent to the definition of the middle class and the rise to hegemony of its self-definition. As I suggested earlier, we cannot examine this form of power as power because this class- and cultural-specific definition locates the family in nature. As a natural unit within the social world, the middle-class family seems virtually impervious to historical or political interrogation.

Although "blood" and "kinship" were once part of the same semiotic universe, McLennan tore them asunder and reinvested them with new and opposite meanings in the service of the new family model. Yet despite the abrupt disassociation, each term retains elements of its former meaning. This semiotic confusion is evident again in Spencer's narrative of the primal scene, which closely resembles McLennan's version. "Though they [the horde] have some common interests, with *some vague notion of general kinship*," he writes, "there lacks that element of strength arising from the interests within groups *distinctly related by blood*" (1898, 649, emphasis added). Note that Spencer describes kinship relations in an imprecise manner, while he defines blood relations in increasingly specific terms, thus broadening the semantic distance between the two formerly unified concepts. In contrast to those groups united by "some vague notion of general kinship," groups related by blood share "distinct" interests in common.

In this first "stage" of civilization, according to the logic of gender, social and sexual disorder are completely equivalent. "In the loose groups of men first formed," Spencer writes, "there is no established order of any kind: everything is indefinite, unsettled. If the relations of men to one another are undetermined, so are the relations of men to women. Like birds or beasts, they pair off according to fancy" (1898, 614). McLennan's treatise goes a step further when it identifies the primal scene with the scene in the city, where "savages are unrestrained by any sense of delicacy from a copartnery in sexual enjoyments; and, indeed, in the civilised state, the sin of *great cities* shows that there are no natural restraints sufficient to hold men back from grosser copartneries" (1865, 69, emphasis added). Chief among the "grosser copartneries" for Spencer is incest, the discussion of which provides another instance of the shift from the political language of alliance to the depoliticized idiom of gender. Of the primal horde, he writes: "Still more are we shown that regular relations of the sexes are results of evolution, and that the sentiments upholding them have been gradually established, on finding how little regard is paid to those limitations which blood-relationships dictate to the civilized" (1898, 618). Yet the primary example he offers to support his argument comes straight from the aristocrat civilization of ancient Egypt, where surely "incestuous" unions were consummated out of the purely political desire to perpetuate the ruling family at any cost.[29]

Most astonishing in this anthropological act of historical appropriation is its erasure of the kinship system from the history of England. Anthropology, that is, rewrites history by relegating the relationship between sexual and political alliance, a very real feature of English aristocratic culture, to the history of the ethnic or racial other. In effect, anthropological writing primitivizes other people's past to legitimate the English middle-class present. In *Principles of Sociology*, to note but one example of this strategy, Spencer declares that "the *marital relations* like the *political relations*, have gradually evolved; there did not at first exist those ideas and feelings which among civilized nations give to marriage its sanctity" (1898, 616). One sees here, apart from the familiar Victorian tendency to moralize, the remarkable way in which the distinction between "marital relations" and "political relations" becomes a feature of so-called "civilized nations," thus differentiating them from their primitive counterparts. Furthermore, Spencer dismantles these two forms of social relations only to reassemble them according to another logic. He brings them together again only to mark the difference between "civilized" nations, those that structurally separate politics from marriage, and those presumably "uncivilized" nations in which marital and political alliances remain as one.

We have seen how the political language of kinship is transformed into the material of nature and primitivized as anthropology produces a division between the interdependent cultural functions of the political and the sexual. This division introduces a new distinction between ties of blood and those of biology. As new definitions of the family get used against older ruling classes and other races, the social fact of gender is shifted from the political domain of kinship to the natural domain. We also noted how the anthropological history of the ethnic or racial other incorporates and transforms the history of the middle-class family. There is, however, one last strategy these texts use to undermine the logic of alliance and so conceal the logic of gender. They attack the social concepts of homogeneity and purity, hitherto invoked to maintain the purity of the aristocratic body. Unlike the logic of alliance, that of gender demands sexual differentiation between bodies that must also circulate freely inside and outside the family. In order to naturalize these culture- and class-specific demands of the gender system, both McLennan and Spencer go to great lengths to imagine the disruption of the initial homogeneity of the "primal horde." McLennan constructs a fictional scene of female infanticide that, he claims, deprives the men of the group sufficient females to mate. When they are forced to look elsewhere, the "capture of women" commences and "foreign" females are introduced into the horde for the first time. For Spencer, the *Sturm und Drang* of primitive warfare initiates the capture of foreign "concubines" or "wives" and so accomplishes the same disruption. "The taking of women," he writes, "is but a part of this process of spoiling the vanquished. Women are prized as wives, as concubines, as drudges; and, the men having been killed, the women are carried off along with other moveables. Everywhere among the uncivilized we find this" (1898, 632). In neither case does the introduction of "foreign" females render the group heterogenous immediately. Until kinship relations are recognized, the children of these females, according to McLennan, simply belong to the horde. Only with the recognition of matrilineage are the children seen as foreign "stock," which reintroduces endogamy.

DISORDERLY MOTHERS

It is significant that *Primitive Marriage* contains two contradictory scenes of the matrilineal recognition, which introduce two opposing figures of the mother—the mother as disorder and the mother as order. Such representations of the female demonstrate the way in which the gender system was made, however unwittingly, as a means of putting gender both first and last. Paradoxically, alliance is located in the past only so that it may be remodeled as an earlier, more primitive version of the modern gender system. To do this, nineteenth-century discourses of "man" put tremendous symbolic weight on females. The first account of the mother blames female sexual disorder, both "promiscuity" and "polyandry," for the "uncertainty of fatherhood" that "led to the system of kinship through mothers only" (1865, 71). The second account, in contrast, credits the innate sentimental bond between mother and child with the power to provoke their mutual recognition. Thus the following moving scene of recognition occurs: "when a system of kinship led the hordes to look on the children of their foreign women as belonging to the stocks of their mothers; that is, when the *sentiments* which grew up with the system of kinship became so strong as to overmaster the *old filiation* to the group . . . of the children born within it" (1865, 92–93, emphasis added). Here the slippage in the term "kinship" produces a new synthesis of the aristocratic notion of the family ("old filiation") united by blood with the middle-class idea of affiliation ("sentiments"). At the same time, McLennan reauthorizes incestuous unions that were previously forbidden by incorporating them into the social system as endogamy renewed. Thus *Primitive Marriage* represents the prehistory of the middle-class family as regulated and restrained by the demands of the alliance system, and as incited by desires encouraged under the system of gender.

The matrilineal moment is represented as one of sexual confusion and illicit combination. "Not to assume that the progress of various races of men from savagery has been a uniform process," McLennan hypothesizes, "we shall be justified in believing that more or less of *promiscuity* in the connection of the sexes, and a system of *kinship through females* only have subsisted among races of men among which no traces of them remain" (1865, 66, emphasis added). It can be no accident that "motherright" is firmly associated with the figures of primitive promiscuity, for out of this set of associations again emerges the negative figure of the mother—the mother as disorder. The practice of polyandry at this stage is further evidence for the disorder of matrilineage, which diminishes as the moment of paternal recognition approaches. "The first advance from a general promiscuity," writes McLennan, "would naturally be to a promiscuity less general—to arrangements between small sets of men to attach themselves to a particular woman" (1865, 70). The text contrasts this "rude species" of promiscuous polyandry in which "the husbands are not relations" with "the less rude polyandry in which the husbands are brothers" (1865, 71). Admittedly McLennan cites several instances, such as Levirate marriage under Hebrew law, where polyandry was serial rather than concurrent and constituted a legal and political obligation ensuring the succession of an heir. Nevertheless, polyandry is depoliticized as soon as it is classified as a species of sexual promiscuity, however less "rude." Spencer's *Principles of Sociology*, on the other hand, does not demure from explicitly connecting polyandry with female promiscuity. "Promiscuity," Spencer declares, "may be called indefinite polyandry" (1898, 654). With the advent of the patrilineage system, according to both McLennan and Spencer, sexual disorder diminishes or disappears entirely. This anthropological representation of the past is crucial to the construction of the gender system. Men must rule women, not to create or maintain economic or political affiliations but to manage individual bodies. When the past is represented as the disorderly disposition of bodies through time, the modern notion of population management becomes nascent within it. The past then creates the need for modern families and for institutions that intervene on their behalf when all else fails.

If one's object were to see nineteenth-century anthropological writing as a "reflection" of Victorian "patriarchy" and its reconstruction of the past as but one more attempt "to show women are inferior to men" (Duffin 1978, 58), then one might stop at this point. However, the means by which the primitive family arrives at the point of organizing itself through a patrilineal system challenges those who represent females as victims in a history dominated by males. For the decisive actor in this event and the agent of cultural transformation is not the male but the female; the figure of the mother as disorder gives way to her positive counterpart, the mother as order. It is the orderly mother who ensures the requisite sexual stability and order necessary for the recognition of patrilineage. "A system of relationship through fathers could only be formed," McLennan reasons, "after a good deal of reflection upon the fact of paternity. . . . There could be no *system* of kinship through males if paternity was usually, or in a great proportion of cases, uncertain" (1865, 65). It is *female choice* not male prowess that imposes order and so brings about the decisive conditions for the recognition of paternity. "The requisite degree of certainty," he continues, "can be had only when the mother is appropriated to a particular man as his wife, or to men of one blood as wife, and when *women thus appropriated are usually found faithful to their lords*" (1865, 65, emphasis added). Female sexual choice represents both the culmination of this argument and the crucial moment of "civilization." In the hands of the female rested the fate of civilization as middle-class culture depicted it; her choice determined either the society's return to "anarchy" or its advance to "culture." Here I want to emphasize one point. Anthropology can bring about the transition from disorder to order, from anarchy to culture, only by using the figure of the mother to describe one thing and its opposite. That is, the libidinous mother represents the sexual disorder of the matrilineal household, while the docile and desirable mother stands for the sexual order of patrilineage. In both cases the gendered identity of this foundational figure is assumed as its most basic characteristic. "Primitive" social organizations are thus inscribed with gendered features from the very beginning of discursive and historical time.

WHEN A WOMAN IS NOT A WOMAN

If nineteenth-century anthropology represented the accomplishments of the "good" female to and for middle-class culture, it also reminded its readers that the bourgeois female and with her the middle class itself were always in imminent danger of slipping back into the chaotic, sensual depths from which they had emerged. Recall how sociological writing relied for moral authority on the contrast between the domestic female and the prostitute. Sexual difference for women was not constructed in opposition to males, but in distinction from females whose sexual conduct marked them as "not female" (Kaplan 1985). This strategy finds its anthropological expression in representations of the African female and of the prostitute. Both are "not female" for one of two reasons: first, they exhibit female sexual features so overdetermined as to make them "masculine," as in the case of the African; second, they exhibit blatantly "masculine" characteristics, as in that of the prostitute. Not only did anthropological writing express "positive femininity" through "hostile and denigrating representations of women" (Kaplan 1985, 166) but it drew a thin line between the primitive and the degraded female.[30] In this section, then, I concentrate on the manner in which anthropological writing constructed sexual difference by virtually effacing female sexual features. To do so, I examine two texts that focus on the African female and the prostitute respectively.

In 1810 a woman by the name of "Sarah Bartmann" or "Saat-Jee," servant of a Dutch farmer near Capetown, was brought to London exhibition at Picadilly. Known to the English and their Continental neighbors as the "Hottentot Venus," Saat-Jee attracted curious crowds from miles around London. One might well ask what they were so eager to see. Not only were they fascinated by this "creature who straddled that dreaded boundary between human and animal" (Gould 1982, 22), but they were amazed and affrighted by the sight of her naked body with its enlarged buttocks and elongated genital flap.[31] After five years of ignominious display throughout Europe, Saat-Jee died in Paris at the age of twenty-five. Even then she would not rest in peace, for before burial her body was autopsied by the well-known French anatomist Georges Cuvier. "The audience which had paid to see her buttocks and had fantasized about the uniqueness of her genitalia when she was alive could, after her death and dissection, examine both." As Sander Gilman explains, "Cuvier presented to 'the Academy the genital organs of this woman prepared in a way so as to allow one to see the nature of the labia' " (1985a, 213–16).[32]

This lurid performance of anatomy was enacted upon the bodies of both male and female Africans throughout the nineteenth century. Gilman offers one explanation for this curiosity, arguing that sexual deviance was necessary and sufficient proof of a more general racial deviance. "The polygenetic argument is the basis for all the dissections of these women," he writes: "If their sexual parts could be shown to be inherently different, this would be a sufficient sign that the blacks were a separate (and, needless to say, lower) race. Similar arguments had been made about the nature of all blacks' (and not just Hottentots') genitalia, but almost always concerning the female" (1985a, 216). He goes on to ex-

plain that sexual features are semantic signs of " 'primitive' sexual appetite and activity," in which "the link established between the ill, the bes-
tial, and the freak (pathology, biology, and medicine)" was embodied
(218). These are significant links in a formidable ideological chain. However, Gilman's answer only raises another question—what was so interesting about the female in particular? Why did female sexual parts excite
the attention of numerous authors, while descriptions of male genitalia
were conspicuously absent from most accounts of such proceedings? In
partial answer to this question, I turn to the record of another dissection,
one performed by English physical anthropologists William Flower and
James Murie.

Two children of the "Bushman" or "Bosjesman" race, a ten-year-old
and a twelve-year-old, followed Saat-Jee to England in 1853 to entertain
and educate London audiences. A few years later, the boy died and was
buried in a cemetery in South Wales. The girl survived until June 16,
1864, when she too succumbed to the ardors of life as a spectacle and
died of "pulmonary phthisis," popularly known as consumption. Before
receiving burial, her body "was sent to the Royal College of Surgeons for
the purpose of dissection" (Flower and Murie 1867, 190). There it fell
into the hands of Flower and his assistant Murie, who performed the
dissection, the results of which were published in the 1867 volume of the
Journal of Anatomy and Physiology under the title "Account of the Dissection of a Bushwoman."

What is remarkable about the case is that this anonymous young
woman, as well as those before her, were objects of knowledge and observation in life as well as in death. That fact does not even register with the
authors, who dismiss her as but a "single instance," the value of which
"may be considered by itself as insignificant, and yielding little result"
(1867, 189). To these men of science, "it is . . . only by an accumulation
of such instances that the materials for the foundation of a scientific system of ethnology can be formed" (1867, 189). Perhaps even more dis-
turbing is the insistent gaze immobilizing the body of the "primitive"
female, so similar to that fixed upon the prostitute by inspectors empowered by the Contagious Diseases Acts. Anatomy itself obviously held a
special fascination for anthropology. To my earlier suggestion that the
anatomy enabled anthropology to produce a notion both of "universal
man" and of white European, I must add another dimension. The grim
fascination exerted upon audiences, be they the eager crowds of Picadilly
or the more solemn faces of health inspectors, by the genitalia of the African woman was reproduced in the anatomy. These gazes sexualize the
body and suggest that the secrets of culture are located in certain parts of
the body—more specifically, in the sexual parts of the female. Displaying
the genitals of females both living and dead, African and prostitute, illus-

trates a cultural logic that used female sexuality as both problem and solution, question and answer. To say this, however, is to do little more than rephrase the question with which we began. Yet if we consider that anthropology effaced ethnic and racial difference by producing sexual difference, we can understand why the female was the focus of the anthropologists' gaze.

With this in mind, it is easy to see how "Account of the Dissection of a Bushwoman" fulfills two interrelated purposes. The report is blatantly racist in its determination to produce physical "evidence" of white superiority, yet as the measurements of the "Negro" body are compared with those of the "beautiful female figure of European origins" (Flower and Murie 1867, 194) something else happens as well. Even as the account uses the female to secure racial boundaries, it produces a standard of "femaleness" from which the "primitive" female deviates not from a *lack* of female features, but from an *excess* of them.

After cursorily surveying the entire body, the gaze of the examiners is drawn to the sexual organs, which become the privileged site of their investigation. The external features of the vagina are particularly fascinating to the scientific gaze, the description of which is especially important here. In clinical language, Flower and Murie describe "the clitoris of moderate size, but with a *well-developed prepuce,* and far more *conspicuously situated* than in the European female, chiefly on account of the want of prominence of the labia majora" (1867, 207, emphasis added). Most obvious about this narration is, of course, the comparative analysis of the European and the non-European female. However, obscured by medico-technical language is the associative link between the clitoris and the penis made by the term *prepuce.* Prior to the nineteenth century, prepuce referred solely to the foreskin, or "the loose fold of integuement which covers the glans penis. . . . " Around the middle of the century the meaning changed, interestingly enough, to include the protective skin of the clitoris.[33] It is not only the "well-developed prepuce" that marks the African female as "not female," but its conspicuous visibility, which so over-determines the clitoris as to discursively identify it with the penis. The Bushwoman's genitals may have looked exactly like a penis to Euro-white observers. The crucial point that needs stressing, however, is that this representation of female sexual "abnormalities" heightens the contrast between males and certain females precisely as it cancels out sexual difference between male and female. The "inside," in other words, is too big and protrudes "outside," violating the distinction between male and female, the domestic and the political, inscribed on the body. Also note the resemblance to the grotesque body, characterized by Bakhtin, where protuberances and permeability alike mark the unenclosed, insufficiently individuated body. "Account of the Dissection of a Bushwoman" concludes, for emphasis, by recounting yet another instance of the elision of difference, this time of a "Hottentot" mother whose labia minora were so long and exaggerated that she could grasp each side and wrap them around her back, where they met at the base of her spine. "I am now perfectly convinced," Flower writes to his great satisfaction, "that the organization is natural and congenital, and not produced, as has been supposed, by the degraded and filthy habits of the tribe" (1867, 208). In this backhanded fashion, then, he attributes to nature the power of culture to create and maintain the sexual difference just engendered by the text itself.

Having begun with *London Labour and the London Poor*, a sociological representation of female sexual disorder, I end with its anthropological equivalent. If Henry Mayhew could be said to have a Continental counterpart, it would certainly be Cesare Lombroso. In the annals of criminal anthropology, Lombroso is famed for his theory of *l'uomo deliquente*, or the criminal man. Lombroso's genealogy of criminality combined the best and the worst of anthropometry and evolutionary theory; as such it is another brilliant example of physical anthropology gone awry. In *L'homme Criminel* (1887), Lombroso argues that criminal behavior is not only an hereditary ill but a Tylorean "survival" from the primitive past. Briefly, Lombroso maintains that criminals are evolutionary throwbacks whose heredity contains the seeds of an unfortunate ancestral past. In some of these individuals the past comes alive again, driving them to behave as a normal ape or savage would. Such behavior, however, is considered criminal in civilized society. Fortunately, born criminals could be identified because they bear anatomical signs of their apishness (Gould 1981).

Lombroso's theory presupposes psychological thinking, thus linking anthropology to that late nineteenth-century speciality. Both disciplines presuppose that germs of an ancestral past lie dormant within us, waiting for the right moment to show themselves. It is easy to understand from this summary how sociological representations of the working classes, based in less precise notions of heredity and biology, gained considerable power and authority in alliance with physical anthropology and evolutionary theory. From the massive amounts of anthropometric data collected throughout the century came the telltale signs of criminal degeneration. Lombroso identified both physical abnormalities—greater skull thickness, large jaws, preeminence of face over cranium, low narrow forehead, darker skin, and such social disabilities as speech characterized by high levels of onomatopoeia similar to that of children and savages and the presence of tatoos, to name but a few. If such criminal stigmata strike a familiar chord, it is no wonder. Thanks to the foundation laid by Lombroso and his colleagues, this typology of the "shady character" has passed into the domain of the cliché, where it still dominates the popular imagination today.

It should come as no surprise that Lombroso subsequently turned his attention to the more sensational phenomenon of female criminality. In 1889, with his son-in-law Guillaume Ferrero, he published *La Donna Deliquente, La Prostituta e La Donna Normale*, only a portion of which was translated into English as *The Female Offender* in 1895. Among the untranslated sections, *Criminologia femminile* is particularly interesting for the way in which it construes the female other by collapsing differences in time and space. It is enough to consider briefly the chapter headings to understand how their anthropo-logic links the working-class female with the non-European female, and both with nature. *Criminologia femminile* begins by cataloging the "crimes" of female animals (*Il delitto delle femmine animali*). This is less astonishing than it may seem, since nature becomes the sole referent for the representations of working-class and non-European women to follow. Lombroso may then attribute the crimes of savage and primitive women (in *Il delitto delle donne selvaggio e primitive*) and those of the prostitute (in *Prostituzione*) entirely to nature rather than to culture. Implicit in this figuration, too, is the warning that the "normal" female is but one step away from the abyss of sensuality and criminality lying deep within her.

Armed with twenty-six skulls, five skeletons, and an unspecified number of photographs, Lombroso continues his investigation of the female offender. As enamoured of numbers as his contemporaries, he measures every facet of the skulls, including their "cranial and orbital capacity, facial angles, nasal index, height of face, and weight of lower jaw" (1895, 85). Well schooled in the science of observation, he diligently searches the photographs for the offending signs of moral and physical degeneracy. Not surprisingly, among "female offenders" it is the prostitute who exhibits the most abnormalities. "Almost all anomalies occur more frequently in prostitutes than in female offenders," Lombroso concludes, "and both classes have a larger number of the characteristics of degeneration than normal women" (1895, 85). Of the anomalous features Lombroso identifies—"moles, hairiness, prehensile feet, virile larynx, large jaws and cheekbone"—several are primarily "masculine" in character; in fact, he even admits as much. "Very often, in women," he writes after closely examining photographs of prostitutes, "the type is disguised by youth with its absence of wrinkles and the plumpness which conceals the size of the jaw and cheekbones, thus softening the *masculine* and savage features" (1895, 97, emphasis added). When is a woman not a woman, one might ask? When she is represented as a figure whose "femaleness" is excessive or erased or diluted by mixture with masculine features. That is, while the figure of the non-European female was "not female" because of the *presence* of exaggerated sexual features, it must be stressed that the figure of the prostitute is similarly "unfemale" precisely because of the *absence* of female characteristics.

It might be concluded that anthropological writing revised the notion of the family to make it both an instrument of alliance and the center of sexual desire. At the same time as it generated a new vocabulary for representing the middle-class family, anthropology assigned certain features of middle-class history to the history of the other. When anthropological writing contrasted the "bad" female, disruptive of familial and sexual order, with the "good" female, the upholder of that order, it pinpointed female choice as the decisive factor in the transition from nature to culture. Anthropology reminded the middle class that the order and stability achieved through good female desire were in constant jeopardy from the bad female, whose features it construed as other than "female." Most important, anthropological writing helped middle-class women to understand their gender as a contradictory phenomenon precisely because it was both crucial to a woman's identity and the gravest threat to it. Being female meant (as it does today) constant self-regulation; neither too little nor too much femininity would do.

Chapter 4

DOMESTIC FICTIONS IN THE HOUSEHOLD:

WUTHERING HEIGHTS

> Literature is itself a heterogenous discourse, which appropri-
> ates, contextualizes, and comments on other
> "languages" of class and gender.
> (*Cora Kaplan, "Pandora's Box"*)

> The novel's realistic bodying forth of a world is to provide
> representational or representative norms selected from
> among many possibilities. Thus the novel acts to
> include, state, affirm, normalize and naturalize
> some things, values and ideas, but not others.
> (*Edward Said, "Reflections on American
> 'Left' Literary Criticism"*)

CHARLOTTE BRONTË, responding to the outraged critical attack upon her dead sister Emily's *Wuthering Heights*, reidentified
its author as a female in 1850. When the first edition appeared in
1847, reviewers of that sensational book condemned it, calling it "coarse
and loathsome," "strange," and "repellant." *Wuthering Heights*, it
seems, had transgressed the borders of good taste and decorum, and in so
doing it had jeopardized its fictional authority. To rehabilitate Emily
Brontë's novel, Charlotte turned to a tradition, forged in the first half of
the nineteenth century, that had already established a female authorial
voice and subject matter as an inviolable cultural domain. Charlotte's
task in the 1850 biographical notice and preface to *Wuthering Heights*
was to secure its place and that of its author within that domain. Under
Charlotte's ministrations, *Wuthering Heights* was transformed into the
product of a distinctively female imagination.[1] It is significant that the
Emily Brontë of the notice is represented as radically separate from the
outside world much as earlier sociological descriptions of the industrial
poor had regarded the self as an interior space distinct from an exterior
world. In this case, however, Charlotte defined that inside as a distinctively female place. In her words, Emily hid "a secret power and fire"
under an "unsophisticated culture, inartificial tastes and an unpretending
outside." Emily Brontë, her sister concluded, possessed "no worldly

wisdom"; in fact, "an interpreter ought always to have stood between her and the world" (1847, 35–36).[2] Novel and author, then, appeared to have no referent in the outside world and no relationship to their historical moment. Charlotte did not trace the source of Emily's (and Ann's) creative powers to imaginations that were shaped through contact with the external world. Unlike the poetic imagination described by Wordsworth, her sisters, according to Charlotte, "had no thought of filling their pitchers at the well-spring of other minds; they always wrote from the *impulse of nature*, the dictates of *intuition*, and from such stores of observation as their *limited experience* had enabled them to amass" (1847, 36, emphasis added). This passage locates Emily's fiction, and by extension all women's writing, in the natural world; thus emptied of cultural or historical features, it seems a product of timeless emotions alone.

Charlotte Brontë's representation of *Wuthering Heights* and its author still dominate Brontë scholarship. Encouraged to look solely to the secrets of the imagination as the key to unraveling its mysteries, critics most often address the novel in those terms.[3] Before 1850, reviewers who were not alienated by the novel praised it for its "unconscious strength," and "rugged power." After Charlotte's disclosure, however, a female commentator labeled the novel "odiously and abominably pagan," while G. H. Lewes described *Wuthering Heights* in 1850 as "sombre, brutal, yet true" and found it strange that such a book, so coarse "even for men," could be the product of a "retiring," "solitary," "consumptive girl" (Allott 1970, 68). The novel was further removed from a cultural or historical tradition and rooted in the pathology of an individual woman. Thus Derek Traversi could still maintain in 1949 that "concentration" and not "maturity" was the "distinctive quality" of the book (Allott 1970, 166). Even more recently, J. Hillis Miller found that "the brilliant stratagems which Emily Brontë devised in *Wuthering Heights* to persuade the reader to accept the world of her novel are striking and even pathetic proof of the powerful need which drove her to communicate her visions" (1963, 163).

To point to Charlotte Brontë's preface to *Wuthering Heights* or to subsequent critical treatment of the novel is not to identify a problem but to outline its parameters and those of this chapter. By imaginatively elaborating the realm of the individual, the family, and the household, *Wuthering Heights* naturalized the notion of an "inside" drained of the materials of the "outside"—social, political, and historical content. In other words, *Wuthering Heights* effectively took itself out of history; Charlotte Brontë and subsequent critics have simply capitalized on that split, elaborating and replicating it in their own work.[4] Since, by definition, it is not in and of the stuff of history, the novel itself cannot explain the nature and importance of the change that detached the novel from history. One might look, however, to a different kind of history that can apprehend the very mechanism of disjunction and enclosure as history, and to a different kind of literary criticism that considers the novel as an agent and document of that history. To situate the novel in cultural history, one must, I believe, consider its role in producing the reproductive realm—that of the individual, the home, the family, and sexual desire—apart and distinct from economic and political matters.

"Inside" *Wuthering Heights*, then, what one encounters is not really "fiction" at all, but rather rhetorical strategies that are also cultural strategies. These organize and make sense of the individual, the home, and the family as gendered and enclosed "spaces."[5] The rhetoric of fiction, I argue further, also organizes the human sciences. For Gaskell and Kay Shuttleworth, McLennan and Spencer, this rhetoric turns social difference on the part of a class or race into forms of deviance that originate in the depths of the self or in the conditions of personal life. More than that, like the official scientific discourses of otherness, fiction relocates sexual desire within the female. It delineates both the "normal" domestic female and the deviant female, who threatens the reproduction of individual, family, and household. Thus, if we reject the distinction between fiction as "inner" text and an "outer" context that becomes "real" by implication, the "inside" of Brontë's novel takes on a surprising resemblance to an "outside" composed of the other discourses and practices of the century. Let me outline briefly the shape of such an interaction between *Wuthering Heights* and nonliterary sources.

As the characters in the novel are doubled, split, transformed, and enclosed within different bodies and houses, "new" figures emerge cleansed of all historic and economic identifiers; what remains are gendered features alone. The main female figure Catherine, for instance, is rewritten into a new "female" body and self with the birth of the daughter who replaces her. In the figure of the daughter, we discover a female who closely resembles the domestic woman described by sociologists. Thus, within this fictional life cycle classed and gendered role prescriptions found within another discourse are normalized, naturalized, and affirmed. Heathcliff, the "other" character of class and race, however, is written out of the story entirely. At a certain moment one realizes he is no longer the dark, attractive lover, but a demon akin to Young's barbarians—never sleeping, never eating, with eyes that do not close even after death. At the same time, the novel confines its characters to similarly differentiated, divided, and enclosed physical and familial "spaces." It does so by manipulating the signifiers of kinship and gender used in anthropological discourse. To create a modern family, the novel must first dismantle an older historical family model responsive to the demands of blood. Only then can the second generation of lovers, Cathy and Hareton, constitute a family organized according to the principle of gendered sexuality.

The body, too, undergoes similar transformations. Catherine Earnshaw is initially identified with the collective, undifferentiated body of the world, to use Bakhtin's figure. By the end of the novel, a metaphysical essence displaces the physical body, and a thoroughly domesticated daughter appears in place of the untamable Catherine. The hermaphroditic unity of Catherine and Heathcliff is replaced by the "male" and "female" of Cathy and Hareton. Passionate desire is not laid to rest in the grave with Catherine and Heathcliff, however. Rather, it takes its place at the very center of both the self and the nuclear family finally formed by Cathy and Hareton. This form of desire also reappears in the ghosts and apparitions of the unearthly lovers that haunt the text.

If one reads *Wuthering Heights* as an historical document, one might understand Brontë's inclusion of several "Catherines" in the text as her resistance to the middle-class forms of desire that the novel calls into being. There is, of course, the "living" Catherine, but also the female child monster desperate to enter the Heights, the disintegrating face of death revealed to Heathcliff when he lifts the coffin lid, and the final apparition of the unearthly couple that magnetizes one's attention at the end of the novel. If one insists on reading the novel in the tradition of Charlotte Brontë and subsequent critics, that is, as a portrait of the pathology of an individual woman, then these recurrent figures must be considered part of a domain of fantasy and belief originating within a damaged female. Read backward from within a culture that believes unquestioningly in such a domain, now called the "psyche" or the "unconscious" in the language of psychology, *Wuthering Heights* seems to confirm, justify, and reauthorize that belief.

I would like to suggest an alternative model, one that implicates the history of psychological thinking in fiction itself. Briefly, psychology was not a new discipline when Emily Brontë wrote *Wuthering Heights* in 1848. It had existed, mostly as a custodial treatment of the insane, at least since the end of the previous century. Yet some time around the middle of the nineteenth century, the benevolent, domestic model of psychological treatment began to disintegrate. Psychology then moved from a concern for the subjectivity of persons in institutionalized settings, a more sociological model, to a focus on the essentialized individual. At the same time, as the following chapter demonstrates, the discipline and its practices began to locate the problem of insanity within the female.[6] When *Wuthering Heights* materializes the "outside" world as the "inside" world of the self and domestic space, it transforms sociological information into psychological information, mirroring the history of psychological thinking. The figure of Catherine, for instance, begins in a family matrix. As the novel shifts from a sociological to a psychological mode, the female is represented as autonomous, essentialized, and, in the case of the dying Catherine, damaged. Thus fiction is writing the history of institutionalized change even as this change takes place partially in fiction.

When *Wuthering Heights* moves from the outside to the inside, from the rhetoric of sociology and anthropology to that of psychology, it also reflects a historical shift within the discourses of the human sciences. As the official disciplines attributed the historical and cultural materials of the other to origins within the self or personal life, psychology gradually emerged as the most authoritative discourse of the self and the other. Perhaps psychological thinking took precedence within the human sciences because it provided the most powerful model for representing the social world as it must be to and for capitalism—divided into gendered components allowing no reference to place or time. While sociology imagined society as composed of classes and anthropology viewed it according to a kinship model, only psychology provided the theoretical justification for construing the social world in terms of the male and the female individual.

In so representing *Wuthering Heights*, I regard it as an unbounded site where various rhetorical and cultural strategies, generated by the human sciences, meet and overlap, interact and establish priorities. The novel, I argue, provided the imaginary means for mediating a series of boundaries—between outside and inside, male and female, public and private, culture and nature—represented in the languages of sociology and anthropology and later given psychic authority within psychology. Brontë's novel, and by extension all domestic fiction, I contend, functioned as the naturalizer, popularizer, and the imaginative means of establishing the collaboration among the discourses of the human sciences. The novel pulled together and gave fictional life to the gendered and classed norms dictated by the sociological thinking that coalesced within statistical societies and in the pages of official journals at the beginning of the century. With the anthropological vocabulary of kinship and gender circulating among the texts and practices of anthropologists and their armchair counterparts, writers such as McLennan and Spencer, the novel constituted a version of the modern family. At the same time, domestic fiction collaborated with psychological thinking, as it would emerge in the writings of Krafft-Ebing, Havelock Ellis, Freud, and others, to represent the self consumed by an interior domain of forbidden desires. In the preceding chapters I read reports on the condition of the working classes and studies of the primitive family with all the attention to detail usually reserved for a literary text; here I read a literary text as a historical document to show that it relies on the same figures of thought as sociology and anthropology and that it prepares the ground for the figures of psychology. By stressing this common discursive and cultural ground, then, I also read fiction as sociology, anthropology, and psychology. In the first two chapters, I dispelled the contradictions that distinguish one genre of writing from another in order to establish their fundamental interrelationship. I showed how the anthropological representation of the Hottentot female, both productive and disruptive of gendered norms, was facilitated by the figure of the prostitute in sociological writing. Here I show how the figures of the oversexed prostitute and the improperly gendered African female reappear in the androgynous Catherine. I focus on one kind of writing to explode generic boundaries from within, to identify the rhetorical and figurative intersections between the discourses of the human sciences and the fictional text.

My point in this chapter is not to make an exhaustive survey of nineteenth-century novels, or even of those novels that appeared after sociology and before psychology emerged as disciplines.[7] I can only establish interconnections between *Wuthering Heights* and scientific writing of man that suggest how fiction must be read by those who want to revise the study of both fiction and social science to make a more adequate history of women. I consider *Wuthering Heights* the crystallization of a historical moment and of a complex social dynamic that cannot be contained within any one text of the nineteenth century. Domestic fiction such as *Wuthering Heights* and the work of Emily's sisters, as well as that of Thackeray, Mrs. Gaskell, Dickens, and others, clearly demonstrates an intensifying compulsion to designate cultural information and to assign function according to gender. The enclosed domestic universe that first appeared in the fictions of Richardson and Austen was modified by the Brontës and their contemporaries to cut the modern family loose from its historical circumstances and make it a model toward which any social function should aspire. The household in which these novels leave us is consequently one that could justify a rapidly changing social world irrevocably divided into public and private to facilitate industrialization.[8]

DESIRE ON THE MOORS

Desire in *Wuthering Heights* undergoes essentially four stages marked by the transformations in the two Catherines and in the different quality of sexual relationship that each produces. The chronological, spatial, generational, and narrative transitions result in relationships that are increasingly differentiated according to gender as the partners are inscribed with sexual difference. At the same time, in Catherine gender undergoes a process of differentiation and refinement both "within" the woman and in the transformation of the household. The novel detaches the body of the female from the collective body of the world; it displaces physicality, materiality, and openness with a sexualized and enclosed body that partakes more of the spirit than of the flesh. At the same time, the novel refigures the household according to a vocabulary of enclosure, division, and difference. By moving between the sociological and the psychological, the household and the figure of Catherine, I intend to show that these components are part of one changing cultural formation. The four narrative stages I delineate constitute a history of desire that participates in an unwitting conspiracy to transform the model of the individual and the family underlying and naturalizing all power relations within middle-class culture.

The first stage is the early, passionate relationship between young Catherine Earnshaw and the gypsy child Heathcliff, the intimacy of which can be gauged when Catherine describes her "greatest punishment" as her separation from Heathcliff. This first stage ends and the second begins with Catherine's initial "accidental" sojourn at Thrushcross Grange when she is bitten by "the devil"—when her leg is literally engulfed by the mouth of a hound named Skulker, "his huge, purple tongue hanging half a foot out of his mouth, and his pendant lips streaming with bloody slaver" (Brontë 1847, 122). Within the physical and social space of the Grange Catherine undergoes her first transformation, doubling and splitting into the beautifully attired and coiffed young lady who returns to Wuthering Heights virtually unrecognizable to her childhood friend. Marriage to Edgar initiates Catherine's second trip away from the Heights and the third stage in my analysis. In the Grange bedroom, removed from the elements and separated from the house on the moors, Catherine is further transfigured when illness doubles her into an unrecognizable mirror image. As she dies, she bears a daughter also named Catherine, and so the final stage begins.

When the novel confines the second Catherine to successively smaller, more enclosed spaces, she is gradually integrated into a domain of female power. There Brontë invests her with the domestic authority to regulate and socialize her partner Hareton that sociology prescribed when it demanded the return of the female to the household. The younger Catherine is a double of her mother, yet significant differences between the two figures are apparent in the adjectives that characterize and so distinguish one generation from the next. First are the adjectives that spatialize desire itself, locating it within an internal landscape of the self that possesses depth and breadth. Whereas Catherine's spirits were "rough," Cathy's are "high," and her love is "deep and tender." Second, *Wuthering Heights* consistently defines Catherine by modalities of being and doing—she is "wild," "defiant," "imperious," one who acts upon the world. Young Cathy, in contrast, is imprisoned by her qualities. Not she, but her "spirit," her "anger," and her "love" are represented; as subject of being and doing, Cathy is absent. Finally, and most important, Catherine is virtually indistinguishable from Heathcliff; they are not "boy" and "girl" but two children. Cathy is gendered, on the other hand, marked as "female" by adjectives that clearly differentiate her from both Heathcliff and Hareton.

At this point, I would like to examine the text more closely to show how Brontë quite self-consciously uses the character of Lockwood as the reader in the text. His function is to register the need to understand the history of desire that defies or eludes any discursive categories by which one attempts to explain or contain it. To Lockwood, the urbane, modern counterpart of Gaskell or Kay Shuttleworth, the undifferentiated and unenclosed house that he enters at the opening of the novel is a dark, secret space of illicit mixture. He attempts to organize this space according to a cultural logic that is no more appropriate for it than was that brought to bear upon the households of the industrial poor by the social researchers. Even though this particular household extends throughout narrative time, it bears all the markings of an earlier historical moment. Most important, the members of the Earnshaw household are not differentiated according to biological or genetic relationships; in other words, they are not a nucleated unit. Rather, the household is organized according to the older notion of kinship, when no word existed that meant "only kin" within a household, and the house could be occupied by servants, lodgers, visitors, pupils, shopmen, or unrelated children (Davidoff and Hall 1987, 31).

As a dwelling, furthermore, the Heights represents an earlier historical moment when the state was a government of families through alliances, rather than a government through the family. The house is more like a hiding place, retreat, and place of familial defense and autonomy than a "home" like the Grange, permeable both to vision and outside interference. Brontë describes the house as a fortress that "happily the architect had the foresight to build strong," whose walls are pierced by "narrow windows" "deeply set in the wall, and the corners defended with large jutting stones" (1847, 46). Compared to the large unshuttered windows of the Grange that allow Catherine and Heathcliff unlimited surveillance of the squabbling children in the parlor, these narrow windows speak of a different cultural code that protected the household from observation and state interference. While the exterior of the Heights prohibits all manner of intrusion, human or natural, the interior is open and functionally undifferentiated; thus, it too announces a way of thinking about space as unbounded combination and mixture, rather than as something enclosed within categories and divisions. It is not surprising, then, that the arrangement of this house and its occupants baffles Lockwood, just as those of the industrial poor baffled municipal officials sent to inspect and organize them.

"One step" brings Lockwood into "the family sitting room, without an introductory lobby or passage," an area called "the house" by its occupants. Akin to both a kitchen and a parlor, "the house" formerly functioned in both capacities without regard to the functional boundaries that give the Grange a nonfunctional and overly elaborate parlor distinct from the kitchen. Lockwood's first experience of this space is a sensuous one as he distinguishes light and heat at one end of the room splendidly reflected "from ranks of immense pewter dishes, interspersed with silver jugs and tankards, towering row after row, in a vast oak dresser, to the very roof" (Brontë 1847, 47). Yet he is convinced by the absence of activity that the kitchen has been forced "to retreat altogether into another quarter," for he could observe "no signs of roasting, boiling, baking, about the huge fireplace; nor any glitter of copper saucepans and tin cullenders on the wall" (Brontë 1847, 46–47).

The Heights is clearly represented as the mediation between one historical moment and the next, between artisanal and middle-class cultures and between conflicting notions of the organization of space. It is a space where features of both cultures meet in a dialogic relationship. The warm, cheerful atmosphere and open hearth Lockwood first encounters, as well as the huge collection of pewter ware for eating and drinking on a massive scale, outmoded now by the more modern copper cookware, for instance, suggest the moment of festival when the household might have hosted the entire community for a bountiful feast. The impression is compounded, furthermore, by the references to size and quantity punctuating Brontë's description evoking the abundant wealth of former days. Still the house is alive with activity; indistinguishable sounds and voices emanate from it, as if from a vast body. Thus, Lockwood hears "a *chatter* of tongues, and a *clatter* of culinary utensils, deep within" (Brontë 1847, 46, emphasis added). When Brontë gives the household a voice that speaks in tongues of chatter and clatter, she clearly links it to the materiality of the physical body. The narrative endows the house with all the features of the mass body as Bakhtin describes it—sensual, permeable, and polyphonous. Despite its strong walls, at this moment in the story, it is neither detached from the world nor articulated solely by the set of individuals within. There are signs, however, of the division of functional or productive space from nonfunctional or unproductive space, part of a larger reorganization of living and work space in middle-class households undertaken in the first half of the nineteenth century. The hearth blazes, for instance, only for heating, while the productive work of cooking, roasting, baking, and boiling has "retreated" into a hidden household core. Thus the novel collapses several stages of a process that ultimately saw the enclosure of the house and family behind gates, drives, hedges, and walls in the new suburbs springing up on the outskirts of manufacturing towns throughout England. In this process, productive work was first banished from the domestic area to a remote corner of the house. As a result, cooking, eating, washing, sleeping, and other "back stage" functions could be separated from polite social intercourse and eventually assigned a special place within the house (Davidoff and Hall 1987).

That the Heights is a site that produces and suppresses contradictions by representing changing relations inside and outside is further heightened by Lockwood's subsequent experiences within it. When he first surveys the rustic simplicity of the room, Lockwood expects to discover a paterfamilias—a powerful male figure like old Father Earnshaw—in charge. The furnishings themselves, as he describes them, lead him to this conclusion:

> The apartment and furniture would have been nothing extraordinary as belonging to a homely, northern farmer with a stubborn countenance, and stalwart limbs, set out to advantage in knee breaches, and gaiters. Such an individual, seated in his armchair, his mug of ale frothing on the round table before him, is to be seen in any circuit of five or six miles among these hills, if you go at the right time, after dinner. (Brontë 1847, 47).

His complacency is immediately disturbed when he discovers Heathcliff rather than the stalwart patriarch of his imagination. Although he is dressed in gentlemanly attire, the gypsy's swarthy complexion and dark visage mark him as the savage foreigner who appeared as the very antithesis of family feeling in the discourse of the early sociologists.

On his next visit to the Heights, Lockwood is even more bewildered and estranged as he futilely attempts to introduce social divisions, as he understands them, into an as-yet-undifferentiated kin group. When he returns to the "apartment" where he was formerly received, Lockwood finds what he takes to be signs of domesticity. The room is "warm and cheerful," glowing "delightfully in the radiance of an immense fire," and it reveals a table "laid for a plentiful evening meal" (Brontë 1847, 52). Yet this is not a domestic scene that Lockwood can comprehend. For one thing, the woman tending the inviting fire is not the "missis" as he expects, even though "he had never previously suspected" the existence of such a figure. For another, this "missis" does not greet him graciously as befits the woman of the house, but she regards him with mute hostility. Finally, Lockwood is unable to interpret correctly the presence of an anomalous young man, whom he first thinks to be a servant by his appearance, but whose free, haughty demeanor and bearing contradict such a conclusion. All this is to say that as he surveys the individuals of the household arrayed before the fire, Lockwood tries to organize them as if they were figures in a domestic novel.

Wuthering Heights, however, is not *yet* a domestic novel, even though the narrative will inscribe its characters into just such a cozy scene by novel's end. Brontë departs from Austen's aesthetics of normalcy to build her fiction on domestic disarray. In this way, the novel partakes in the ideology that ungenders the female, making female pathology its starting point and rationale. Lockwood simply seems all the more fatuous as he persists in this attempt to fashion a domestic scene, sanctimoniously lecturing "Mr. Heathcliff" as to the virtues of home and hearth. " 'Many could not imagine the existence,' " he rapturously intones, " 'of happiness in a life of such complete exile from the world as you spend; yet I'll venture to say that, surrounded by your family, and with your amiable lady as the presiding genius of your home and—' " (Brontë 1847, 55). Although Heathcliff does not permit Lockwood to finish his sentence or his soliloquy, Lockwood is not easily discouraged, so strong is his desire to imagine a "pleasant family circle." While such an enclosed domestic configuration is achieved in the union of Cathy and Hareton later in the story, this group cannot be circumscribed within the limits of a nucleated family. It is Lockwood's function, to reiterate the point with which I began, to register the dissonance between older figurations of the family and desire and those categories that cannot contain them.

I move now to an analysis of the relationship between Catherine and Heathcliff and the resultant transformations in the character of Catherine. In these formations, I contend, the fictional landscape both naturalizes and universalizes the figures of anthropological and sociological thinking, and it introduces more completely those figures of female pathology that psychological thinking would embody more fully a few years later.

Years earlier, instead of the whip that young Catherine had asked her father to bring her from his journey, Mr. Earnshaw brings home a dirty, ragged boy, a gypsy from the slums of Liverpool. The child belongs to another class and race, yet he quickly replaces the legitimate son in the affections of the father and head of household. This event is not as simple as it would seem, for the child's incorporation into the family radically disturbs primogeniture and exacerbates the dependency of the other heirs. Nonetheless, the family is sufficiently flexible, its boundaries permeable and undifferentiated enough, to allow Heathcliff to become a member of the family precisely as if he were biologically related to it. The usurper immediately forms a strong bond with the young daughter of the family; together they constitute an inseparable unit unmarked by gender distinctions. Catherine is similarly undifferentiated within the family unit, since she is identified only as a willful *child*, and not as *female* child. Her body is also intimately connected to the communal body of the world, refusing to remain enclosed for long. She and Heathcliff freely roam the moors, unhampered by boundaries or fences of any kind. According to Bakhtin, the physical body so depicted is not understood as separated from the world by clearly defined boundaries; it is not a closed, completed unit but it blends with animals and objects in the stream of life. Desire, too, does not observe boundaries of a social nature. Thus it comes into the world essentially "adulterous" because it is as yet unconnected to procreative desire.

When one of their rambles brings them to the unshuttered parlor windows of Thrushcross Grange, Catherine and Heathcliff, in one of their final moments "together," take in the plush interior with its crimson carpet and gold and white ceiling interrupted by "a shower of glass drops hanging in silver chains" (Brontë 1847, 89).[9] Their revery is interrupted by the shrieks and tears of the children in this gilded cage, who "had nearly pulled [a dog] in two between them" (Brontë 1847, 89). The luxurious, over-decorated, even gaudy room is contaminated further by the presence of these two spoiled "petted things," as Catherine and Heathcliff maliciously dub them. Both Catherine's abrupt separation from Heathcliff and her entrance into this enclosed "paradise" are similarly self-divisive. Because he is of a different race and class, Heathcliff is instantly othered and excluded.

I stress the fact that self-division and division of an earlier mode of family life are two facets of the same cultural move. Both rely upon the principle of gender to articulate the productive and reproductive spheres and to organize the individuals suitable to inhabit a world so divided. Once the physical separation of Catherine and Heathcliff is accomplished, the Grange begins to transform her into an individual other than Heathcliff, but "same" to her class, sex, and race. At the Grange, Catherine's treatment is specifically governed by the gendered and classed categories lived by the middle-class Lintons; they assume she is a delicate "young lady" and proceed to treat her accordingly. "The entire Linton household cossets the wounded (but still healthy) girl as if she were truly an invalid," as Sandra Gilbert and Susan Gubar observe (1979, 273).[10] Enclosed not only within the drawing room but also within a set of gendering, infantilizing clothes, manners, and rituals, Catherine is endowed with a classed and sexed body. The metamorphosis that the female body undergoes "inside" is inextricably linked to the transformation of the domestic space outside; they are bound up in a mutually authorizing relationship. Catherine receives a bounded and gendered body only within the confines of a domestic space that both creates and contains it. Maturity for her does not mean the loosening of these boundaries, but, to the

contrary, their refinement and intensification within ever-narrowing domestic space, culminating in her death at Thrushcross Grange.

In Catherine's marriage to Edgar Linton, I argue, the figures of anthropological discourse are thought out most clearly in the logic of fiction.
Like the history of the family as written by McLennan and Spencer later
in the century, *Wuthering Heights* revises the materials of the family to
incorporate features both of kinship and gender. That is, the novel makes
the family both exogamous and endogamous, both an instrument of alliance and the center of sexual desire.[11] To illustrate this point and, more
specifically, the way in which the signifiers of kinship and sexuality overlap and interact, I would like to detour into literary critical territory for
a moment to review one analysis of the marriage episode written from
an anthropological perspective. William Goetz's "Genealogy and Incest
in *Wuthering Heights*" (1982) relies upon the vocabulary of kinship—
incest, endogamy, and exogamy—to make sense of a representation of
the family organized both by the demands of kinship and by gender. In so
doing, Goetz reifies the very language that enabled intellectuals and professionals to represent the middle-class individual, family, and household
as different from both the aristocratic and artisanal models. For, as I have
argued, it was in anthropological and fictional writing, above all, that
these categories were first formulated. Even more interesting is the way in
which anthropological thinking cancels out the historical dimension of
the family in *Wuthering Heights*, even as it does in *Primitive Marriage
and Principles of Sociology*.

Catherine's marriage to Edgar, according to Goetz, is an "agreement"
to participate in the circuit of exchange of women that he, after Lévi-
Strauss, mandates as the basis for culture itself. In this way, Goetz argues,
the temptation toward incest represented by the first half of the novel is
overcome.[12] Research on the early modern family (Medick 1976; Trumbach 1978), as well as on representations of the household in both domestic fiction and sociological writing, however, has indicated that the
boundaries between inside and outside the family, and hence between
exogamy and endogamy, are shifting terms. Yet Lévi-Strauss, and Goetz
after him, assume them to be ahistorically fixed markers. If the family is
placed in historical perspective, Catherine's earlier relationship to Heathcliff is in fact radically exogamous since he clearly comes from a different
race and class. Her marriage to Linton—a man of her own class and
race—is the first step toward realigning her misdirected desire with endogamy. *Wuthering Heights*, then, retrieves desire from its asocial, lim-
inal position outside the family and secures it for the purpose of repro-
ducing the family and, consequently a certain kind of household. Desire
among family members compels each to reproduce those relations with
someone else. The marriage is also an exogamous alliance between fami-

lies, as Goetz rightly maintains. This is so in that the novel, like anthropological writing, revises the materials of the family, making it both endogamous and exogamous, both an element in the kinship network and the locus of sexual desire.[13]

Marriage to Edgar brings Catherine to the more highly organized and enclosed space of the Grange. Situated in a valley, sheltered from the elements and surrounded by a fenced park, Thrushcross Grange is clearly organized according to a different spatial logic than that of Wuthering Heights. Yet unlike the domestic female imagined by sociological writing, the new mistress of the Grange refuses to be similarly reordered by this division of space, the social nature of which becomes apparent upon Heathcliff's visit to her there after an absence of three years. Beseeching Edgar to maintain a hospitable posture toward her old friend, Catherine petitions her husband for permission to bring her guest "up" into the parlor. Unlike the Heights, where functional and spatial boundaries between the kitchen and the sitting room are virtually nonexistent, space at the Grange is hierarchical; therefore, the kitchen is "below" the parlor, indicating the strict divisions observed between tasks, time, and personnel in this middle-class household. Edgar is surprised, even rendered uncomfortable, by his wife's request, since for him Heathcliff's proper place is similarly "below" in the kitchen:

> "Shall I tell him to come up now?"
> "Here?" he said, "into the parlour?"
> "Where else?" she asked. (Brontë 1847, 134)

Catherine quickly understands her husband's "fastidiousness" and uses it against him, ordering Nelly to remedy social inequities with an ingenious scheme designed to shame him into relenting. "Set two tables;" she says, addressing Nelly, "one for your master and Miss Isabella, being gentry; the other for Heathcliff and myself, being of the lower orders" (Brontë 1847, 134). Victorious, Catherine rushes off to gather up Heathcliff; Edgar, for his part, still cannot bear Catherine to welcome the "plough boy" in front of all the servants. Bidding Nelly to have him step up, he cautions Catherine to "be glad, without being absurd." Invoking a now-revised conception of what constitutes a household, he says: "The whole household need not witness the sight of your welcoming a runaway servant as a brother" (Brontë 1847, 134–35). The point is that *this* household can no longer tolerate an individual who represents an earlier historical moment of the family, when its members were not thoroughly differentiated.[14] If Heathcliff and Catherine's relationship is ignorant of boundaries of race, class, and sex, it is precisely because it was formulated out of an entirely different definition of "family." Edgar's words, however, like those of the social researchers, impose order where there was none, dividing and enclosing the relationship within a new set of categories that overrides any original unity. Greetings by the "lady" of the house, according to this logic, are reserved for family members, or members of the same class body, but not for a servant who is a brother or a brother who is a servant; such a pollution of boundaries Edgar cannot tolerate. His words, like the household itself, spatialize and compartmentalize desire, confining it to its proper place. Heathcliff is a figure of undifferentiation—one who does not respect such boundaries and who disturbs the hierarchy of the household, along with the "master's" prerogatives.

In addition to providing the fictional landscape in which to negotiate the demands of kinship and gender, Catherine's marriage to Edgar initiates a crucial segment in the transformation of the female figure, beginning with her first entrance into the Grange. As this metamorphosis culminates in the birth of a daughter and the apotheosis of the heroine, the aesthetics for representing the female are rewritten. Shortly after Heathcliff's return, Catherine suffers her second bout of illness, brought on by a furious argument between Edgar, Heathcliff, and herself. Whereas the first illness deprives her of her sunny spirits, subjecting her to uncharacteristic fits of depression, the second illness deprives her of her body and ultimately her life. Catherine's body is etherealized, fading into the air as she is doubled and split once again. As she "dies into art,"[15] the revision of the wild, undifferentiated object of Romantic desire is completed: "No angel in heaven could be more beautiful than she appeared; and I [Nelly] partook of the infinite calm in which she lay" (Brontë 1847, 201). It is crucial to note here the way in which the narrative moves from the sociological mode emphasizing the structure of the household to the psychological focus on the internal structure of the female mind and desire.

I want to stress that doubling does not simply produce an exact replication, but rather it creates a double with a difference—a supplement—that is, in some basic ideological way, incompatibly other.[16] As she looks in the mirror in her delirium, Catherine is doubled and split as she misinterprets the sight of her own body. She cannot identify the image reflected in the mirror, yet as she gazes upon the image, she also defines it as object of her gaze. The image of herself is the product and the expression of self-alienation. She becomes the Victorian woman who embodies not only the self, the woman who is culturally acceptable, but also the other, the woman who is both the authentic object of desire and the one whom it is forbidden to desire. The gaze in the mirror privileges the enclosed and bounded body. So transformed, curiously enough, her material body disappears as she slowly starves herself to death.[17] It is at this point, too, that

Brontë "replaces" her heroine with a more saintly and recognizably Victorian figure:

> Mrs. Linton sat in a loose, white dress, with a light shawl over her shoulders, in the recess of the open window, as usual. Her thick, long hair had been partly removed at the beginning of her illness; and now she wore it simply combed in natural tresses over her temples and neck. Her appearance was altered, . . . but when she was calm, there seemed unearthly beauty in the change. (Brontë 1847, 192)

Formerly characterized by her insistence on physical oneness with Heathcliff, this Catherine is *unearthly*. As she is beatified before our eyes, the spirit subsumes all traces of the material Catherine, creating a new self, which the novel endows with superior beauty. This passage shows her thus dying into art:

> The flash of her eyes had been succeeded by a dreamy melancholy softness: they no longer gave the impression of looking at the objects around her; they appeared always to gaze beyond—you would have said out of this world. Then the paleness of her face—its haggard aspect having vanished as she recovered flesh . . . added to the touching interest which she awakened. (Brontë 1847, 193)

Several features of this passage warrant particular attention. First, the fully transformed Catherine, literally and figuratively unrecognizable from the wild, saucy child that ruled the Heights, incorporates many of the characteristic features of "femininity" that exist today in the form of powerful clichés and stereotypes. In place of a spirited, desiring subject, there is now a dreamy, soft, melancholic, mad, damaged female deprived of material reality. Second, this figure mediates the configuration of female/not female by incorporating that contradiction into one body. Both sociological and anthropological writing represent the identical contradiction in the form of two figures—the domestic woman and the prostitute, and the European and non-European female, respectively. Fiction goes one step further; it has the capabilities both to materialize a single, naturalized figure that mediates opposing notions of the female without sacrificing either and to capture the popular imagination in the process. Third, as the interior of the self is articulated, the physicality of the context recedes; as a physical entity the household itself becomes irrelevant and loses substantiality. The narrative includes fewer and fewer references to the materiality of the house, which, after this point, essentially becomes a state of mind—that place defined by the presence of the female.[18] Domestic space, furthermore, is identified completely with its occupants. Finally, the splitting of the self, I contend, allows for the production of the essential woman as something apart from and other than her body. The production of the enclosed and individuated body is also the hollowing out of the material body, which is filled, then, by a new metaphysical self. In the transformation of soul to psyche, the novel constitutes and materializes a new domain of gendered information, which psychology will extract from the individual and endow with sense later in the century.

DESIRE AT HOME

Young Catherine enters the novel into a new historical problematic. In order to form the "family" that the narrative demands, the materials of the first family, based on an older notion of kinship, must be torn apart and reformulated according to the new logic of gendered sexuality.[19] An entirely different woman, the second Catherine inhabits a completely different space from that of her mother. The wild, natural landscape that Catherine and Heathcliff roamed gives way to a park, an enclosed and organized cultural space, seen in the nineteenth century as an extension of the home "proclaiming the values of privacy, order, taste, and appreciation of nature in a controlled environment" (Davidoff and Hall 1987, 370).[20] Thrushcross Grange dominates this space and Cathy's universe as well. Until she is thirteen she never ventures beyond the park. "She was a perfect recluse; and, apparently perfectly contented" (Brontë 1847, 225). Not only is her body spatially contained within a domesticated environment, her movements closely watched, but her desire is also bounded by the limits of that tamed place where only "imaginary adventures" can be experienced.

The sexual desire between Cathy and her sickly, ill-humored cousin is highly mediated and explicitly tied to discursive formations. Armed with the cultural power of language, Cathy begins a communication with Linton that requires her significantly to confine herself to nooks and crannies in order to compose secret epistles: "she grew wondrous fond of stealing off into corners by herself, and often, if I came near her suddenly while reading, she would start, and bend over the book, evidently desirous to hide it; and I [Nelly] detected edges of loose paper sticking out beyond the leaves" (Brontë 1847, 258). Her desire for Linton is secret and interiorized, hidden in a drawer or, ironically, in the folds of the book, most likely a novel, that she reads. Since words have become the only possible connection to a space outside herself, her desire seeks gratification within a world of signs rather than referents. Where there were "real" objects of desire in the drawer—trinkets and baubles—there are now bits of paper with words written all over them. In Brontë's words, "the playthings and trinkets, which recently formed its contents, were transmuted into bits of folded paper" (1847, 258).

It is worth speculating for a moment why desire, as figured in the relationship between Cathy and Linton, is doomed to failure—why it becomes "bad" desire. Several possibilities seem to me worth bearing in mind. If gendered desire is being articulated in this text as the coming together of different "things"—that is, "male" and "female"—then Linton, with his sickly frame, peevish nature, and general effeminacy, is not sufficiently differentiated physically and sexually from Cathy to make their coming together an instance of "good" desire. In addition, if the newly figured "female" is being gradually confined and enclosed within domestic space, as I have argued is true both in written representation and cultural practice, then "she" must be provided with a "he" that will display the effects of her domesticating power. Linton is not such a male; already a subject in culture, he does not have that uncultured, undomesticated imprint that Hareton bears like a cross until Cathy's intercession. Furthermore, the mismatch between the two cousins highlights the mismatch between the two overlapping cultural functions of alliance and gender. "Good" desire is no longer entirely synonymous with the fact of alliance between families; the first son is no longer the best or strongest candidate for a "good" marriage. In this way, once again, cultural specifications for the formation of the family are called into question by this fictional gesture naturalizing the terms of anthropological discourse. While the fact of alliance will be a feature of "good" desire as written between Cathy and Hareton, just as it was in the texts of McLennan and Spencer, it will not be the only one. Their relationship must also include an element of sexual desire, which permits the new family to conform to the demands of both kinship and gender. Moreover, Cathy's marriage to Linton deprives her of economic support, since her inheritance is ceded to Heathcliff. Yet this loss provides her with an occasion for the eventual exercise of domestic power, because her domestic authority eventually restores Hareton to his rightful position as heir to the estate. Desire is once more brought into alignment with kinship.

As Foucault has argued in *Discipline and Punish* (1979), the dark, fortresslike "house of security" is replaced by a "house of certainty" when self-regulation replaces external force as the major method of social control. When Lockwood returns to the Heights after a prolonged absence, it is not the familiar "house of security" that he finds but a "house of certainty." Unlike his first entrance into the Heights, this time his approach is considerably easier; he "had neither to climb the gate, nor to knock—it yielded to my hand" (Brontë 1847, 338). Inside the gate, Lockwood is greeted by the pleasant smell of flowers and "homely fruit trees."

Domesticity, as this description makes abundantly clear, has tamed the formerly wild, unruly quality of the Heights. It is crucial to note the similarity between Lockwood's language in characterizing the house and that used in Victorian manuals of domestication. The resemblance between this new domestic space and that called forth by the following instruction issued to housing inspectors in the 1850 French manual *Catéchisme d'hygiène a l'usage des enfants* emphasizes the manner in which the novel pulls together and fuses representations from other cultural areas. Thus, the authors write on the subject of flowers: "One must be strict and show no leniency in proscribing excessive decoration, obscene or degrading images, in order to replace them with flowers about the house" (Donzelot 1979, 41). Lockwood can immediately spy the inhabitants of the house, who are seated by an open kitchen window. This is a house fit for the landscape imagined by such urban professionals as Stonestreet, Kay Shuttleworth, and Gavin. Here nothing can be hidden, no secret hatched without detection; before he enters the house, Lockwood can "both see them and hear them talk." Open space, accessible to penetration by the gaze of power, is characteristic of the nineteenth-century prison, hospital, factory, or public housing unit. "He who is subjected to a field of visibility," in Foucault's formulation, "and who knows it, assumes responsibility for the constraints of power; he makes them play spontaneously upon himself; he inscribes in himself the power relation in which he simultaneously plays both roles; he becomes the principle of his own subjection" (1979, 202–3). It is clearly no accident that the representational use of space has shifted with shifts in representations of desire and the family. Once closed to outside visibility, the novel opens domestic space and avails it to supervision, just as sociological writing and practice penetrated and reorganized the working-class household.

The voice that emanates from within the house is now not the gruff tones of Joseph, the manservant, but rather the silken notes of the female educator. Here Cathy is discovered in the act of exercising her domestic authority by disciplining a willing Hareton:

> "Con-*trary*!" said a voice, as sweet as a silver bell—"That for the third time, you dunce! I'm not going to tell you,—Recollect, or I pull your hair!"
>
> "Contrary, then," answered another, in deep, but softened tones. "And now, kiss me, for minding well."
>
> "No, read it over first correctly, without a single mistake." (Brontë 1847, 338)

Hareton's pleasure in this scene of punishment is distinctly evident: "His handsome features glowed with pleasure," the author tells us, "and his eyes kept impatiently wandering from the page to a small white hand over his shoulder, which recalled him by a smart slap on the cheek, whenever its owner detected such signs of inattention" (Brontë 1847, 338). The relationship between pleasure and pain, as well as between pleasure and linguistic mastery, in this scene is unmistakably obvious. Note, too, how different pleasure becomes as Brontë transfers erotic pleasure from the release of natural desire to its constraint, and as intercourse between male and female is conducted at the level of words. As Catherine teaches Hareton to read, the harsh power of the punisher and the rewarder becomes indistinguishable from the restorative power of the domesticator and bearer of culture.

FICTION, DESIRE, AND SELF-REGULATION

As an agent that imaginatively redefines, restructures, and produces cultural materials on the family, the self, and sexual desire, the novel also functions as an agent of history, rewriting and redefining history itself. Viewed in this way, *Wuthering Heights* can be said to have participated directly in a cultural redefinition that occurred both inside and outside the domain of fiction. The discourses of sociology viewed the household, the family, and the individual from outside and moved steadily inward to locate the causes of social disorder ultimately within the newly defined domain of the self. As it did so, sociological writing simultaneously identified the domestic female as the solution to the ills besetting the industrial classes. Anthropological writing reformulated discourses of the family, kinship, and gender in order to imagine a family suitable to reproduce and maintain the modern individual. The novel, I have argued, followed a similar path, rewriting the materials of the social and historical world into those of the interior to produce a distinctively modern notion of the self. By naturalizing, popularizing, reformulating, and mediating cultural categories imagined within the human sciences, fiction talked about areas of culture and history as if they had always been about truths of self and sexuality. Later in the century psychological discourses, as I discuss in chapter 5, extracted gendered information from the self, represented among other places in the novel, and endowed it with new cultural sense, consistent with a logic of the self as an interiorized place of fantasy and belief unconnected to the outside world.

Wuthering Heights consequently presents readers with two families and two radically opposed forms of desire. Ruled by Father Earnshaw, the paterfamilias, the family that dominates the first half of the novel is organized according to the older model of blood kinship. The family that emerges in the second half is formed out of these materials but founded on the notion of the couple with clearly differentiated gender roles. Cathy and Hareton's relationship as glimpsed through the window is the logical culmination of the reformation of the family also imagined in sociological and anthropological tracts. More important, the fictional representation infuses the new model of human relationships with pleasure. Securely lodged within the governable and bounded interior, the new couple is subject to social regulation, not by any mechanism of law but by the limits fiction places on desire.

Growing speculative, one might feel inspired to claim that fiction's success can be seen in Matthew Arnold's 1869 contention that the most efficient means to a docile population lay nowhere if not within the self and its desires. Referring to individuals of the new industrial classes, Arnold writes:

> Now, the Philistine's great defect is delicacy of perception, to cultivate in him this delicacy, to render it *independent of external and mechanical rule, and a law to itself*, is what seems to make most for his perfection, his true humanity. And his true humanity, and therefore his true happiness, appear to lie much more, so far as the relations of love and marriage are concerned, in becoming alive to the finer shades of feeling which arise within those relations, in being able to enter with tact and sympathy into the subtle instinctive propensions and repugnances of the persons with whose life his own life is bound up, to make them his own, *to direct and govern* in harmony with them *the arbitrary range of his personal action*, and thus to enlarge his spiritual and intellectual life and liberty. (1869, 154, emphasis added)

Only through the regulation of desire, then, does the middle-class individual becomes a law unto himself. Domestic relationships by implication subordinate the worst impulses of the "ordinary" self to the "better" self, who is capable of rule that will not overturn but perpetuate the existing social order. It is necessary to point out that the regulation of the body versus desire is a very recent thing and particularly suited to an economy that sexes labor. To the labor that seems least valued, that is, domestic supervision, middle-class culture has delegated this task. Only the history of the reproductive realm, as written in texts like *Wuthering Heights* and those of sociology, anthropology, and psychology, can adequately capture the cultural moment when internal regulation of the self became more crucial for control of the population than "external and mechanical" rule could ever be.

In conclusion, I return to the question of the author with which I began. If there is one individual who is generally thought to have failed to regulate her desires, it is the author of *Wuthering Heights*. Since Charlotte Brontë's first descriptions in the biographical notice, Emily Brontë has frequently been transformed into an improperly socialized, pathological, or "damaged" female—overemotional, childish, undisciplined. *Wuthering Heights*, I have argued, has similarly been removed from history and culture and turned into an intricate, convoluted mystery resembling the female self. Surely one of the most common methodological approaches to the novel in the twentieth century has been to identify its "strange power," "energy," and "uniqueness" with those of its author. As recently as 1987 Harold Bloom wrote, "the three Brontë sisters . . . are *unique* literary artists whose works resemble one another's far more than they do the work of writers before or since"(1987b, 1, emphasis added). Bloom's statement not only illustrates the tenacity of this critical approach, it also wraps the "weird" sisters in a familial, almost incestual embrace that encloses author and work within the parsonage household and removes them from any "outside" influences.[21]

It should not surprise us that Brontë and her novel are most often interpreted according to a psychological hermeneutic that collaborates with the novel to erase its history. In the twentieth century a plethora of Brontë criticism and biographical work has been devoted to psychologizing author, text, and characters.[22] Much of it identifies author with text until their complete confusion makes it impossible to tell one from the other. According to this way of thinking, the author is her text, the text her psyche. After disavowing any attempt to "psychoanalyze the biographical Emily Brontë," Margaret Homans writes, for example, that there is "a psyche available to the reader, Brontë as she presents herself in the text, intentionally or not" (1987, 101).

If author and novel have been conflated and confined to a psychic room where history and culture never enter, so too have author and characters. It is astonishing to note the similarity, for instance, between this description of Brontë at seven from Edward Chitham's 1987 biography and Brontë's depiction of the young Catherine. "She is a precocious, volatile, ardent seven, whose eyes reflect the emotional mobility of her selfhood," Chitham narrates: "She is far from being able to control these racing moods. . . . If she becomes angry the whole family begins to wonder whether she may be unbalanced, and she knows herself as a potentially destructive creature, who can annihilate with her scornful wit and physical strength" (244). So Brontë's Catherine is a high-spirited "wild wick slip" whose tongue is "always going." Yet Brontë's characterization of the young Catherine is free of the language of deviance Chitham so readily deploys. His narrative is redolent with pathological associations; young Emily is quintessentially "female"—out of "control," "angry," "unbalanced," and "potentially destructive."

If I draw attention back to the critical treatment *Wuthering Heights* has received, it is to stress the way in which author, novel, and characters have lost historical and cultural specific meaning; instead they have become signs of pathological, female, psychic life. As *Wuthering Heights* and other novels of the 1840s and 1850s created the discursive conditions for the emergence of an internal domain of the self, they became the repositories for material no longer locatable in or identifiable with the outside world. This gendered domain, then, would become the focal point and incitement for the discourse of psychology—a new language of self and sexuality. Early nineteenth-century sociology, anthropology, and fiction, I have argued, broke up and reordered social and economic information to formulate an extensive language of gender. With psychology and later with psychoanalysis, I show in chapter 5, this process reverses itself: its self-assigned task was to extract gendered information from the individual and endow it with sense.

Chapter 5

PSYCHOLOGY: THE OTHER WOMAN AND
THE OTHER WITHIN

> The female patients in the Retreat are employed, as much as
> possible, in sewing, knitting, or domestic affairs. . . . Of all
> the modes by which patients may be induced to restrain
> themselves, regular employment is perhaps
> the most generally efficacious.
> (*Samuel Tuke*, Description of The Retreat)

> . . . the patient shall feel absolutely free to tell her own story
> and so [Freud] proceeds from the surface downwards, slowly
> finding and piecing together such essential fragments of the
> history as may be recovered, in the same way . . . as the
> archeologist excavates below the surface and recovers
> and puts together the fragments of an antique statue.
> (*Henry Havelock Ellis*, Studies in the Psychology of Sex)

BY THE MIDDLE of the nineteenth century the English country
house had become a madhouse.[1] In 1844 thirteen out of every ten
thousand English citizens had been officially classified as insane
(Scull 1979), with more added to the rosters every year. So designated,
they were kept in one of the numerous asylums built throughout the
country during the first half of the century, institutions ranging from the
sublime to the ridiculous. The largest, most modern, and most costly asylum in England, Colney Hatch Lunatic Asylum, opened its doors in 1851,
the same year Queen Victoria inaugurated the Great Exhibition at the
Crystal Palace. Colney Hatch boasted an ornate italianate facade nearly
a third of a mile long, with campaniles, cupolas, cornices, and decorative
trimmings. Built to accommodate 1,250 mostly poor patients within its
six miles of wards and corridors, it included a chapel, a stable, a farm,
and a cemetery on the grounds. To Dr. Andrew Wynter, distinguished
editor of the *British Medical Journal*, Colney Hatch presented "the appearance of a town," its wards and corridors an urban sociologist's
dream, so similar were they to "streets inhabited by distinct classes"
(Showalter 1985, 24). Other madhouses retained the gracious facades of
the stately homes they had once been, yet inside dark corridors and damp,

airless rooms resembled those of prisons. The poor were not the only ones to suffer from a growing list of mental "diseases," as they came to be called in the language of medicine that so dominated the business of madness. The middle and upper classes had their madhouses too, although theirs were more luxurious and commodious than those reserved for the laboring classes. Samuel Tuke's advice concerning the treatment of female patients confined within these new madhouses, the initial epigraph to this chapter, represents the first of two points in a discursive process that I argue witnessed a fundamental shift in the conception of femaleness. This chapter traces the path of that cultural revision in the use of the female body from the beginning of the modern madhouse to the discovery of the unconscious, to which Ellis alludes in the second epigraph to this chapter.

Historians of psychiatry have called the period that began in the late eighteenth century and witnessed the enormous growth in numbers of madhouses and madpeople in England and France the "rise of the asylum" or the "age of the asylum" (Doerner 1981, Foucault 1967, Scull 1979). Whereas most conservative historians long associated this period with the "liberation" of the insane from their chains, progressive historians debate the merits of the so-called emancipation. They represent this revolution as a new period of incarceration characterized by more insidious, if less brutal, methods of treatment. Among the two most important recent critiques of psychiatry in the nineteenth century are Andrew Scull's *Museums of Madness* (1979) and Elaine Showalter's *The Female Malady* (1985). As each study chronicles the swift, sure rise of psychiatry to professional power and social acceptance, entirely contradictory sketches of the discipline emerge. A brief outline of the contradiction between their respective analyses of similar data not only identifies a cultural event but outlines the parameters of this chapter.

Museums of Madness takes one into a grim world where insanity and incarcerations proliferate at a staggering rate with every passing year. Nineteenth-century psychiatry, as Scull represents it, constituted an unprecedented expansion in the techniques of intervention in the lives of the working-class individual. In his view, psychiatry in the nineteenth century was a powerful means to modify "socially undesirable behavior" (1979, 266). In other words, *Museums of Madness* represents psychiatry as a form of population management. To support such a claim, the author amasses persuasive data, including the most damning evidence of all: by 1844, according to official statistics, 80 percent of those consigned to madhouses came from the ranks of the disreputable and "respectable" poor (Scull 1979, 201). As the psychiatric profession refined diagnostic techniques and invented new classification systems, the madhouse population grew proportionately. By mid-century English asylums were filled to the brim with "pauper lunatics"—those too poor, too ill, or too crazy to remain in the care of their already-overburdened and impoverished families once asylum keepers began actively recruiting patients to fill their burgeoning facilities. Inside the walls of the madhouse, new techniques changed the face of madness, forever altering its "cultural meaning" (Scull 1979, 68). Those techniques, delineated below, enclosed madness further within the bosom of the middle-class family, where it would be rediscovered by psychoanalysis at the end of the century. The advent of moral therapy was the first of two important shifts in the treatment of insanity to occur roughly within the first half of the nineteenth century. For this and other reasons that will become apparent shortly, I would like to take a moment to review this new technique.

By the early nineteenth century many English asylums had abandoned the coercive and often brutal treatment of the insane prevalent in the seventeenth and eighteenth centuries in favor of a new system called "moral management" or "moral treatment," modeled after the technique devised at the York Retreat by the Quaker William Tuke at the end of the eighteenth century.[2] One of the most celebrated features of the new treatment was that it substituted supervision, observation, and self-discipline for the chains, leather muzzles, handcuffs, and manacles previously deployed to control the insane.[3] Psychological thinking, as manifested in moral management, relied on many of the same figures of separation and division that gave sociology and anthropology their rhetorical and practical power. This convergence of techniques and strategies is illustrated quite clearly in the following excerpt from Robert Gardiner Hill's 1857 report on asylum conditions:

> I made *statistical tables* with great labour; . . . I considered the cases *individually*; I *lived amongst the patients*; I *watched* their habits. . . . At length I announced my confident belief that under a proper system of *surveillance*, with a suitable building, instrumental restraint was in every case unnecessary and injurious. (Doerner 1981, 92, emphasis added)[4]

While Hill's initial task was to investigate the "non-restraint system," he both organizes his task and represents the new system in terms of the identical strategies of the system in question. That is, to organize his material and research into the nonrestraint system, he makes "statistical tables" and separates and divides the patients into individual cases, the better to subject them to observation and surveillance. Such procedures closely resemble those used by the social researcher and the anthropologist to gather knowledge about and organize the urban poor or the "natives."

If the English lunatic asylum looked like a house on the outside, inside moral management structured it like a family that organized the insane and their keepers. Tuke's mode of management reconstituted around the insane a half-real, half-imaginary family—a simulated family to be sure, an "institutional parody" as Foucault observes in *Madness and Civilization* (1967, 254), but a real situation nonetheless. Thus moral management removed the individual and the family from their historic circumstances and isolated them within a "fictitious" family. Early modern psychiatry, as embodied in the discourse and practice emanating from the asylum, posited the middle-class family as the most basic and natural social arrangement; within this family madness was then enclosed and domesticated. As Foucault observes, Tuke's moral treatment "isolated the social structure of the bourgeois family, reconstituted it symbolically in the asylum, and set it adrift in history" (1967, 254).

The family as represented within the context of the asylum was governed, most importantly, by a notion of female domestic benevolence. This domestic model, which Showalter aptly calls the "domestication of insanity" (1985, 28), was materialized in asylums in several crucial ways. First, public asylums were generally managed by a resident medical superintendent and his wife, who usually served as the matron. They presided over an establishment whose look and feel were designed to evoke a "homish" atmosphere. Second, asylum work observed strict gendered divisions of labor that reproduced in miniature the productive and reproductive spheres of home and factory. Females labored at tasks inside the "house" such as laundering, ironing, and cleaning, while males toiled outside the "home" as gardeners and laborers (Tuke 1813). Third, the asylum staff ideally constituted a nucleated family unit, where the superintendent and matron approximated the roles of father and mother kindly tending to their crazy children. The lunatic then was subjected entirely to the authority and discipline of the "adult." "There is much analogy between the judicious treatment of children, and that of insane persons" (1813, 150), wrote William Tuke's grandson Samuel Tuke in his 1813 *Description of The Retreat.*

Clearly the model of female domestic benevolence that infused the asylum—along with such other institutions as the workhouse, school, hospital, and prison—with a new type of authority, did not rely solely on the actual presence and participation of women. Instead, it was a mode of governance that took the reproductive sphere as its model and female domestic authority as its desired form. Madness was domesticated insomuch as it was brought "inside" both the household and the individual and assigned a new set of gendered and individualized features. Moral management, I suggest, was not part of a "paternalist tradition," as Showalter argues, in which " 'humanitarianism was inextricably linked to the practice of domination' " (1985, 50). Quite the contrary, it was a vital experiment with a mode of power modeled after female authority in the domestic sphere within an institutional setting. This type of power, I argue, materialized first in the formation of the domestic sphere in the first half of the nineteenth century. It was later extended beyond the home and institutionalized in the factory, the school, and the hospital, as well as in the asylum in the 1830s, 1840s, and 1850s.[5] Simply to dismiss this transference and technique of power as "paternalism" is to miss this point entirely.

While moral management appeared to deliver the insane from bondage into a promised land of kindness and compassion, in reality, according to Scull, its consequences were far more insidious. In the seventeenth and eighteenth centuries, madmen and madwomen were considered beasts who could be restrained or coerced into outward conformity alone. What moral therapy accomplished was to link madness to the domain of correction. According to earlier historical thinking, the body of the lunatic was an "outside" subject to rudimentary disciplinary measures alone. With the advent of moral management and the collaborative efforts of the companion human sciences, the body was gradually refigured as an "inside" filled with bad desires susceptible to remediation and therapeutic intervention—not surprisingly, by middle-class professionals, psychiatrists, or "alienists." "Instead of merely resting content with the outward control of those who were no longer quite human," Scull writes, "moral treatment actively sought to *transform* the lunatic, to remodel him into something approximating the bourgeois ideal of the rational individual. From this viewpoint, the problem with external coercion was that it could force outward conformity, but never the necessary internalization of moral standards" (1981b, 111). Moral treatment addressed lunatics as subjects, inculcated in them a sense of their own responsibility for controlling their madness, and managed them according to the twin principles of self-restraint and fear. That fear was addressed to the patient directly, not by instruments of coercion, but in speech alone.

To illustrate this interrelationship between verbal coercion, fear, self-discipline, and the domestic scene, I would like to reproduce in some detail a story proudly recounted by Samuel Tuke, grandson of York Retreat founder William Tuke and author of *Description of The Retreat* in 1813. He tells a story of "a man, about thirty-four years of age, of almost Herculean size and figure" who was brought to "the house" in manacles clapped upon him during a fit of violent behavior. As soon as the madman entered The Retreat, the offending restraints were taken off; he was ushered into the superintendents' apartment, who were discovered "supping." The domestic scene in Tuke's representation then takes on transformative powers. When the vision of home reproduced within the mad "house" is artfully revealed to the madman, it magically arrests his attention, calming him sufficiently to allow him to sit down to supper with the good bourgeois and his wife. "After it [supper] was concluded," the author recounts:

> the superintendent conducted him to his apartment, and told him the circumstances on which treatment would depend; that it was his anxious wish to make every inhabitant in the house, as comfortable as possible; and that he sincerely hoped the patient's conduct *would render it unnecessary for him to have recourse to coercion.* The maniac was sensible of the kindness of his treatment. He promised to restrain himself. . . . (1813, 146, emphasis added)

Like the scene of punishment and pleasure enacted between Hareton and Cathy at the end of *Wuthering Heights*, the therapeutic scenario unfolds within a domestic space saturated with "female" benevolence. The superintendent is portrayed as a kind "hostess" desiring to make "her" house guest "as comfortable as possible," yet also as someone possessing the power to make that guest quite miserable if "she" so chooses. Moreover, just as Hareton finds pleasure in Cathy's disciplinary measures, so here the madman derives pleasure not from the gratification of his desire, but from the constraint of it by the contractual agreement. Here too, the power of punishment and reward becomes indistinguishable from the restorative power of the domestication embodied in the feminized figure of the asylum superintendent. Finally, something in this scene is ignored by both Scull and Showalter with their respective models organized by class or gender alone: not only the superintendent, as Showalter denies, but the patient, as Scull ignores, is feminized.

The quintessential nineteenth-century lunatic, as represented in *Museums of Madness*, was a poor, working-class male. Yet as the madhouse was gradually transformed into a domestic space during the first part of the century, the number of female lunatics increased dramatically. By the middle of the century, women constituted the majority of the inmate population (Showalter 1985, 17); the madman had become the madwoman. While this fact is only glancingly acknowledged by Scull, to Showalter in *The Female Malady* it is of the utmost importance. Highly critical of "even the most radical critiques of psychiatry [which] are concerned with class rather than with gender as a determinant of the individual's psychiatric career and of the society's psychiatric institutions," she proposes "to supply the gender analysis and feminist critique missing from the history of madness" (1985, 6). When *The Female Malady* "adds women and stirs,"[6] a picture of the psychiatric discipline emerges that is virtually unrecognizable from that described by Scull. I would like to stress a few of its features briefly in order to understand the nature and importance of this strategical and rhetorical divergence of *The Female Malady* from *Museums of Madness*. Such a divergence is itself a consequence of the nineteenth-century construction of madness, where the category of gender conceals the operation of class, and the category of class conceals that of gender.

"Even when both men and women had similar symptoms of mental disorder," Showalter writes, "psychiatry differentiated between an English malady, associated with the intellectual and economic pressures on highly civilized men, and a female malady, associated with the sexuality and essential nature of women" (1985, 7). Both the world of psychiatry, as Showalter characterizes it, and her mode of analysis are inscribed within a gendered model from the outset so different from Scull's classed model. Showalter does not understand the division of madness into male and female categories as another instance of the cultural production of the gendered individual. Instead, she allows that representation of gender to produce her reading of the history of women and madness. It is a history where male doctors wage relentless war on female patients, and "images of female insanity" are "the stories that the male culture told about the female malady" (1985, 17). Not only does this model build in gender as a given, but it allows little room for historical change. "As the nineteenth century went on," Showalter concludes, "English psychiatry and English culture created new stories about the female malady, but the themes remained essentially the same" (1985, 17). Showalter's task then, within such fundamental historical and cultural immutability, is to trace the long and admittedly shameful history of psychiatry's war against women. Guided by a historically essentialist construct of gender, she cuts a long chronological swath through the history of madness, beginning with its domestication in the nineteenth century and ending with the "culture of antipsychiatry" in the twentieth.

If Showalter argues that the history of madness is one with the history of patriarchy's war against women, Scull contends that the lines of battle were drawn by distinctions of class, not gender. As Scull and Showalter explore psychiatry in the nineteenth century, one must ask, why do they end up with accounts based on mutually exclusive categories of class and gender? Perhaps the most obvious answer is that both depend upon a different cultural and theoretical model to shape their investigations. *Museums of Madness* describes the history of psychiatry in terms of the techniques of population management developed in the early nineteenth century to ensure the reproduction and maintenance of capitalism.[7] This model of history necessarily excludes the female and the household from any representation of the strategies by which the working population was made suitable for the demands of capitalism. Since capitalism, according to this logic, originates outside the household in the "real" economic world, power is any relationship in which men are managed by other men. *The Female Malady*, to its credit, understands that working- and middle-class females ultimately experienced the most nefarious effects of psychiatric management and mismanagement. Throughout the century, working-class women continued to make up the bulk of the asylum population. Middle-class women were gradually confined to the household, where, for reasons I will enumerate, they too became objects of moral management. Showalter's critique, admirable though it may be in this respect, ultimately suffers from its own malady. It falters under the weight of essentialism, as any model must when gender is assumed to be the main determinant of power relations. Most interesting for my purposes in these two accounts is that in describing the history of madness each omits consideration of one factor to talk about the other. Yet I contend that one cannot historicize psychiatry adequately unless one considers both categories of class and gender.

As my histories of sociology and anthropology have illustrated, class and gender are in fact interwoven in the fabric of middle-class history and must be accounted for together. Thus, I consider the history of psychology in light of a third model, which represents gender and class in a mutually constituting relationship within a discursive system. Having argued for the interrelationship between gender and class in the history of psychology, I provide first a brief summary of the figurative strategies by which the human sciences collaborated to organize a social world irrevocably divided by class according to the principle of gender. Then I examine in detail two psychological texts that represent a disciplinary shift away from a focus on the working-class lunatic to one emphasizing the pathological nature of middle-class female sexuality. In doing so, the two texts reveal the interrelationship between sex and class in the history of psychology.

The human sciences surveyed thus far, I have argued, were all concerned in some way with the management of disruptive populations vis-à-vis the female or according to a notion of female domestic authority. Sociological writing and practice penetrated the lives of industrial workers through its portrayal of the factory as an organization divided and separated like a household. At the same time, sociology reorganized the "disorder" of the working-class home according to a middle-class domestic model that presupposed a social role for women as household supervisors. Anthropological writing, on the other hand, portrayed the middle-class family within the family of man according to the norms of heterosexual monogamy, and it located the female within all kinship relations on the basis of her sexual desire. In the asylum milieu of the first halfcentury, psychiatry appropriated the notion of female domestic authority to underwrite a benevolent "state" for the government of lunatics. The domestic imagery that controlled the theory of moral management is made plain in the following 1841 remarks of a doctor who noted the resemblance of a lunatic asylum to

> a nursery or infant school. The patients in it have, like children, their whims and tempers, and are governed by a similar kind of discipline, the same mixture of kindness and authority which is necessary to preserve order in a family. All of them require to be managed, that is, made to feel that they are subject to a superior, who must and will be obeyed. (Showalter 1985, 28)

Such disciplinary measures both produced and reproduced gendered divisions of bodies, spaces, and labor when they subjected the mentally disturbed individual to the kind of observation and regulation that characterized the kind of household in which people were supposed to develop normally. If the logic of gender was a feature of early psychology, then that of class also figured prominently as the discipline focused upon "pauper lunatics"—both male and female—whose social visibility middle-class professionals needed "as a problem of public order, as an object of emancipation" (Doerner 1981, 304), and as an impetus for professionalization.

Sociology's female in the home and anthropology's female in culture, I have argued, paradoxically jeopardized and guaranteed middle-class culture. As a desired object within a social system, the female had the power to preserve the home and the community. As a desiring subject, her unregulated desires threatened the stability of both social formations. With the mid-century shift away from the asylum and into the home, as I will demonstrate, psychology contributed the female in the self. According to this model of psychosexuality, desire in the middle-class female actually bore all the same features as desire in the working-class woman and the savage, which both ensured and threatened home and family. Not only was the "other" woman to be found in the dark tenements of Manchester or the steamy jungles of Africa, she was inside the self. The "other" woman and the other within the self converge in the late nineteenth-century model of the female mind as divided against itself by conflicting "primitive" sexual impulses.

When the human sciences represented the female as the problem, they also established control of the reproductive realm as the solution. Sociology proposed bringing order to the disorder created by poverty by encouraging the poor to form middle-class households. Anthropology envisioned the primitive past as a struggle to establish a proper domestic environment for the nucleated family. Mid-century domestic fiction of the kind that *Wuthering Heights* exemplifies imagined the household and the female within it as the site for the resolution of social and economic problems requiring change only within the individual and the household. Finally, psychology enclosed the lunatic within the mad "house" and madness within the family as part of a therapeutic technique devised along the domestic model. As narratives of progressive improvement, these models augmented and contributed to one another in significant ways. By analogy, the primitive is "lazy," a nonworker like the poor; poor people are undeveloped like the savages. The middle-class household model enabled analogical thinking by serving as a base from which to measure the deviance, and hence degeneration, of the poor and the undeveloped. The household enters into social thinking in another respect as well when both the poor and the primitive are seen as children in relation to more developed "adults." Finally, this analogy is further cemented by the treatment of madness within the middle classes.

Sociology, anthropology, and psychiatry, most importantly, represented the other of class, race, and sex to and for middle-class culture according to the principle of gender, which erased social, cultural, and economic difference. Each discipline, moreover, defined its notion of what the other should be according to its own peculiar logic. Sociological writing, I have argued, was responsible for presenting and representing a notion of the "poor" that circulated as truth through middle-class England. Anthropological writing, as many critics have argued, facilitated colonialism with its representation of the "primitive" or racial other. Especially from 1850 onward, this chapter contends, psychiatric representation provided a natural basis for the subordination of women to men and developed the institutional procedures of enforcing this law. When considered as functions of a single discourse, then, the human sciences were both "colonialist" and "imperialist" in that they were fundamentally concerned with managing "disruptive" populations such as the working class, colonial peoples, and women, and they were deeply involved in writing the subjectivity of the other of class, race, and sex.[8]

PROSTITUTE AND HOTTENTOT: THE OTHER WOMAN

No one can say exactly why moral management went into a profound decline around 1850 or why the Victorians lost faith in domestication as a solution for virtually every social problem of the 1820s, 1830s, and 1840s.[9] The fact remains that they no longer believed in the power of domestication to seat every mother by a happy household fire, to control colonized populations, and to calm lunatics. With the demise of the household remedy came the complete collapse of the asylum's pretension to cure insanity. While asylum populations continued to grow by leaps and bounds throughout the second half of the century, the "house" became a warehouse for the defective and the decrepit. Almost every county in England built mammoth psychiatric institutions that increasingly restricted admission to pauper lunatics. With the failure of the domestic model, moral therapy was replaced by custodial care at best, and by neglect and outright abuse at worst. One must conclude that the use of the household as a model for population management had changed dramatically.

From the 1850s onward, psychiatry came out of the asylum, moved into the private office, and from there penetrated the most "private" recesses of the middle-class home and individual. It might be said that when Marx foresaw a "spectre haunting Europe" in 1847, what he envisioned was not the collective resistance of an oppressed class that would primarily occupy middle-class culture for the next fifty years, but the fantasm of the mind located within the deepest recesses of the individual. Discovered inside the very frontier of the self, this terra incognita threatened to overrun the borders of culture, wracked as it was by storms of impulse, winds of instinct, and torrid summers of desire. This domain, ultimately named the unconscious or the psyche,[10] became the focal point, incitement, reason, and impetus for the multitude of representations of the self and the mind that dominate middle-class culture even today. And even as middle-class Europe consolidated its conceptual mapping of the peoples of Asia, Africa, and Latin America, just as it had surveyed those who inhabited the slums of Manchester and London, so its psychological practices at home firmly focused on the female body.

With loss of faith in the domestic model, the politics of the female body underwent a profound change. To imagine this fabric of transformation, one has only to begin with some of the most familiar, often clichéd, images of the therapeutic scene. We generally associate psychiatry, and its modern offshoot psychoanalysis, with upper- or middle-class women, sitting pale and languid in plush, upholstered chairs among potted palms pouring out sexual secrets to the likes of Freud and Breuer. Or perhaps we see a woman, her bosom heaving, swooning into the arms of a famous psychiatrist. He holds her while lecturing on hysteria at his clinic in La Salpetriere. Over to one side, earnest, bespectacled men observe the scene with rapt attention.[11] Finally, we might remember half-told tales of female desire curtailed by nineteenth-century doctors and their "cures" of constant surveillance, ice cubes inserted in the rectum, and amputation of the clitoris.[12] It is no accident that the scenes that come to mind are dominated by female figures. That the female body was the subject of legal, medical, and scientific debate in many different media, each with its own professionals, well into the second half-century is evidence to suggest that with the breakdown of the domestic procedures as social policy came an unprecedented redefinition of female sexuality and nature.

In the 1860s the prostitute came to occupy a prominent place in the public consciousness. The 1861 publication of Henry Mayhew's extensive study of the prostitute in England, the world, and history, *London Labour and the London Poor*, coincided with a series of statutes passed by Parliament providing for the sanitary inspection of prostitutes (Walkowitz 1980). Under the Contagious Diseases Acts, prostitutes could be identified by a plainclothes policeman and forced to submit to demeaning fortnightly examination if suffering from venereal disease. Such attempts to deal with prostitution located the origin of prostitution in the defectiveness of the women themselves. Bad desires within the female self, not economic necessity, made women "loose." If such representations of working-class women saw class difference as a function of bad female sexual desire, other developing bodies of knowledge linked racial difference to female sexuality in a similar way. Particularly significant were anatomical studies of the aborigine, which accorded a prominent place to the female body. Of that body, certain parts such as the face and the genitals received special consideration. "Account of the Dissection of a Bushwoman," published in 1867 by Flower and Murie, exemplifies a genre that circulated widely in England during the 1860s. Like the madwoman and the prostitute, the Bushwoman of these anatomical accounts deviates from her white middle-class counterpart by virtue of an excess of sexual features, chiefly her protruding genitals.[13] In England, meanwhile, proponents of the new biologically based science of madness urged husbands to examine the faces of their future wives for physical symptoms of degeneracy, specifically malformations of the head, face, mouth, teeth, and ears (Showalter 1985).

When Victorian culture superimposed a class body and a racial body on a female body, it produced a body that distinguished what was docile and desirable in a woman from what was degenerate and desirous. Separate but inseparable, then, the one always called the other to mind. It was for this hybrid body that psychology of the 1870s and 1880s devised private treatment. When doctors and therapists failed to make their upper middle-class female patients sufficiently pliant with intense domestic supervision or extreme physical measures, they began to situate the disorder in female sexuality itself. Moral management returned with a vengeance in a new psychiatric model of female sexuality as "mind" bearing all the deviant features identified in the savage and working-class woman. This model, as I conceive it, took shape in the countless volumes devoted to sexuality that emerged during the last thirty years of the century. Researchers in England, France, and Germany—Henry Maudsley, Edward Carpenter, Charles Frere, Alfred Binet, Albert Moll, Magnus Hirschfield, Wilhelm Fleiss, and Wilhelm Stekel—their names a distant memory now to all but their acolytes, accumulated "a great archive of the pleasures of sex" (Foucault 1978, 64).[14] Among these "pioneer" sex writers, Richard von Krafft-Ebing and Henry Havelock Ellis stand out as particularly representative of what traditional histories of sexuality usually characterize as two opposing moments—"Victorianism" and "modernism."[15] Since Krafft-Ebing's German work *Psychopathia Sexualis* (1886), and its English response, Ellis's *Studies in the Psychology of Sex* (1898), are divided by major disagreements, there would seem to be little common ground between them. Yet if one acknowledges the assumptions the arguments share, one can discern a model of female sexuality authorized by the very disagreements between them.

According to champions of sexual modernism, Ellis broke new ground when he reorganized Krafft-Ebing's categories of "abnormal" sexual behavior into forms and peculiarities of "normal" sexuality.[16] In liberating deviant sexuality from its prison of abnormality and returning it to everyday sexual life, I argue, Ellis makes deviance a *requisite feature* of the normal self. Enclosing pathology within the individual, more importantly, paves the way for a reformulation of female sexual nature as more pathological than its male counterpart. Ellis's *Studies* incorporates the paradigm of female nature developed in *Psychopathia Sexualis*, which closely follows Darwin's *The Descent of Man and Natural Selection in Relation to Sex*. Briefly, Krafft-Ebing imagines the male as the civilizer of nations and empires and the female as the civilizer of the male. When his highly developed competitive instincts threaten to destroy those same nations and empires, it is she who intervenes. If *Psychopathia Sexualis* envisions a restorative role for the female, the *Studies* imagines her as both the restorer and the disrupter of civilization. While the male may be more animalistic, the female is ultimately more primitive according to Ellis, and so she threatens the very stability she enables. Thus while the middle-class woman inhabits a body that *must* be represented in anthropology and sociology, as well as in visual, sexual iconography of the Victorian period, as contrasting with other bodies, psychology links her to the madwoman, the prostitute, and the Hottentot. The middle-class female body is potentially out of control because it encloses primitive sexual impulses that threaten to disrupt the order of things. The female nature of the woman's body is her link to these "other" women and thus it authorizes and shares their subjection. It demands some kind of internal regulation. To show more specifically how a psychosexual model of female mind emerged in the last thirty years of the century, I would like to trace the movement from the depiction of abnormal sexuality in *Psychopathia Sexualis* to its incorporation into the self as an abnormal part of the normal female in the *Studies*.

As the title suggests, *Psychopathia Sexualis* concentrated on abnormal sexuality to the exclusion of so-called normal phenomena. As a medico-forensic study aimed at physicians and specialists, it conformed to a set of formal expectations characteristic of the new discourse of the expert. It is these signs that signify "science" and so lend legitimacy and authority to the relatively new field of psychology. Interestingly, in his 1939 introduction to the authorized English translation, Victor Robinson emphasized these scientific lineaments[17] when he wrote, "Krafft-Ebing was a physician who wrote for physicians. He did not want the public to read his book, so he gave it a *scientific title*, employed *technical terms*, and inscribed the most exciting parts in *Latin*"(i, emphasis added). Its scientific title, unfamiliar terminology, and reliance on Latin—the language of the aristocracy—guaranteed *Psychopathia Sexualis* a scientific readership to the virtual exclusion of even an educated middle-class reading public. Yet the public was undaunted; Krafft-Ebing's study read like an absorbing novel and so won a tremendous readership. The public "swooped down" on Krafft-Ebing, Robinson announces, and "for a half-century have held it to their collective bosom" (1886, iv). Such an overwhelming response to a scientific discourse suggests that theory was fast displacing fiction as the most important source for the language of the self. That is, masculine, professional knowledge took over from the language of common sense and the body of female knowledge that had underwritten domestic fiction earlier in the century. As a result, the professional as expert gradually came to stand in for mother and wife as the privileged purveyor of everyday knowledge.[18] By 1939 Robinson could confidently include scientific prose—"masculine," "muscular," "forthright," and "authoritative," as he characterizes Krafft-Ebing's—in the domain of the male professional.

When Krafft-Ebing wrote *Psychopathia Sexualis* he was deluged by confessionary epistles, testimonials, and autobiographical accounts as sordid and strange as any that found their way into his study.[19] This suggests a population whose sexuality had already been pathologized and problematized in the years preceding the publication of the work. Apparently many were eager to lay bare in exquisite and endless detail the sordid narratives of their "inner lives." Thus "they read and stumbled and read on," Robinson writes, "for after all the bulk of the book was in the vernacular, and to thousands of readers, fascinated and horrified, there was revealed the entire realm of sex turned upside down" (1886, iv–v).[20] The book both required its readers to supply meaning where it was denied to them by Latin inserts and pirated their everyday experience and language. Psychology, in this instance, appropriated the "vernacular" in order to produce a truth text guided by a set of formal requirements characteristic of the language of experts. Yet Krafft-Ebing, as Robinson tells it, "did not want the general public to read his book"; he deliberately mystified it to render it inaccessible to a middle-class readership, and yet the book was still read avidly.

How then did *Psychopathia Sexualis* ensure its professional, scientific status? How did it create the conditions for a professional readership while still requiring interpretation by a specialist? These questions can be answered by turning to the Latin words, phrases, and paragraphs inserted into and surrounded by the idiom of daily life. Such inscriptions are significant because they transform representation into a surface that must be excavated to uncover meaning hidden "below." A section from one of Krafft-Ebing's case histories serves to illustrate this point. "B. claimed to have always been delicate and sickly," Krafft-Ebing writes: "His *vita sexualis* awoke at the age of eight. He began to masturbate and derived much pleasure from *penem aliorum in os arrigere. . . .* He masturbated daily thinking of some man he loved. His ambition was always *penem viri in os arrigere*, which thought caused ejaculation accompanied by the utmost lust" (1886, 386). Neither the subject of the case history, who has told his truth to Krafft-Ebing, nor the reader unfamiliar with Latin, controls the truth of this narrative. As Foucault observes in *The History of Sexuality*, such truth as constituted here is "present but incomplete, blind to itself, in the one who spoke it, it could only reach completion in the one who assimilated and recorded it" (1980, 66). The reading public, moreover, was implicated in the production of meaning as it was called upon to supplement such Latin gaps with its own explanations, suspicions, and theories. Semiosis then is disrupted momentarily by foreign bodies in the text; these lacunae appear to open onto a realm that cannot be captured in language—a realm apparently beyond, below, outside of language, and thus of representation. This occurs in much the same way that Catherine's eerie transformation in *Wuthering Heights* seems to leave her in a domain beyond the expressive potentialities of language itself. In this way, both texts, the fictional and the psychological, suggest the materiality of the unconscious.[21] Even though it remains unnamed as such, both posit something there to be uncovered and named within the self.

Stuff-fetishists, slaves of scatology, defilers of statues, despoilers of children, *frotteurs, renifleurs,* pageists,[22] and satyriasists all parade through the pages of *Psychopathia Sexualis*, as presumably they did through British drawing rooms and bedrooms. After its publication and translation into English, the editor informs us, countless households concealed a volume of Krafft-Ebing "behind innocent rows of Shakespeare and Dickens" (Krafft-Ebing 1886, v). Of course, the novel was no more "innocent" of the language of subjectivity than was psychology. However, the notion of psychology as a lurid book tantalizing the household is a significant one for two reasons. First, it suggests the degree to which psychological thinking permeated domestic space and usurped the power of the novel to imagine the self; second, it is indicative of the notion that both the household and the individual concealed sexual pathology unaware in their midst. The tales told to Krafft-Ebing intimated that enclosed within each individual were illicit and abnormal desires; the self had become its own worst enemy.[23]

Ellis's *Studies in the Psychology of Sex* retrieves deviance from the domain of abnormal sexuality and plants it firmly in that of the normal. Given this, it is significant that the first volume of the *Studies* Ellis readied for publication was devoted to a classic "abnormality"—"sexual inversion" or homosexuality. "It was not my intention to publish a study of the sexual instinct before discussing its normal manifestations," apologizes Ellis in the preface to the first edition. "It has happened, however, that this part of my work is ready first"(1898, 2.1.v). What Ellis regards as coincidence is further evidence suggesting that the "normal" both relied upon and subsumed the "abnormal."[24] The two pairs of lovers in *Wuthering Heights* illustrate well this exquisite paradox. The first pair, Catherine and Heathcliff, are grandly eccentric and quite unable to fit into the social world as such. Cathy and Hareton, in contrast, are subjects of correction by disciplinary processes; Cathy is disciplined by Heathcliff, and she in turn tames Hareton. In the transition from one generation to the next, abnormality is incorporated into "ordinary" deviance that no longer withstands corrective or disciplinary measures. Much as the abnormality of the first pair of lovers paved the way for the subsequent representation of normalcy in the second, so it was through the lens of the abnormal that Ellis believed the normal might be apprehended and focused. He lamented the common description of his work as "pathological." "It was true of the earlier books on the subject of sex," Ellis concedes in the foreward:

> notably of the best-known of these, Krafft-Ebing's, in which the whole field of normal sexuality was dismissed in half a dozen feeble and scrappy pages. The original inspiration of my own work, and the guiding motive throughout, was the study of normal sexuality. I have always been careful to show that *even abnormal phenomena throw light on the normal impulse*, since they have their origin either in an exaggeration or a diminution of that impulse. (1898, 1.1.xxi, emphasis added)

Ellis never questions the existence or validity of abnormal sexuality. Rather, he includes abnormalcy within normalcy by placing them side by side on a continuum of sexualities that both highlights the average and gains from the inclusion of "abnormal phenomena."

The concept of normalcy was upheld by "the facts"—those things that Ellis took to be natural and self-evident. To verify their objectivity, Ellis adopts an ingenuous pose as he relates his own sexual confusion in the following passages from *Studies*. Here the figure of Ellis the individual depicted in a "state of nature" requires the intervention of Ellis the social scientist. In this brief narrative account of the triumph of scientific knowledge, Ellis the scientist provides the solution to problems besetting Ellis, the already-gendered individual. "I determined," he writes: "that I would make it the main business of my life to get to the *real natural facts of sex* apart from all the would-be moralistic or sentimental notions, and so spare the youth of future generations the trouble and perplexity which this ignorance had caused me" (1898, 1.ix, emphasis added). Later he adds, "I have tried to get at the facts, and, having got at the facts, to look them simply and squarely in the face (1898, 1.1.xxvii–xxviii).

Ellis's project was simple; he would uncover a hidden truth of sex and expose it to public view. He admitted the task was not without its obstacles—undue "sentiment" and misguided "moralism" among them. Still, "facts" were necessarily true, and if they could only be discerned the congeries of "ignorance," "trouble," and "perplexity" that had plagued the scientist in Ellis could be painlessly avoided. While sociological or anthropological thinking took as its object of knowledge the other of class or race, who was then constructed in opposition to the middle-class individual, psychological thinking incorporated the self almost immediately into its language. Thus Ellis was concerned from the outset with the "common individual," the poor sod dealt his share of sexual troubles just like everybody else. "Very few middle-aged men and women," Ellis notes, "can clearly recall the facts of their lives and tell you in all honesty that their sexual instincts have developed easily and wholesomely throughout" (1898, 1.1.xxviii).[25] Significantly, the individual, who both justifies and authorizes Ellis's discourse, is reconstituted as a particular field of knowledge whose identity is neither social nor genealogically determined because its fate or development is propelled by sexual instinct. What must be emphasized is that late nineteenth-century psychology signs a contract with the common individual returning sexuality to him or her in exchange for sovereign interpretative authority and expertise. This contract both universalizes psychological theory and secures its position in the hierarchy of scientific knowledges.

Those who glanced furtively at the sordid tales revealed by Krafft-Ebing's study of sexual perversity were only required to identify marginally with the nightmarish world of abnormal sexuality they found inside the covers. Readers of Ellis's *Studies*, however, were dramatically incorporated into psychological thinking about the self when they were contractually obligated as subjects and objects of sexual knowledge. We are all abnormal, Ellis told his readers, albeit some are more abnormal than others. And so the *Studies* addressed itself to all readers quite self-consciously, since they too contained alluring yet potentially disruptive desires in need of therapeutic regulation. This all-embracing analytic stance, I believe, lends Ellis's text its modern feel, familiar also to readers of psychoanalytical theory. For this reason, too, many have hailed Ellis's work as "liberal" or "progressive," a landmark in the struggle to liberate sexuality from the dark dungeon of repression.[26] Such euphoria, however, disguises the fact that any representation of sex as something that has been misapprehended and must be known, something that has been hidden and must be brought to light, and something enchained that must be liberated, itself functions as a component of the discourse of sexuality that produces a truth of sex, even as it claims to discover that truth.

MAIDS AND MADWOMEN: THE OTHER WITHIN

When Havelock Ellis superimposed abnormal onto normal sexuality, it became virtually impossible to tell the difference between the two sexual categories. Since Ellis thought everyone was capable of deviance, he rendered the distinction, so carefully crafted by his German predecessor, almost irrelevant. There was, however, no danger of mistaking a woman for a man. There was also no chance of confusing the female sexual "impulse" with that of the male in Ellis's theory of sexual nature, which he derived in part from that of *Psychopathia Sexualis*.[27] This theory specified exactly what was "male" about men and "female" about women.

Sexual instinct, as described in Krafft-Ebing's study, is a "mighty irresistible impulse" that drives the species to reproduce itself. Propelled by "impulse," incited by desire, instigated by instinct, humans must copulate or die. Yet the desire that guarantees the survival of the species paradoxically threatens its very existence, for sexual instinct is both a lust that cannot be denied and a "lust which must be curbed." "Love unbridled," Krafft-Ebing warns, "is a volcano that burns down all—honour, substance and health" (1886, 2). Thus, to appease this primordial appetite, individuals must actually deny a part of the very desires they wish to indulge, because only the socialized component of sexual desire can become the "mighty factor" in individual and social relations, the acquisition of property, the establishment of a home, and all "altruistic sentiments towards the opposite sex" (1886, 1). There are several things one should notice about this model. First is the way it splits sexual desire within the self into two distinct parts: healthy/unhealthy, bridled/unbridled, civilized/uncivilized, or socialized/unsocialized. The individual is composed of desires that must be regulated if civilization is to grow and prosper. Suffice it to say, the concept of the docile and the dangerous self becomes extremely important in Ellis's analysis of female sexuality, since the female is the domesticator of others as well as herself. Second, in this model sexuality achieves centrality in the narrative of growth and development attributed to individuals and civilizations. Sex subsumes economy, history, and culture in Krafft-Ebing's narrativized account of the origins of the social world as the Victorians knew it. *Psychopathia Sexualis* emulates both McLennan's *Primitive Marriage* and Spencer's *Principles of Sociology* as it locates culture in the midst of a nature redolent with sexuality. Sexual feeling, moreover, lies at the root of ethics, aestheticism, and religion; in short, Krafft-Ebing claims nothing less for sexuality than that it forms "the basis upon which social advancement developed" (1886, 1).

According to the logic of the human sciences, as I have endeavored to show, desire emanated from within an individual defined first and foremost as a sexual being, to the detriment of political or social motivations that conditioned sexual demands, desires, and alliances at an earlier historical moment.[28] Good sexual desire was figured in sociological, anthropological, and fictional writing as the coming together of sufficiently different "things"—male and female. During the first half of the nineteenth century, male and female were differentiated primarily by a set of personality traits bounded and enclosed within a sexed body. As the century progressed doctors, scientists, and anthropologists began to scrutinize living and dead bodies of criminals, prostitutes, lunatics, and Hottentots, avidly seeking signs of physical and sexual degeneracy. As a result, they mapped the gendered body in increasing physical detail, their skills a testimony to their newfound professional status.

Psychological thinking about the individual intensified this trend as it produced a more exact psychosexual language of the self. It was an idiom of difference endowing bodies with biologically gendered features and minds with a sex. "Secondary sexual characteristics," in Krafft-Ebing's assessment for instance, include *both* somatic and psychical manifestations. In his formulation, somatic features such as the size of the skull, the skeleton, and the hair type are complemented by "sexual consciousness," which is "the knowledge of a special sexual individuality as man or woman and a congruous sexual instinct" (1886, 32). This spectacular claim constitutes a truth unencumbered by the usual facts so dear to social scientists. Because Krafft-Ebing can rely upon a metaphysics of self as sexual essence, he extends this logic to include innate distinctions between essences of the opposite sex. That he can blithely substitute essence for substance, metaphysic for fact, is a measure of the success of the human sciences in establishing the self as a form of subjectivity within and bounded by and yet distinct from the body.[29] His strategy also represents psychological aspects of gender as nature as it naturalizes the gendered mind. Moreover, "human nature" is called into being as something attached to but not the same as biology. The "natural psychology of love," *Psychopathia Sexualis* triumphantly announces, is based in the psychical characteristics of the sexes: male desire is active, female desire is passive; males want sex, females want love; sexual desire is strong in males, it is absent in females; males are aggressive, females are modest (1886, 15). One should not be surprised to encounter in the nineteenth century such familiar expressions of sexual identity. Rather, one should wonder at the power of these clichés to dictate the terms by which we understand the modern individual even today.

Given the disruptive nature of male sexuality in Krafft-Ebing's account, how was it to be made to do its work for culture? Like its anthropological counterparts *Primitive Marriage* and *Principles of Sociology*, *Psychopathia Sexualis* maps the route from nature to culture in terms similar to those elaborated in *The Descent of Man and Natural Selection in Relation to Sex*. There Darwin proposes a developmental model for the progress of civilizations based upon the competitive "nature" of the sexual instinct. "The sexual struggle is of two kinds," he explains:

> in the one it is between individuals of the same sex, generally males, in order to drive away or kill their rivals, the females remain passive, whilst in the other, the struggle is likewise between individuals of the same sex, in order to excite or charm those of the opposite sex, generally the females, which no longer remain passive, but select the more agreeable males. (1871, 398)

"Woman is the common property of man," Krafft-Ebing writes in a simplified restatement of this formula, "the spoil of the strongest and mightiest, who chooses the most winsome for his own, a sort of instinctive sexual selection of the fittest" (1886, 2). Male competition, not female choice, this model suggests, is the motive propelling cultural development. A woman is a "chattel," "an article of commerce, exchange or gift, a vessel of sensual gratification, an implement of toil"; in other words, it would seem the female is merely an object—a gift, a container, a tool. Indeed, some readers might stop here, having confirmed their belief in universal, biologically determined patriarchy. But in reading further, I have found that the female occupies a pivotal position both within this model in the movement from nature to culture and in the construction of the modern self. The transformation of nature into culture—of man's mastery over desire—is largely due to woman's mastery over man. It is her choice that pushes the state of nature into culture; once she is driven, in Krafft-Ebing's words, "to bestow her favors as inclined, traces of ethical sentiments pervade the rude sensual appetite, and idealisation begins" (1886, 3). The development of civilization is spurred on by the monogamous drive of the female. By logical extension, the domesticating female would appear to be the more civilized of the two sexes, because she is the first to sublimate her desires and those of her partner to the rudimentary pleasures of civilized life. Nomadic life, to cite one instance, "yields to a spirit of colonization, where man establishes a household. He feels the need for a companion in life, a housewife in a settled home" (1886, 2). While it is the male who feels the lack of a domestic environment, it is the female who chooses the male to move into her home. From that point, it is only a brief interval in Krafft-Ebing's narrative until the "monogamous Christian nations" establish their imperial hold, assuming "mental and material superiority over polygamic races, and especially over Islam" (1886, 5). Once again, one finds here the anthropological impulse first demonstrated in Mayhew's *London Labour and the London Poor* to use monogamous sexuality as the measure of cultural development. Despite the tendency to dismiss such Victorianism as Victorian, one cannot over-estimate the power of such representations to fashion an individual and a family organized by sexuality alone. Indeed, the familiar note Krafft-Ebing's conclusion strikes on the contemporary ear is a tribute to its immense power and effectivity.

Given that the difference between nature and culture is always culturally defined, it is equally true that constructs of nature, such as that modeled in *Psychopathia Sexualis*, uniformly function as forms of self-authorization. Sociological writing locates decayed nature within the individual, while anthropological writing discovers the origins of the Victorian family in the sexual conduct of "primitives." All such constructs of nature, I contend, take their place among an array of collaborative representations that indicate a middle class aware of itself as a class. Given this, one might ask what type of culture is authorized by nature as imagined in Krafft-Ebing's psycho-logic? First, when cultural practice is placed in the domain of nature, culture itself is removed from the exigencies of the social, political, and historical world. Illustrating this point is Krafft-Ebing's historiography, which is a sordid record of sexual perversity and woe, where great cities decay from episodes of "effeminacy, lewdness, and luxuriance," and powerful nations fall from pathological sexual excess (1886, 5–6). Yet while Krafft-Ebing locates sexual instinct in the midst of culture, he places it within instinctual and biological limits, where it remains untouched and unresponsive to history or culture.[30] "Sexual instinct" destroys differences between unrelated classes, races, and cultures by conceptually unifying them within "nature." Thus this concept permits the author to compare "the greater sensuality of the southern races" with the "sexual need of those of the north," and to compare both with the "heightened sexuality" of female city dwellers (1886, 25). Such comparisons reposition the racial other as represented by the figure of "races in the south," and the class other as represented by working-class women in the cities, within a new sexual hierarchy. This occurs in much the same way that the anthropological construct of the "family of man" provided a consensual base from which scientists could make further differentiating judgments between individuals and groups of individuals. "Culture" in *Psychopathia Sexualis*, moreover, is a bricolage made from radically decontextualized bits and pieces of social, political, and historical information. The study blithely yokes together observations about lunatics and "men that have been hung," reports from "experimenters with animals," and anecdotes such as one recounting Henry III's sexual arousal from a scent of perspiration on a lady's handkerchief (1936, 28–31) to make a new notion of culture defined by sexuality. Most important, culture as imagined in this mid-century bestseller is originated and maintained under the watchful eye of the female, whose sexual choice propels nature into culture. That is, only when female choice supercedes the more animalistic demands of male competitors can the social order achieve and maintain stability worthy of the name "culture."[31] Indeed, this model implies that women are the more civilized of the two sexes precisely because they restrain aggressive male impulses that threaten to destroy what men build, and so women safeguard the advances of civilization.

If *Psychopathia Sexualis* suggests the female is the more civilized of the sexes, *Studies in the Psychology of Sex* shows she is ultimately the more sexually primitive, and so liable to disrupt the very civilization she ensures. In the *Studies*, one finds a psychological model of female sexuality bearing all the features that in the savage and working-class woman threatened to overthrow gender difference, and with it social order. To assemble his model, Ellis marshalls "factual," anecdotal, and confessional materials, all of which are made to tell the identical story. Female sexuality, the story goes, is always too little or too much, never just right. When the middle-class woman is good, she sublimates excessive desires acted out unabashedly by prostitute, primitive, or madwoman. In doing so, she becomes "excessively prudish," "morbidly sensitive to sexual impressions," or simply "frigid." When she is bad, she lets loose passion for her unlawful lover, desires "to see masculine nudity," or cohabits with twenty-five men in one night (1898, 1.2.189–224). Either way it seems, female sexuality is always in need of a little tinkering here and a bit of fixing there to keep it properly regulated. Sociology and anthropology, as I have attempted to show, divide the female into two bodies according to the presence or absence of female features; psychology, I argue, encloses both bodies within one. Woman is a kind of desire, according to Ellis, that is deeper, more primitive, more elusive, and more complex than man. To be female is to contain within the self uncivilized or degenerate desires perpetually in need of control, lest they deprive one of "femaleness."

The good psychologist begins his study of "the sexual impulse in women" to rectify the wrongs of woman. To the many who think women are "sexually frigid," or who believe that "sexual anesthesia" is natural in women, Ellis will reveal a world turned upside down. In this other world, the daughter of a country vicar offers herself *"virgo intacta"* to a "man of science," while a respectable young woman proffers first ankle, then "pudenda," to an astonished yet obliging young man (1898, 1.2.224). Thus intent on revealing that which remains hidden from view within the female, Ellis begins his quest. And it is indeed a quest, for the female sexual impulse does not lie on the surface of the body as the male impulse does, but far below it. "A special and detailed study of the normal characters of the sexual impulse in men seems unnecessary," he writes, ". . . if only because it is predominantly open and aggressive" (1898, 1.2.189). Despite his best intentions, Ellis inscribes male and female sexuality within a surface/depth model that assumes that which it should prove. If male sexuality is open, aggressive, superficial, and simple, female sexuality is closed, passive, deep, and complex. "The sexual instinct in women," Ellis recites predictably:

> is much more elusive. This, indeed, is involved at the outset in the organic psychological play of male and female, manifesting itself in the phenomena of modesty and courting. The same elusiveness, the same mocking mystery, meet us throughout when we seek to investigate the manifestations of the sexual impulse in women. (1898, 1.2.189)

It is interesting that this passage represents Ellis the psychologist in the same relation to the female figure as a prospective lover might be. Both pursue her, both desire access to her sexual "secrets." Ellis's language positions the sexual body beneath the female body and then proceeds to discover it in much the same way that Catherine is buried and exhumed in *Wuthering Heights*. That act suggests how fiction earlier positioned the deep, sexual woman (Catherine) beneath the domestic surface (Cathy). In this manner, too, narrative strategies of fiction enter into scientific thinking.

Female sexuality eludes the scientist/lover for two main reasons: it is deep "inside" the body, and it permeates both body and mind. Yet it is everywhere and nowhere at the same time. Illustrating the first point is the following description of one of the most fundamental characters of both male and female sexuality, which Ellis calls "tumescence." Whereas tumescence is a straightforward biological manifestation of arousal in the male, its infinite complexity in the female suggests it belongs more to the psychological than the biological domain. "In man the process of tumescence and detumescence is simple. In woman it is complex," the psychologist explains patiently:

> In man we have the more or less spontaneously erectile penis, which needs but very simple conditions to secure the ejaculation which brings relief. In women we have in the clitoris a corresponding apparatus on a small scale, but *behind*

this has developed *a much more extensive mechanism,* which also demands satisfaction. . . . Naturally the more complex mechanism is more easily disturbed. (1898, 1.2.235, emphasis added)

This passage takes us into female depths not quite identifiable with the biological body. The sense is that the intricate, internal female organs are so distant as to fade into an ill-defined psychological domain. Interestingly, that the female sexual response is more biologically or psychologically complex does not signify that the female herself is more civilized; on the contrary, it means just the opposite. "In coitus the orgasm tends to occur more slowly in women than in men," Ellis continues. "It may easily happen that the whole process of detumescence is completed in the man before it has begun in his partner, who is left either cold or unsatisfied. This is one of the respects in which *women remain nearer than men to the primitive stage of humanity*" (1898, 1.2.236–37, emphasis added). Surely it makes as much sense to argue that prehistoric man had to copulate quickly for fear of discovery or attack by wild beasts, while a slower sexual response would have developed with time and civilization. How then, one must ask, does Ellis jump from the greater swiftness of the male to the greater primitivity of the female? Why, given all he has said to this point, is speed a civilized and not an animalistic, or at least an atavistic, feature of male sexuality? There can be no satisfactory answers to these questions unless one understands that the truths formulated here and in similar psychological studies of the 1870s, 1880s, and 1890s subordinated female to male by establishing the greater primitivity of female nature. In Ellis, woman remains a savage who is never completely civilized.

That female sexuality is everywhere and nowhere at the same time is amply illustrated by the example of the woman Ellis describes who is and is not a desirous female. This woman may "unquestionably be without any conscious desire for actual coitus," Ellis explains. "But if we realize to how large an extent woman is a sexual organism, and how diffused and even unconscious the sexual impulses may be," he continues, "it becomes very difficult to assert that she has never shown any manifestation of the sexual impulse" (1898, 1.2.206). The implications here are twofold: first, and most important, the female is liable to act out sexually at any time, possibly without her knowledge, understanding, or control; and second, what seems to be a lack of sexual desire in actuality may turn out to be an excess of it.

The female is filled with conflicting desires, some of them potentially unregulatable, that paradoxically enable or endanger other desires for home and family. This motif becomes abundantly clear in the following vignettes, which I recount in some detail for that reason. The first describes what happens to "a young girl" when she reaches puberty. " 'On the psychic side,' " writes Hammer, Ellis's German source:

> "there is a feeling of emptiness and dissatisfaction, a need of subjection and of serving, and . . . the craving to see masculine nudity and to learn the facts of procreation. Side by side with these wishes, there are at the same time inhibitory desires, such as the wish to keep herself pure . . . for a man whom she represents to herself as the 'ideal.' . . . " (1898, 1.2.220)

What exactly does this say about female sexuality? The female harbors desires, we are told, that threaten the very domestic stability she seeks; an impure woman cannot find a husband or make a happy home. The desirous female, however, is inseparable here from the docile female who needs to be dominated, the one who feels "a need of subjection and serving."

There can be little doubt that the illicit desires that fill this young woman are meant to be understood as identical to those enacted by maids and madwomen. In a second illustration, Ellis makes this point after regaling the reader with innumerable accounts of bawdy servant girls, including one who sucks a "boy's little dangle" to cure her of "pains in her stomach," another who masturbates children, and a third who "enjoys the spectacle" of male exhibitionism (1898, 1.2.221–22). "The prevalence of such manifestations among servant-girls," he concludes, "witnesses to their prevalence among lower-class girls generally." "In judging such acts," Ellis continues:

> even when they seem to be very deliberate, it is important to remember that at this age unreasoning instinct plays a very large part in the manifestations of the sexual impulse. This is clearly indicated by the phenomena observed in the insane. . . . Among girls of better social position these impulses are inhibited, or at all events modified, by good taste or good feeling, the influences of tradition or education. . . . (1898, 1.2.223)

It is crucial to note in this formulation how working-class women act out their worst impulses while middle-class women subordinate them to better ones because *they regulate themselves*. If maids act out their desires in middle-class houses, madwomen pursue theirs in madhouses. "Insanity tends to remove the artificial inhibitory influences that rule in ordinary life," writes a French source Ellis quotes, "and there is therefore significance in such a fact as that the sexual appetite is often increased . . . to a notable extent in women" (1898, 1.2.251).

A third illustration of the twofold character of female sexuality as defined by the *Studies* comes from "Dr. King" and his description of a condition he calls "sexual hysteria in women." "Sexual hysteria," in Dr. King's words, is " 'a temporary modification of the nervous government of the body ... occurring for the most part ... in prudish women of strong moral principle, whose volition has disposed them to resist every sort of liberty or approach from the other sex' " (1898, 1.1.230). What happens to sexual hysterics once their "nervous government" has been overthrown is similar to what happens to the "prude" whose body contains potentially disruptive, unconscious sexual desires. In both cases, female body and mind betray themselves in unpredictable and uncontrollable ways. Here, the "reproductive ego" " 'overrules the government by volition, and ... forcibly compels the woman's organism to so dispose itself, at a suitable time and place, as to allow, invite, and secure the approach of the other sex, whether she will or not, to the end that Nature's imperious demand for reproduction shall be obeyed' " (1898, 1.1.230).[32] That the female, by implication, must breed at any cost is a need that threatens her civilized self, despite the fact that she may be unaware of her own desires. Paradoxically, there is a fundamental contradiction here: all women are the same, but lower-class women are worse. It seems Ellis must show how some women act out, in order to demonstrate the existence of, a desire requiring repression. What is said about the repressed "prude" makes little sense without working-class and savage women who exhibit other sexual behavior that is supposedly more natural, but still abnormal.[33]

One can see the transformation of female sexuality into female mind in Ellis's discussion of modesty. Ellis provisionally defines modesty at the beginning of the first volume as an "almost instinctive fear prompting to concealment and usually centering around the sexual processes." While "common to both sexes," modesty is "more peculiarly feminine, so that it almost may be regarded as the *chief secondary sexual character* of women on the *psychical side*" (1898, 1.1.1, emphasis added). Female sexuality, that is to say, is all in the head. Interestingly enough, Ellis reverses himself two hundred pages later; modesty, he concludes, is not really what it appears to be. "The seeming reluctance of the female is not intended to inhibit sexual activity either in the male or in herself, but to increase it in both," he decides. "The passivity of the female, therefore, is not a real, but only an apparent, passivity" (1898, 1.2.229). Just as normal is abnormal, and absence is really presence, so in the logic of the *Studies* modesty is anything but timidity, while concealment amounts to exposure. "The true nature of the passivity of the female is revealed," Ellis continues, "by the ease with which it is thrown off, more especially when the male refuses to accept his cue" (1898, 1.2.232). In the game of courtship the first move may be the male's prerogative, but make no mistake—under the female's blush lurks an aggressive contender for his love.

Taken together, then, both definitions of modesty reproduce the very contradiction implicit within Ellis's model of female sexuality. That is, how can women by nature be repressed and openly aggressive? How can both be true if the savage and working-class woman are abnormal human beings, although closer to nature, and if the middle-class woman in a normal state keeps her savage self under control? Simply put, this is how late nineteenth-century psychology constitutes a woman whose female-ness, although closer to nature than male sexuality, is unstable and de-stabilizing. It is this femaleness that theories of hysteria will confirm, thus positioning all those whose gender, race, or ethnicity endows them with features in common with the middle-class woman in some relationship to the rational middle-class male. This point cannot be emphasized too much. One has only to look at the following passages from Freud and Darwin to understand that in the time intervening, psychological theory repositions the woman under the man with all the attendant conse-quences. "The sexual struggle is of two kinds," writes Darwin in a pas-sage from *The Descent of Man* quoted earlier:

> in the one it is between individuals of the same sex, generally males, in order to drive away or kill their rivals, the females remain passive, whilst in the other, the struggle is likewise between individuals of the same sex, in order to excite or charm those of the opposite sex, generally the females, which no longer remain passive, but select the more agreeable males. (1871, 398)

In contrast to this crucial role Darwin imagines for the female in the tran-sition from nature to culture, Freud virtually effaces her almost sixty years later in his revision of Darwin's theory in *Civilization and Its Dis-contents*:

> One may suppose that the founding of families was connected with the fact that a moment came when the need for genital satisfaction no longer made its ap-pearance like a guest who drops in suddenly, and, after his departure, is heard of no more for a long time, but instead took up quarters as a permanent lodger. When this happened, the male acquired a motive for keeping the female, or, speaking more generally, his sexual objects near him; while the female, who did not want to be separated from her helpless young, was obliged, in their inter-ests, to remain with the stronger male. (1930, 46)

By creating the under-woman in the image of the underclass and the racial underdog, psychology accomplishes two things. It not only subordinates woman to man but it also contains and effaces other, more clearly politi-cal, forms of oppression within that of gender.

The representation of hysteria, finally, is the most powerful means by which psychological thinking shifts away from a biological to a psycho-logical model of female sexuality. The study of hysteria had an old and venerable history by the time Ellis and Freud began their work late in the nineteenth century. In fact, the science of psychology was founded upon and periodically replenished by research into hysteria.[34] What distinguishes late nineteenth-century enquiries into hysteria, however, from earlier research is a decided shift from the biological to the psychological nature and manifestations of the disease. Quite deliberately, Ellis denounces older theories of the physical etiology of hysteria. "It is clearly demonstrated that the physical sexual organs are not the seat of hysteria," he announces. "It does not, however, follow," he continues, "that even physical sexual desire, when repressed, is not a cause of hysteria" (1898, 1.1.216). I would like to draw attention to several crucial features that follow from this redefinition of the hysterical female. While biological symptoms may still translate into psychological ones through the agency of repression, hysteria is represented above all as a psychological malady. Moreover, the female hysteric represses illicit sexual desires that, once again, are acted out by working-class women and primitives. This much one may infer from Ellis's quotation of A.F.A. King's list of the twelve characteristics of hysteria, leading one to believe that middle-class women are among those who lead the "idle, purposeless life" so conducive to hysterical attacks (1898, 1.1.229n.). The hysterical phenomena he considers to be "facts" common to women appear only under the "artificial conditions of civilized life." Neither "primitive" women unencumbered by the burdens of civilization[35] nor factory women who incorporate the rhythmic motions of pedal sewing machines and other mechanical devices into autoerotic episodes are repressed or, by extension, hysterical (1898, 1.1.176). Ellis locates hysteria in the psychosexual pathology of the female, which to a greater or lesser extent is *always* hysterical.[36] The analysis of hysteria, then, provides the perfect discursive occasion to prove that female sexuality is not only more elusive, more complex, and more primitive than male sexuality, it is also more pathological.

Ellis argued that hysteria arose from a sexual scar etched into consciousness by a traumatic experience in early childhood. In nearly every case, "the intimately private nature of the lesion causes it to be carefully hidden from everyone," so that even the subject remained virtually unaware of its existence (1898, 1.1.222). This scar or "primary lesion" acted like a "foreign body in consciousness," causing a morbid change in the structure of consciousness itself. Thus scarred, the hysterical individual can only be cured by materializing the original experience in language. "The mere act of confession," writes the English psychologist, "may greatly relieve hysterical symptoms produced by this psychic mechanism [the lesion], and in some cases may wholly and permanently remove them" (1898, 1.1.223). One should note several important features of this model of hysteria. First, experience apparently exists prior to its representation in the confessional narrative. Yet confession itself, as Foucault has shown in *The History of Sexuality*, materializes forms and peculiarities of the self and social relations that he claims do not exist prior to their representation in language. Throughout the nineteenth century, myriad confessional experiences focused on the sexual act—thoughts, obsessions, images, and desires were formulated in memoirs, autobiographies, letters, or consultations between priest and sinner, parent and child, teacher and student, doctor and patient. This mass of information, Foucault argues, accumulated into an intricate language of sexuality, a "sexual mosaic," requiring, even demanding, scientific intervention to extricate what was hidden from the one who spoke.

Ellis implies that part of the mind may be expelled from consciousness of necessity once it has been imprinted with the pathological experience. That "foreign body" does not disappear; it simply moves to a different psychic address, where it awaits transposition into the physical idiom of the symptom. "Something is introduced into psychic life," Ellis writes, "which refuses to merge in the general flow of consciousness. It cannot be accepted simply as other facts of life are accepted . . . and so submitted to the slow usure by which our experiences are worn down and gradually transformed" (1898, 1.1.222).[37] If one reads backward through the culture of psychoanalysis, it is easy to name the unconscious as the domain that awaits the "something" "which refuses to merge in consciousness." The unconscious is not named as such, I believe, primarily because the *Studies* remains deeply immersed in the mechanistic figures of biology. If not specifically identified in content, however, Ellis's impenetrable prose certainly evokes the apparently impenetrable depths of the unconscious. This account of the fate of the hysterical symptom fades away into grammatical and logical oblivion. Further, since the passage is abstract and entirely lacking in sense, it suggests the amorphous and nonsensical character of the unconscious. Finally, such a syntactic and semantic vacuum requires the intervention of the specialist equipped with "scientific" and hermeneutic instruments of decipherment. Only the highly skilled techniques of the auditor, among which Freud's are the best according to his English admirer, can translate nonsense into sense. Freud "simply tries to arrange," Ellis observes in the passage that also serves as the second epigraph to this chapter:

> that the patient shall feel absolutely free to tell her own story, and so proceeds from the surface downwards, slowly finding and piecing together such essential fragments of the history as may be recovered, in the same way he remarks, as the archeologist excavates below the surface and recovers and puts together the fragments of an antique statue. (1898, 1.1.222)

Here the psychological method as characterized in Ellis's depiction of Freud's work assumes the existence of an originary signified that can only be reclaimed as a signifier. Simply put, the "statue" can only be recovered and its original existence verified through its discursive re-creation from fragmented shards of clay.

Impressive as it is, the analogy of the ruined statue is flawed, and Ellis knows it. Even within the psychoanalytic model he so admires, impressions in the unconscious do not remain static awaiting the scientist-archeologist; they constantly metamorphose into new shapes and figures. Because of this instability, Ellis is highly mistrustful of any semantic content unearthed as a result of such analytic procedures. Meaning to him always remains elusive and deceptive, and it often screens yet a deeper layer that must be explored by the therapist. "Much of the material found," the *Studies* warns, "has only a symbolic value requiring interpretation and is sometimes pure fantasy" (1898, 1.1.222). The depths of the self, this model suggests, provide endless justification for psychological meddling with the individual unaware of her own psychic profundity. In the course of the therapeutic encounter the female patient cedes information to the observer that, by implication, loses its authority. She is ignorant of her self until that self is rendered visible in the language of the professional. And who is the woman she finally sees in psychology's mirror? She is both a woman and not a woman, a figure who represents the logical culmination of Matthew Arnold's notion of a "better" self responsible for subordinating the worst impulses of the "ordinary" self to internal regulation. Because she contains within her the other woman, who poses a constant danger to the social order, she must be ever vigilant lest the savage, the prostitute, or the madwoman escape.[38]

By the end of the nineteenth century, then, gender is no longer a physical thing that can be opened up and debated, but the metaphysical basis of professional expertise available only to a few. Along with gender, the body where it resides has become a metaphor for talking about the modern industrial state.[39]

Chapter 6

EPILOGUE: MODERNISM, PROFESSIONALISM, AND GENDER

I N 1898 HAVELOCK ELLIS rescued sexual fact from "moralistic and sentimental" fiction when he vowed to make it the "main business" of his life "to get to the real natural facts of sex apart from all would-be moralistic or sentimental notions" (1898, 1:ix). His narrative of personal sexual darkness called forth Ellis the psychologist to dispel this gloom of ignorance with the shining light of science, implying that only Ellis the professional could solve the problems besetting Ellis the already-gendered individual. Yet in substituting scientific "facts" for sentimental "notions," and so rewriting the terms by which individuals understood their sexuality, he did something more than invite science into the dark closets of the mind. I have argued that throughout much of the nineteenth century, so-called moralistic and sentimental notions underwrote a model of female domestic authority that governed the middle-class debate on the individual, the family, and sexuality, as well as on the working class, the criminal, and the insane. When *Studies in the Psychology of Sex* dismissed this familiar nineteenth-century language of domestic power as mere morality and sentimentality, it also declared it to be outmoded and thus quaint, even cranky. Most important, Ellis's study appropriated the self from the feminine domain of knowledge for masculine, rational, scientific discourse. While the object of psychological discourse remained female, the discourse became masculine.[1] And masculine, scientific models of the female continue to dominate medical textbooks and popular descriptions today. These models even permeate the very language women use to talk about themselves (Martin 1987).

These conclusions may startle those who regard turn-of-the-century psychology as an emergent science in hot pursuit of the secrets of mind and the psychologist as an explorer venturing into terra incognita. On the contrary, far from creating knowledge anew, psychology, like sociology and anthropology, constructed it by force when it reorganized older cultural materials into new categories. Specifically, psychology dismantled an older language of female domestic power and incorporated it into the masculine language of the professional expert, much as anthropological writing both integrated and overturned the language of kinship in favor of that of gender to represent the modern family. Such appropriative behavior is entirely consistent with patterns of professionalization Dietrich Rueschemeyer identifies in *Power and the Division of Labor*. "Exaggerated claims of validity and effectiveness, selective development of knowledge . . . as well as protective maintenance of mystique and complexity and the *derogation of alternative approaches*," he writes, "are indeed among the tools of professional self-advancement" (1986, 118, emphasis added). Thus, psychological knowledge depowered and subordinated the domestic model even as it elaborated and updated it in professional terms. On this basis the culture of the expert made new inroads into modern life as psychological professionals increasingly won the right of all professionals to determine "what constitute[d] a problem fit for, and in need of, expert intervention" (Rueschemeyer 1986, 118).

The relationship between the masculine culture of experts and the female language of sentiment is a suggestive one. It does much to illuminate the more problematic bond between the modernist novel and nineteenth-century realist fiction. I would like to suggest a few of the more enticing possibilities for reading the modernist novel in light of the history of gender in domestic fiction and the human sciences as I have represented it.

Modernism as a visual and verbal aesthetic has provoked raging fights ever since it set foot on the historical stage in the early years of this century. Pound's imperative to "make it new," Woolf's vehement rejection of the "Edwardian" realists—"Mr. Wells, Mr. Bennett, and Mr. Galsworthy"[2]—have been met by equally strenuous denunciations of modernist aesthetics. While competing critical evaluations of the movement have flooded the intellectual marketplace, two rival positions, according to Fredric Jameson, have set the terms for the debate. Among the most famous is the bitter attack by Marxist philosopher Georg Lukács, who argued that the new movement, in Jameson's words, amounted to nothing less than a "symptom of the reification of late capitalist social relations" (1979, 13). "Ideologists of the modern,"[3] on the other hand, argued that "the formal innovations of modernism are to be understood as essentially revolutionary acts, and in particular as the repudiation of the values of a business society and of its characteristic representational categories" (Jameson 1979, 13). The "truth" of modernism, one suspects, lies somewhere between a slavish subjection to capitalist social relations and the complete rejection of the literary status quo. This would suggest, as Jameson does, that "the concept of modernism [is] realism's historical counterpart and its dialectical mirror image" (1979, 198). Provisionally, then, I contend that the modernist novel is like the realist novel, but to be like realist fiction, modernist fiction must turn against it.

Bearing this formulation in mind, let us return to the equation between modernism and realism and Ellis's discourse and the female language of morality. It is fair to say that psychology consciously cultivated a professional idiom, setting it apart from what had become common knowledge by the end of the nineteenth century. I suggest, by way of conclusion, that the modernist novel, like psychology, behaves like a professional discourse, and for two primary reasons. First, modernist fiction of the type represented by Virginia Woolf's *Mrs. Dalloway* and D. H. Lawrence's *Lady Chatterley's Lover* appropriates the materials of female subjectivity to make a professional language of art; second, it too finds its object of knowledge in the moralism and sentiment that constituted a form of middle-class power not fifty years before. As such, modernist fiction carries out the same political project that psychology had—albeit in a different rhetorical, thematic, and stylistic form—which rendered the model of female domestic benevolence anachronistic.

I am aware, of course, that to call modernist fiction a professional language and the modernist author a professional is a radical departure from much critical thinking about the movement. This is especially true for those accustomed to think reverently of the avante-garde writer as "the immured priestess [or priest] in the temple of art—dedicated, solitary, out of touch with the life of her [or his] time" (Zwerdling 1986, 9). Let us take a closer look at the ways in which modernism belongs to the culture of experts. In addition to leaving behind the enduring notion of the isolated artiste, modernism has bequeathed another, less famous legacy to the twentieth century. Modernist fiction changed the way people read novels. Behind new modernist techniques, to put it another way, was a new relationship to the audience (Zwerdling 1986). Novels written in the language of art, like *Mrs. Dalloway*, required special rules and categories of plot, setting, narration, and character. One must admit that to follow Woolf's novel through various transformational rules from the conventions of standard English to the specialized rules governing fictional discourse and ultimately to those of a highly individualistic style is no easy task for the untrained reader. Yet if *Mrs. Dalloway* is inaccessible to the common readers, it is not because of their incompetence, as Mr. Bennett or Mr. Bloom would insist.[4] On the contrary, it is because the novel updates the rules of ordinary competence and so goes beyond the reaches of common knowledge to the more rarified environs of art. And art in our culture, as many of us know but won't often acknowledge, belongs to the few who can afford to purchase it or to their children endowed with the costly private education that enables them to make sense of it. Thus, modernism behaves like a professional language because it sets itself apart from the reader and so dictates the conditions for the intervention of the specialist (critics and academics like myself included).

In this light, it can be no accident that literary criticism underwent intense professionalization in England at the same time that modernism flourished. Shortly before F. R. and Q. D. Leavis began to demand formal rigor and self-consciousness from novelist and reader alike in the pages of *Scrutiny*, the middle class formalized English literature curriculums at Oxford (1893) and Cambridge (1917) (Batsleer 1985). Modernism, growing institutionalization of English literature, and professionalization of literary criticism cannot be separated. Together they attest to one of the most important political realities that I have tried to demonstrate in my readings of domestic fiction and the human sciences in the nineteenth century: namely, that the institutions and representations of cultural hegemony and the ideological struggles they articulate "are no less 'material' than guns and prisons" (Batsleer 1985, 19) in the constant struggle to maintain middle-class power.

Modernist fiction belongs to the culture of experts in another crucial respect. It is motivated to a considerable extent by the will to observe and to know the female. Both Mrs. Dalloway and Lady Chatterley are objects of knowledge within the novels that bear their names, much as knowledge of the female justified practices and discourses from the Contagious Diseases Acts to *Studies in the Psychology of Sex*. If Woolf and Lawrence claim to make art, then, it is in some way due to their depiction of the beautiful woman who comes to life either in the absence of the penis (Mrs. Dalloway) or in its presence (Lady Chatterley).

Not only is it unusual to compare modernism to the language of experts, it is also odd to talk about the fiction of Woolf and Lawrence in the same breath. After all, the differences that seem to divide them apparently outweigh any potential similarities. Woolf's rich, languid prose of female consciousness, her clever critical essays, and Mrs. Dalloway hardly seem to occupy even the smallest bit of common ground with Lawrence's gritty, masculine evocations of working-class life, his cosmic sexual mythology, and Lady Chatterley, or her lover, for that matter. If the fiction of Woolf and Lawrence apparently speak from entirely different aesthetic moments, perhaps it is because the modernist novel demands to be read as an expression of "personal styles and private languages" (Jameson 1979, 2) bearing little relation to their historical moment. This is the case because the modernist novel distinguishes itself from Victorian fiction precisely when stylistic and thematic individuality replaces attention to narrative convention as the distinctive mark of the new novel (Armstrong 1983, Jameson 1979). By resisting normative categories of style, narrativity, and grammar, the modernist novel revises Victorian fiction, making each novel a "signature of the author" (Armstrong 1983).[5] Significantly, the rhetoric of modernism bears a striking similarity to that of Ellis's psychological writing. Both incorporate abnormality into their discourse, which then becomes a component of a newly defined normality. Psychological writing, that is, redefines normal sexuality as inherently pathological; modernist writing cultivates rhetorical and stylistic deviance to form a new set of conventions.

Since the modernist novel, is by definition a highly individualized cultural form, resistant to historical appraisal, it raises the problem of how to historicize writing apparently alienated from history. "The most influential formal impulses of canonical modernism," Jameson writes in *Fables of Aggression*, "have been strategies of inwardness, which set out to reappropriate an alienated universe by transforming it into personal styles and private languages; such wills to style have seemed in retrospect to reconfirm the very privatization and fragmentation of social life against which they meant to protest" (1979, 2). Jameson remains well within a paradigm of individualism when he interprets modernist rhetorical and stylistic personalization as inherently different, *individualized* responses to the social fragmentation of the capitalist world. Yet it is precisely the very fact of difference, ironically, that makes things the same. In other words, if such seemingly disparate novels as *Mrs. Dalloway* and *Lady Chatterley's Lover* are to be historicized adequately, I contend, we must resist the temptation to interpret them in their own individualistic terms. More specifically, since the modernist novel represents itself as a private discursive space referenced only to the gendered individual, it implicitly demands to be interpreted on those grounds. To do so, I insist, would be to accede to a dangerous cultural logic, a logic that depoliticizes discourse by detaching it from the social world to locate it in the ahistoricism of the gendered self. Mrs. Dalloway and Lady Chatterley are markers of historical change. They came into being at a moment when the authority granted to women's feelings and experience in the nineteenth century was undergoing drastic revision within the new culture of the expert. If it is difficult to comprehend the significance of this transformation, perhaps it is because we cannot remember what we have been made to forget—that representations of gender have a political and historical meaning inseparable from the meaning of middle-class power. What has been lost or misplaced and what must be rediscovered is the political and social information that would allow us to make sense of such representations as forms of cultural power.

NOTES

CHAPTER 1
INTRODUCTION: THE MAKING OF DOMESTIC CULTURE

1. For an analysis of the political unconscious as constituted in and through narrative, see Fredric Jameson, *The Political Unconscious: Narrative as a Socially Symbolic Act* (1981).

2. In *The Great Arch: English State Formation as Cultural Revolution* (1985), Philip Corrigan and Derek Sayer identify a similarly selective process as central to the formation of the bourgeois state:

> Out of the vast range of human social capacities—possible ways in which social life could be lived—state activities more or less forcibly 'encourage' some whilst suppressing, marginalizing, eroding, undermining others. . . . Certain forms of activity are given the official seal of approval, others are situated beyond the pale. This has cumulative and enormous, cultural consequences; consequences for how people identify (in many cases, *have to* identify) themselves and their 'place' in the world. (4)

3. This is but one way in which this suppressed or marginalized material reappears. "Because society is not factually a unity these [other ways of seeing, other moralities] can never be finally erased" (Corrigan and Sayer 1985, 6).

4. What these women lost, over the course of a century, was the right to an experience-based language that would have allowed them to make sense of the world in their own terms and to integrate that understanding into their everyday life in a culturally authorized fashion. "Whether a worker experiences his or her physical reaction on the assembly line as a personal biological deficiency," Jochen Schulte-Sasse writes, "or whether he or she learns, through reflection and discussion, to see those experiences as part of a collective, social phenomenon, depends on the availability of institutions that allow ordinary members of society to develop 'languages' that provide them with a medium for transforming what is merely lived into experiences that have been comprehended and integrated into their consciousness" (1988, 196).

5. See Doerner, *Madmen and the Bourgeoisie: A Social History of Insanity* (1981); Gilman, *Difference and Pathology: Stereotypes of Sexuality, Race, and Madness* (1985b); Foucault, *The History of Sexuality*, vol. 1 (1980) and *Discipline and Punish* (1979).

6. In so doing, I join a growing array of historians, new anthropologists, and literary critics whose analyses break up traditional modes of historical causality and focus instead on the role of language and writing in the history of modern culture. See Michel Foucault, *The History of Sexuality*, vol. 1 (1980); Leonore Davidoff and Catherine Hall, *Family Fortunes: Men and Women of the English Middle-Class 1780–1850* (1987); Joan Wallach Scott, *Gender and the Politics of History* (1988); Johannes Fabian, *Time and the Other: How Anthropology Makes Its Object* (1983); Jean Comaroff, *Body of Power, Spirit of Resistance*

(1985); Nancy Armstrong, *Desire and Domestic Fiction: A Political History of the Novel* (1987a); Page DuBois, *Sowing the Body* (1988); Masao Miyoshi, "Against the Native Grain: The Japanese Novel and the 'Postmodern' West" (1988); Edward Said, *Orientalism* (1979); and Leonard Tennenhouse, *Power on Display: The Politics of Shakespeare's Genres* (1986).

7. For a further discussion of this professional group see chapter 1. Also see Davidoff and Hall (1987), Perkin (1989), and Perkin (1969).

8. For a detailed discussion of the early modern or protoindustrial family, see Armstrong (1987a), chap. 1; Hans Medick, "The Proto-Industrial Family Economy: The Structural Function of the Household and Family during the Transition from Peasant Society to Industrial Capitalism" (1976); and Randolph Trumbach, *The Rise of the Egalitarian Family* (1978).

9. Trumbach's history of the aristocratic family in the eighteenth century (1978) quite explicitly identifies the historical shift that placed the responsibility for the health, welfare, and education of the family exclusively in the domain of the female. He outlines, in particular, the role of the doctor and medical literature in this shift. See also Jacques Donzelot, *The Policing of Families* (1979), and Foucault, *History of Sexuality*, vol. 1 (1980).

10. For an example of an early feminist discussion of the interrelationship between capitalist and patriarchal relations implied in my brief formulation, see Heidi Hartmann, "The Unhappy Marriage of Marxism and Feminism: Toward a More Progressive Union" (1981). More recently, in their introduction to *Feminism as Critique* (1987), Seyla Benhabib and Drucilla Cornell critique what they call an "earlier stage of feminist thinking [about] the confrontation between Marxism and feminism." They criticize "such calls for a more progressive union" because they were themselves "vitiated by the fact that the Marxism appealed to by feminists and considered paradigmatic was itself 'orthodox Marxism' "(2). "Feminist theorists formulated their demands for a more progressive union between feminism and Marxism," Benhabib and Cornell maintain, "without challenging the primacy of production implied by the orthodox model" (2).

11. " 'Production' and 'reproduction,' work and the family, far from being separate territories like the moon and the sun or the kitchen and the shop," writes Rosalind Petchesky,

> are really intimately related modes that reverberate upon one another and frequently occur in the same social, physical . . . spaces. . . . Not only do reproduction and kinship, or the family, have their own historically determined products, material techniques, modes of organization, and power relationships, but reproduction and kinship are themselves integrally related to the social relations of production and the state. . . . (1979, 376–77)

12. Here I am relying only peripherally on the Lacanian notion of the imaginary defined as a specific stage or instance in the constitution of the self. "The 'Imaginary' is a stage prior to linguistic competence . . . where the child begins to find a coherent sense of self by observing his/her bodily image (in a mirror, in relation to the body of the mother)" (Kavanagh 1985, 101). The image is not simply a reflection of a preexisting subject, but a tool for the creation of self supplied by an external figure such as the mirror image or the mother.

13. In her introduction to *Sea Changes: Culture and Feminism* (1986), Cora Kaplan insists that "cultural expression," "subjectivity," and the "quality of social . . . life," issues that I consider part of the reproductive sphere, remain on the agendas of socialism and feminism. She sees "a narrowing of the political vision of the left to traditional issues of economics and politics in the face of a massive shift to the right in western societies" as simply "part of a conservative retrenchment" (5). Yet feminism, like the political left in general, has also been shaped by the massive historical shift fostered in part by the human sciences, and so it often does not include the household in history or the female in the home as an historical agent. However, if politics and history have been put back into a home drained of all political meaning in the nineteenth century, it is largely due to both the contemporary feminist movement and feminist criticism.

14. Cultural critics have only recently begun to conceptualize the individual, familial, and sexual practices of everyday life that collectively constitute "middle-class culture." Davidoff and Hall, *Family Fortunes*; Linda Nicholson, *Gender and History* (1986); and Peter Stallybrass and Allon White, *The Poetics and Politics of Transgression* (1986) are among the most recent studies that flesh out the historical specificity of middle-class culture in England. My understanding of this complex notion is highly indebted to the imaginative way in which these and other studies cross and recross traditional disciplinary boundaries to construct new and vital ways of seeing writing as a cultural product constituted and constituting of power relations. In addition, Raymond Williams's extensive work on class and culture in *The Long Revolution* (1961), Roland Barthes's delineation of the "mythical" character of the middle class in *Mythologies* (1972), and Edward Said's stunning research on "Orientalism" have served informally as my inspirations and models for politically responsible academic work on aspects of middle-class hegemony.

15. See *The Political Unconscious: Narrative as a Socially Symbolic Act* (1981).

16. See Scott, *Gender and the Politics of History*, for a brilliant reevaluation of the interrelationship between these categories.

17. Following Marx's lead, E. P. Thompson's highly respected exhaustive study, *The Making of the English Working Class* (1966), for example, does not interrogate the boundary between the productive and the reproductive.

18. In *The History of Sexuality*, Foucault redefines "repressive" in the usual sense by directly opposing it to "productive." He goes as far as to suggest that in modern culture the production of human subjectivities may be more "basic" to the class hierarchy than production in the classical sense. Foucault thus provides the possibility for inverting or dissolving the base/superstructure distinction, a move that is becoming even more necessary to theorizing power as we encounter the "postmodern condition."

19. Teresa de Lauretis criticizes Foucault's work in *The History of Sexuality* on the grounds that it lacks a serious consideration of what she calls, after Foucault, " 'the technology of gender'—the techniques and discursive strategies by which gender is constructed" (1985, 18). While this point is well taken, I attempt to build gender back into Foucault's model as a component of sexuality and so return it to historical and semiotic consideration.

20. Ernesto Laclau and Chantal Mouffe, *Hegemony and Socialist Strategy—Toward a Radical Democratic Politics* (1985), has been especially important in allowing me to imagine hegemony as an "articulatory practice" where contesting forces attempt to appropriate, rearticulate, and rerepresent the signs and symbols of a culture. "The general field of the emergence of hegemony is that of articulatory practices," Laclau and Mouffe write, "that is, a field where the 'elements' [any difference not discursively articulated] have not crystallized into 'moments' [differential positions articulated within a discourse]. In a closed system . . . in which the meaning of each moment is absolutely fixed there is no place whatsoever for a hegemonic practice" (134). Their work challenges several basic Marxist assumptions, including economic and historical determinism, and the notion of the autonomous and unified identity of the subject. "What is now in crisis," Laclau and Mouffe argue:

> is a whole conception of socialism which rests upon the ontological centrality of the working class, upon the role of Revolution, with a capital 'R', as the founding moment in the transition from one type of society to another, and upon the illusory prospect of a perfectly unitary and homogenous will that will render pointless the moment of politics. The plural and multifarious character of contemporary social struggles has finally dissolved the last foundation for that political imaginary. Peopled with "universal" subjects and conceptually built around History in the singular, it has postulated "society" as an intelligible structure that could be mastered on the basis of certain class positions and reconstituted as a rational, transparent order, through a founding act of a political character. (2)

On this point, see also T. J. Jackson Lears's "The Concept of Cultural Hegemony: Problems and Possibilities" (1985).

21. To this brief discussion of Gramsci's theory of the intellectual, it might be useful to inject the cautionary note sounded by Stanley Aronowitz in "Postmodernism and Politics" (1988). He argues that to speak in strictly Gramscian terms is to deny professionals and intellectuals their own specific interests. "[E]mbedded in Gramsci's idea of hegemony," Aronowitz writes:

> is the assumption that intellectuals as a social category do not bring to social movements any interests of their own. This explicit denial of intellectuals as a "class" is rooted in the notion of an intellectual as a person of "ideas," who represents national culture but is not directly linked to its economic and political life. For Gramsci, as for Lenin, intellectuals affiliate with various classes, playing the role of cultural mediator on behalf of these classes. While Gramsci recognizes that intellectuals are vital actors in the historical process, their importance stems from their function rather than from their position within the social structure. (1988, 111)

For these reasons, Aronowitz prefers to speak in terms of an "alliance" of "ingredients" within the technical and the intellectual strata "that populate all state-driven industrializing societies" (1988, 110).

22. My brief treatment of this issue barely evokes a long and complex debate among twentieth-century Marxists focused on the relative autonomy of the economic and cultural spheres. Much of it attempts to reconcile strict deterministic modes with cultural artifacts such as writing. I would include in this category

Louis Althusser's *Reading Capital* (1970), Jameson's *The Political Unconscious*, and Laclau and Mouffe's *Hegemony and Socialist Strategy*, the last of which seems particularly successful in proposing a new model that can account for cultural determinism.

23. For an illuminating discussion of professionalism see also Dietrich Rueschemeyer, *Power and the Division of Labour* (1986), chap. 6.

24. For an example of this literary-critical strategy, see Mary Poovey, *The Proper Lady and the Woman Writer* (1984).

25. See Mikhail M. Bakhtin, *The Dialogic Imagination* (1981). According to Bakhtin, this dialogic relationship is made possible by:

> the novel's special relationship with extraliterary genres, with the genres of everyday life and with ideological genres. . . . the novel often crosses the boundary of what we strictly call fictional literature—making use first of a moral confession, then of a philosophical tract, then of manifestos that are openly political, then degenerating into the raw spirituality of a confession. . . . These phenomena are precisely what characterize the novel as a developing genre. After all, the boundaries between fiction and nonfiction, between literature and nonliterature and so forth are not laid up in heaven. Every specific situation is historical. And so the growth of literature is not merely development and change within the fixed boundaries of any given definition: the boundaries themselves are constantly changing. (33)

26. See Armstrong (1987a) for an extensive discussion of this point, and Raymond Williams, *Keywords* (1976), on the historical specificity of that category of writing known as "literature."

27. This enormous and complex issue has been rightly the subject of much discussion among scholars. See, among others, Tania Modleski, *Loving with a Vengeance* (1982); Janice Radway, *Reading the Romance* (1984); and Jochen Schulte-Sasse, "Can the Disempowered Read Mass-Produced Narratives in their Own Voice?" (1988).

CHAPTER 2
SOCIOLOGY: DISORDER IN THE HOUSE OF THE POOR

1. "I was accused by Gertrude Himmelfarb," Gareth Stedman Jones confesses in his 1984 preface to *Outcast London*:

> of using the same body of primary sources, both to construct my picture of successive middle-class mythologies about the casual poor, and as quarry of factual information, by which to highlight what was mythological in such accounts. Certainly in my use of sources such as . . . Mayhew, this charge is true." (1984, xxiv)

In addition, both Thompson in *The Making of the English Working Class* (1966) and Asa Briggs in "The Human Aggregate" (1973) find Mayhew useful to support their arguments.

2. They shared this faith with other human scientists of the early nineteenth century. As Stephen Jay Gould remarks in *The Mismeasure of Man* (1981), an irresistible trend "swept through the human sciences—the allure of numbers, the faith that rigorous measurement could guarantee irrefutable precision, and might

mark the transition between subjective speculation and a true science as worthy as Newtonian physics" (74).

3. The founders of the Manchester Statistical Society, for example, were all engaged in philanthropy, banking, or cotton manufacture; in addition, many were members of the same family. See Elesh 1972.

4. To illustrate this point, one only has to recall the semiotic battle waged over various terms denoting the character of the middle classes in their struggle to distinguish themselves from the upper classes at the turn of the nineteenth century. Lacking traditional prerogatives for power such as titles, landed wealth, or genealogical connections, the aspiring middle classes often depicted their enthusiasm and ability for industry as their best qualifications for moral and cultural authority. Thus, "productive," "industrious," and "useful" were often adjectives used by middle-class writers "who were pleased to think of themselves as productive, industrious and useful, and who proudly distinguished themselves from the landed aristocracy in these respects. There was the implication that the aristocracy was unproductive, idle and useless" (Himmelfarb 1985, 293).

5. "This kind of semi-voyeuristic fact-gathering," according to Michael Cullen:

> reached its ridiculous limit when the Central Society of Education found that in Marylebone 166 parents were "able to sing a cheerful song" while 871 could not. The accompanying rural survey found that 197 families cultivated flowers against 244 which did not. In neither survey, supposedly designed to reveal the condition of the working classes, was there any attempt to assess the effects of low wages or unemployment. (1975, 137)

6. On this point see also Frank Mort, *Dangerous Sexualities* (1988).

7. Here Medick cites a forgotten portion of Weber's own *The Protestant Ethic and the Spirit of Capitalism*.

8. The example given by the *Oxford English Dictionary* (*OED*) for this usage recorded from the 1797 text of one M. Baillie is intriguing in and of itself: "The hymen is sometimes found without a perforation in it, so that the vagina is completely shut up at its external extremity."

9. Between 1830 and 1880, street clearance accounted for the displacement of an estimated hundred thousand persons (Jones 1971). "It was no accident that the poor were the main victims of this form of civic pride," Gareth Stedman Jones writes. Jones cites a section of the Select Committee report of 1838, calling attention to the fact that

> "there were districts in London through which no great thoroughfare passed, and which were wholly occupied by a dense population composed of the lowest class of persons who being entirely secluded from the observation and influence of better educated neighbors, exhibited a state of moral degradation deeply to be deplored." (1971, 166).

10. To this day working-class neighborhoods are still governed in part by this nineteenth-century logic. In San Diego, California, for instance, an extensive freeway system cuts straight through a Latino area known as the South Bay, dividing the community in half. Fortunately, residents responded defiantly to this intrusion by painting brightly colored political murals on the concrete pillars supporting the roadway overhead.

11. For a fascinating discussion of the cultural construction of the self and the emotions, see Catherine A. Lutz, *Unnatural Emotions* (1988).

12. The issue of race becomes a central one to mid-nineteenth-century anthropology as the construction of the racial other elaborates, extends, and complements the construction of the classed other within sociological writing. On this point, see chapter 3.

13. While earlier theoreticians of the family imagined the household as a polity administered by a sovereign authority, Gaskell imagines society as a replica of the family when he makes the household responsible for the production of the "citizen." Here I have in mind seventeenth-century household governance tracts such as *The Good Hows-holder* (1607), a genre that originally constituted part of the resistance to authoritarian models of governance advanced by the patriarchalists. Despite its origins, household governance literature ultimately contributed to the discursive constitution of the household as a separate domain from the state. This model represented the household as apparently insulated from the demands of the state even as it became increasingly subject to its interventions throughout the seventeenth and eighteenth centuries. For a further discussion of this point, see Donzelot (1979).

One should also note the concept of the "citizen" as it emerges in Gaskell's thinking to diffuse and dilute the nascent class character of the household and the family. According to this logic, the aim of the family is not to make the individual conscious of his or her status as a member of a class, in this case the working classes. Instead, it is to produce "citizens" who may merge as anonymous and classless members into a polity constituted of many social groups. The working class, then, becomes just one among other groups of citizens. As the Chartist movement grew in size and strength in the early nineteenth century, the working classes increasingly demanded and appropriated the right to name themselves. Thus, while they referred to themselves frequently as "the people," they were just as frequently represented by the middle class as "citizens" (Yeo 1981).

14. That the household and the factory were imagined as analogous spaces is illustrated in Mrs. Ann Martin Taylor's practical advice to householders included in her 1815 manual, *Practical Hints to Young Females on the Duties of a Wife, a Mother and a Mistress of a Family*. "That house only is well conducted," she declared, "where there is a strict attention to order and regularity. To do everything in its proper time, to keep everything in its right place, and to use everything for its proper use, is the very essence of good management" (Davidoff and Hall 1987, 176). The orderly arrangement and management of time, space, and bodies were as much features of the nineteenth-century household as of the family enterprise. Such discursive and practical intersections belie the strict separation of public and private, productive and reproductive domains generally attributed to the middle class in the nineteenth century by historians, economists, and literary critics alike.

15. The foundation of the new middle-class economy of the body is represented in many eighteenth-century novels. Pamela, in Richardson's novel of the same name, furnishes Mr. B. with just such a new body as he is transformed from libertine into bourgeois husband. In the same manner, the strange twist of fate at the conclusion of Henry Fielding's *Joseph Andrews* gives Joseph an aristocratic

father, thus informing the hero's strong lower-class body and moral character with an aristocratic bearing and more important, an aristocratic pedigree.

16. In " 'The Mother Made Conscious': The Historical Development of a Primary School Pedagogy" (1985), Carolyn Steedman delineates how teaching as a "conscious and articulated version of mothering" (155) was established within British educational thought in the nineteenth century. Thus she elucidates another facet of the partnership between women and institutional culture that I have described only briefly. She too insists that women have not been excluded from social practices, but they must share in the responsibility for them. Noting that "the feminine has been made official" within prescriptive educational literature, Steedman warns of the dangers of those doctrines that see only women's exclusion:

> To deny this presence, to see female experience only as rejected experience, lying outside the public realm, is to fail to take hold of the analytic devices which may help us recover the historical experience of women. . . . In other words, we're already in that place [within the educational realm]. There's little point in trying to regain territory that we already occupy in so many problematic and convoluted ways. The task that faces us is to discover how, and in what manner, we've been made to fit there. (1985, 161)

17. As a liberal, Gaskell believed that he wrote on behalf of the working class. Thus, when he expressed the belief that women should be in the home not in the factory, he thought he was simply echoing the sentiments of working-class men who resented females in the factory taking their wages. The division of labor, however, was and still is essential to capitalism. Certain productive work must be done for free in order for the system to maintain and reproduce itself. For an historical overview of this issue see Sonya O. Rose, " 'Gender at Work': Sex, Class and Industrial Capitalism" (1986), and Mariarosa Dalla Costa and Selma James, *The Power of Women and the Subversion of the Community* (1972), for its modern implications.

18. In *Discipline and Punish* (1979), Foucault articulates such an intersection of sanitary measures and power offering the ruling class a model for controlling the urban masses when he recounts the measures instituted against the plague. Perceived as disorder, "the plague was met by order," which, according to Foucault:

> lay down for each individual his place, his body, his disease and his death, his well-being, by means of an omnipresent and omniscient power that subdivided itself in a regular, uninterrupted way even to the ultimate determination of the individual, of what characterizes him. Against the plague, which is a mixture, discipline brings into play its power, which is one of analysis. (1979, 197)

19. It is interesting to note that Kent (1981) also observes this figure of "penetration" in the more radical work of Frederick Engels, *The Condition of the Working Class in England in 1844.*

20. This argument is astonishingly similar to that oft-repeated accusation made against welfare recipients. They, too, are accused of sacrificing bread for Cadillacs—another instance of "bad" or unsocialized desire.

21. What was perhaps simply a rhetorical gesture for the nineteenth century towards the working-class population, at least, became a reality in the twentieth. In *The Mismeasure of Man*, Gould recounts the following harrowing tale illustrating how Kay Shuttleworth's nineteenth-century suggestion gets translated into a twentieth-century solution:

> In 1927 Oliver Wendell Holmes, Jr., delivered the Supreme Court's decision upholding the Virginia sterilization law in Buck v. Bell. Carrie Buck, a young mother with a child of allegedly feeble mind, had scored a mental age of nine on the Stanford-Binet [intelligence test]. Carrie Buck's mother, then fifty-two, had tested at mental age seven. Holmes wrote, in one of the most famous and chilling statements of our century:
>
> > We have seen more than once that the public welfare may call upon the best citizens for their lives. It would be strange if it could not call upon those who already sap the strength of the state for these less sacrifices. . . . Three generations of imbeciles are enough. (1981, 335)

22. As the pace of slum clearance accelerated in mid-century, and their residents were rendered homeless, the governing classes grew increasingly anxious over prospects of social disorder provoked by these careless measures. In response official, philanthropic, and commercial efforts were directed toward the amelioration of housing conditions in central London (Jones 1971, 178–79). Gavin's singular focus on the housing problem may be understood as one contribution to this project.

23. The numerical disparity between the sexes—"the surplus of women" in contemporary terms—was a popular topic at mid-century. For a bibliography of works dealing with this issue, see S. Barbara Kanner, "The Women of England in a Century of Social Change, 1815–1914" (1972).

24. The 1851 census of Great Britain gave demographic and statistical life to the domestic female when the registrar general introduced a new fifth class, exclusively made up of married women:

> The 5th class comprises large numbers of the population that have hitherto been held to have no occupation; but it requires no argument to prove that the wife, the *mother*, the *mistress* of an *English family*—fills offices and discharges duties of no ordinary importance; or that children are or should be occupied in filial or household duties, and in the task of education, either at home or at school. (Davidoff and Hall 1986, 272)

As for women themselves, they were not always as eager to abandon single life to join the ranks of the married as the mid-century "surplus women" crisis would lead one to believe (Davidoff and Hall 1986, 325). Lest one think sociological explanations figured in terms of female sexual pathology are a thing of the past, one has only to turn to a recent review by Adolph Reed, Jr., of sociologist William Julius Wilson's *The Truly Disadvantaged: The Inner City, the Underclass, and Public Policy* (1988). Wilson locates the "problem" of the poor, Reed notes, in the "shortage of marriageable men." Like nineteenth-century sociologists and statisticians, Wilson locates his problem and its solution in the domestic relations of the poor. Furthermore, a "shortage of marriageable men" translates into nothing more or less than a "surplus of marriageable women," that population problem which so preoccupied Mayhew and others. Finally, like that of his nineteenth-century predecessors, Wilson's "very definition of the underclass," Reed discovers, "focuses almost exclusively on women's [sexual] behavior. If it were not for violent crime, pathology would be recognizable only among females" (1988, 168).

CHAPTER 3
ANTHROPOLOGY: THE FAMILY OF MAN

1. The degree and range of classifications in this four-volume work is astonishing; it remains a testament to the extensive systematization of sightings and observations required by sociological and anthropological discourse (Coetzee 1985). Under " 'sneaksmen,' or those who plunder by means of stealth," for example, in "Those Who Will Not Work," there are no less than fourteen such unfortunate varieties. Among them are " 'sawney-hunters,' or those who go purloining bacon from cheesemongers' shop-doors" and " 'dead-lurkers,' or those who steal coats and umbrellas from passages at dusk, or on Sunday afternoons" (1861, 4:25).

2. Until the 1870s "anthropology" was the term describing the study that gave priority to physical differences among men, and the one that classified men into distinct types using models supplied by pre-Darwinian comparative anatomy. As the result of a semiotic and ideological struggle between "anthropology" and "ethnology," "anthropology" emerged as the victor and so came to signify the entire discipline (Stocking 1987, 238–73). Given this, I refer to the various mid-century anthropological writings as "anthropology," even though to do so is to give them a posterior unity they did not possess, according to historians of anthropology. Since I treat anthropology as a language with certain characteristic features, I think there is good reason in this case to minimize differences in order to highlight similarities.

3. However, some contemporary anthropologists would proudly claim Mayhew as one of their own. In his introduction to *Writing Culture: The Poetics and Politics of Ethnography*, James Clifford, for example, writes: "Ethnography's traditional vocation of cultural criticism . . . has reemerged with new explicitness and vigor. Anthropological fieldworkers can now realign their work with pioneers like Henry Mayhew in the nineteenth century" (1986, 23).

4. This is precisely what George Stocking does when he traces the intellectual roots of this trend in nineteenth-century anthropology to the "Enlightenment" "Science of Man":

> It is important to insist on the embracive singularity of this prototypical "Science of Man": it was the laws and potentialities of human nature that focused attention. . . . This focus on generic human nature had important implications for "anthropology" of the Enlightenment. By and large, eighteenth-century anthropology did not seriously question the basic unity of all the diverse groups who had been contacted in the age of discovery—a unity which was also the heritage of the Christian tradition. (1987, 17)

5. Roland Barthes discusses the disappearance of the bourgeoisie as an "ideological fact" in *Mythologies* (1972).

6. These two terms are in quotation marks here to indicate their ambiguous disciplinary status in the nineteenth century. From this point on, quotation marks will be implicit in any reference to either discipline.

7. It is interesting to note that ethnological data itself was highly textual. Besides a few bones and artifacts, ethnologists such as James Prichard relied almost exclusively on printed sources—letters from correspondents abroad, books on the experience of travelers, naturalists, missionaries, explorers, and colonial officials (Stocking 1987).

8. The ruthless honesty of the "anthropologicals," however distasteful, is documented albeit anecdotally in their revealing response following Governor Eyre's violent suppression of a revolt of Jamaican peasants in 1866 that left 608 Jamaicans dead. Condemned by liberals and radicals alike, Eyre's actions were celebrated at a public meeting of the society at which

> Captain Bedford Pim gave a paper on "The Negro and Jamaica." Pim's racist diatribe was greeted "with loud cheers" and a unanimous vote of thanks, after which one member of the audience after another got up to offer comments on "the true art of governing alien races"—one even advocating killing savages as "a philanthropic principle": when trouble broke out, there was "mercy in a massacre." (Stocking 1987, 251)

For a further discussion of the controversy between the monogenists and the polygenists see Stocking, *Race, Culture and Evolution* (1986); Ronald Rainger, "Race, Politics, and Science" (1978); Gould, *The Mismeasure of Man* (1981); and T. K. Penniman, *A Hundred Years of Anthropology* (1935).

9. As Homi K. Bhabha observes in his critique of Said's notion of Orientalism, "the suggestion that colonial power and discourse is possessed entirely by the colonizer . . . is an historical and theoretical simplification"(1986, 158). Both the colonizer and the colonial subject, he explains, are unified by the colonial enunciation.

10. There is also an expanding body of literary theory focusing upon the colonizing behavior of language and the constitution of the discourse of colonialism. To a great extent, this important and fascinating work stems from Frantz Fanon's groundbreaking explorations in colonialism from the perspective of the colonized in *Wretched of the Earth* (1969) and *Black Skin White Masks* (1970), although Fanon's influence often remains unacknowledged within the sections of the English literary institution most concerned with these issues. Until recently, English colonialist discourse has received attention primarily from Renaissance scholars, those in the best position to trace the semiotic interchange between Old World and New World. See, for example, Paul Brown, " 'This thing of darkness I acknowledge mine': *The Tempest* and the Discourse of Colonialism" (1985); Peter Hulme, "Hurricane in the Caribees: The Constitution of the Discourse of English Colonialism" (1981); Stephen Orgel, "Caliban and Carthage, Dido and Virginia" (1985). It is perhaps due to the influence of Said's *Orientalism* (1978) that theorists have gradually begun to explore the discursive implications of colonialism, especially for the study of nineteenth-century texts. See *Europe and Its Others* (1984), vols. 1 and 2.

11. These examples are by no means inclusive of all the objections to anthropological theory and practice. Johannes Fabian is another important theorist who

has reinforced the critique of colonialism in *Time and the Other* (1983), an excellent study of the limits of representation itself, an issue, incidentally, not only for anthropologists but for literary theorists, sociologists, and historians as well. One particularly important collection of anthropologically oriented essays that has emerged out of this trend is James Clifford and George E. Marcus, eds., *Writing Culture* (1986).

12. My survey of recent critiques of anthropology is by no means exhaustive. See also Kathleen Gough, "Anthropology and Imperialism" (1968); Susantha Goonatilake, *Aborted Discovery* (1984); Jack Stauder, "The 'Relevance' of Anthropology to Colonialism and Imperialism" (1986); as well as all the essays in Dell Hymes, ed., *Reinventing Anthropology* (1974a).

13. For an extended discussion of the way contemporary feminist theory incorporated nineteenth-century thinking see Nicholson, *Gender and History* (1986), 69–104.

14. Rosalind Coward's *Patriarchal Precedents* (1983) similarly assumes Victorian society did not produce notions of gender but simply manipulated preexisting categories. Nonetheless, Coward's text brings to the feminist critique of anthropology an important dimension neglected in earlier works on the subject as its vision broadens to include a wider notion of power relations. Coward concludes that the struggle over patriarchal and matriarchal theories of origin was not about sexual relations per se, appearances notwithstanding. "The real subject," she observes, "was that of the nature of political and social alliances. The real question asked of the data on sexual and familial organisations was what function they fulfilled in relation to wider social bonds" (1983, 12). Although Coward does not provide a specific analysis of the question posed, it remains a crucial one for my purposes.

15. To illustrate this last observation, I offer the following analogy humorously, yet in all seriousness. A liberal choice in consumer culture is one between Coke and Pepsi. Minor differences aside, these rival soft drinks are bought and sold as alternative choices, while the manufacturers get to set the terms of the deal. The discourse of liberalism is like the soft drink industry because it defines the grounds on which it is to be challenged.

16. Kinship data collected by early ethnographers later became "central both to evolutionary theory and functionalist social anthropology" (Stocking 1987, 105). In Sir George Grey's ethnology on Australia and Polynesia, the "benevolent [colonial] administrative despot" began to unravel the complicated social structure of the area. While his conclusions have been dismissed since as overwhelmingly ethnocentric, he did call attention to kinship laws—"the phenomena that were long to be the foci of anthropological inquiry and debate" (Stocking 1987, 83).

17. In *The Family, Sex and Marriage in England 1500–1800* (1979), Lawrence Stone describes what he terms "the rise of the companionate marriage" in the eighteenth century. Although Stone does make a distinction between older and more modern forms of marriage, he does not understand the crucial distinction between kin and family and between blood and biology, and so he ultimately represents the aristocratic family in terms of the middle-class family. See, for ex-

ample, his description of the aristocratic family in *The Crisis of the Aristocracy 1558–1641* (1965), chap. 11. Also see Davidoff and Hall 1987 and Foucault 1980.

18. The shift from kinship to sexuality, from alliance to domesticity is identifiable in the changing attitude toward money and marriage. While marriage for money had always been a perfectly acceptable part of the system of alliance, by the mid-eighteenth century, as Trumbach notes, "it had become distasteful [to the aristocracy] to use marriage for financial gain. Marriage had become, instead, the cornerstone of domesticity" (1978, 71).

19. Anthropological writing, as Homi Bhabha writes, "turns on the *recognition* and *disavowal* of racial/cultural/historical differences" (1986, 154, emphasis added).

20. In "Images of the Sixteenth and Seventeenth Centuries as a History of the Present" (1986), Simon Barker demonstrates how middle-class England continues to colonize the culture of the other, in this case Elizabethan culture, for its own political and social purposes.

21. That archeology is the politics of the present is made especially clear in modern Israel. There biblical archeology predominates to the exclusion of pre-Islamic Arab archeology because the former authorizes Zionist claims to an ancient mandate. See G. W. Bowersock, "Palestine: Ancient History and Modern Politics" (1988).

22. "However far back one traces the origin of anthropological thought," writes the editor of *Primitive Marriage*, "McLennan represents an all important stage in its modern development because it is with him that the continuing topics of anthropological concern such as marriage forms, incest, exogamy . . . , and totemism originated. . . . Its [*Primitive Marriage's*] qualification as a classic is undisputable since today's anthropologists are still heirs to McLennan's genius" (1865, vii).

23. I am not alone in identifying these notions as pervasive in nineteenth-century anthropological writing. However, they have almost always been characterized as recurrent "themes" vaguely reflective of a "Victorian history" located somewhere outside the text. See Conway 1972 and Stocking 1987.

24. More specifically, McLennan is critical of Peter Simon Pallas's *Voyages dan plusiers provinces de l'Empire de Russie et dans l'asie septentrionale* (1794) and Philip Johan Strahlenberg's *A Histori-geographical Description of the Northern and Eastern Part of Europe and Asia* (1736). In "Anthropology and the Hottentots" (1985), John Coetzee lists twenty categories he considers of significant interest to seventeenth- and eighteenth-century protoanthropologists. At the top of the list are physical appearance, dress, and diet. Entirely absent from this set of concerns is any mention of sexual behavior or gender difference.

25. See Hodgen (1964) and Coetzee (1985) on protoanthropology to understand fully the contrast between nineteenth-century anthropological concerns and those of the three preceding centuries.

26. "As the words endogamy and exogamy are new, an apology must be made for employing them" (McLennan 1865, 22). The *OED* records McLennan's 1865 usage as the first in English. The terms next appear in *The Origin of Civilization*

and the Primitive Condition of Man (1870) by John Lubbock. Although Lubbock and Tylor subsequently incorporate the notion of exogamy/endogamy, I consider McLennan's formulation the model for subsequent usages as it is the first.

27. Specifically, Adam asks: "Love not the heav'nly Spirits, and how their Love / Express they, by looks only, or do they mix / Irradiance, virtual or immediate touch?" (1667, 7.1.615–17).

28. On this point see Armstrong and Tennenhouse, "The Imaginary Puritan." I would like to thank the authors for generously allowing me to see the manuscript in progress.

29. Specifically, Spencer writes: "That the restriction, prohibiting marriage with a uterine sister, was not observed in Egypt, we have sufficient evidence from the sculptures of Thebes" (1898, 618).

30. This line, as Cora Kaplan remarks, is "habitually elided in dominant discourse and practically used to limit the civil and political rights of all three subordinate categories: blacks, women and the working class" (1985, 167).

31. "It is well known that with many Hottentot women the posterior part of the body projects in a wonderful manner," Charles Darwin wrote in 1871: "they are steatopygous; and Sir Andrew Smith is certain that this peculiarity is greatly admired by the men. He once saw a woman who was considered a beauty, and she was so immensely developed behind, that when seated on level ground she could not rise, and had to push herself along until she came to a slope" (345–46). The enlarged buttocks or *steatopygia* and genital flap or *sinus pudoris* are both features of the people now called the Khoi-San and other related groups (Gould 1982).

32. Gilman is quoting from Georges Cuvier, "Extraits d'observations faits sur le cadavre d'une femme connue à Paris et à Londres sous le nom de Venus Hottentote," *Memoirs du Museum d'histoire naturelle* 3 (1817): 259–74. With some poetic justice, Saat-Jee's genitals are still preserved in the Natural History Museum in Paris on a shelf adjacent to Cuvier's brain (Gould 1982).

33. The OED records the first use of "prepuce" in conjunction with female anatomy in Bell's 1878 edition of *Gregenbaur's Comparative Anatomy*. We know from Flower and Murie's example that the term was in use before that date.

CHAPTER 4
DOMESTIC FICTIONS IN THE HOUSEHOLD: *WUTHERING HEIGHTS*

1. On this point see Armstrong (1987a).

2. It is worth pointing out that the sisters' gender is established once and for all with this piece. If Charlotte were not eager to claim for her sister's novel the territory of female discourse, why else would she reveal the gender of its author? Clearly she hoped that, far from weakening its reception, the revelation would secure the novel an audience. As if to make good the gamble, the 1850 edition significantly reawakened public interest in the novel.

3. See Kavanagh (1985), for an extensive discussion of this critical tradition. While I agree with Kavanagh that Brontë has not been historicized adequately, we disagree on the means to this end. In my view, Kavanagh's reliance on late nineteenth-century psychoanalytic interpretive models further exacerbates the prob-

lem he so rightly identifies. *Wuthering Heights*, among many mid-century texts, establishes the conditions by which psychoanalytic models will make sense to late nineteenth- and early twentieth-century Anglo-European culture.

4. Dorothy Van Ghent, for example, is exasperated by the absence of a moral lesson in *Wuthering Heights*. As she sees it, "*Wuthering Heights* so baffles and confounds the ethical sense because it is not informed with that sense at all" (Allott 1970, 181). Yet if the novel is constructed as the product of a female imagination severed from its political and historical roots, then it should not be asked to make critical sense on those very same grounds.

5. As I understand it, a "space" is a sociocultural construction, be it literal or figurative. It is a cultural organization of nature, just as a house is an organized cultural space, the arrangement of which carries certain specific consequences for the arrangement of its occupants.

6. For a complete analysis of this transformation see chapter 5. Also see Doerner, *Madmen and the Bourgeoisie* (1981); Michel Foucault, *Madness and Civilization* (1967); Andrew Scull, *Museums of Madness* (1979); and Elaine Showalter, *The Female Malady* (1985).

7. Among the most provocative recent histories of the novel is Armstrong, *Desire and Domestic Fiction*. Also see Michael McKeon, *The Origins of the English Novel 1600–1740* (1987).

8. In *Capitalism, the Family and Personal Life* (1976), Eli Zaretsky maintains that the split between public and private domains was generated *by* capitalism. My own view approaches that of Davidoff and Hall who suggest in *Family Fortunes* (1987) that such a division both preceded and enabled capitalist expansion.

9. The overfurnished parlor at the Grange is contrasted by the stark, functional simplicity of the kitchen at the Heights. As middle-class families increasingly turned living quarters into homes, functionality gave way to both comfort and gentility, making the home a showplace of wealth, respectability, and rank. "The early nineteenth-century taste which favoured lightness and space," Davidoff and Hall note, "was giving way to the heavy upholstered cluttered effects of the mid and late Victorians. . . . sparse domesticity, the sofa, shutters and tea urn, had now burgeoned with carpets, curtains, redesigned grates, mahogany furniture, wallpaper, chintz covers and bedsteads" (1987, 375).

10. To Gilbert and Gubar, the grooming that makes Catherine into a "female" once she is enclosed within the Grange—the washing of feet, the combing of hair, being dressed in "enormous slippers"—represents "some sinister ritual initiation, the sort of ritual that has traditionally weakened mythic heroines from Persephone to Snow White" (1979, 273). Unfortunately, literary parallels to myth or fairy tale only remove the text further from its historical moment, and so make it impossible to comprehend how this female figure might be historically different from those of Greek legend, the Brothers Grimm, or Walt Disney.

11. The "free choice" supposedly exercised by middle-class desire was regulated by the frequent overlap between marriage and business affairs. It has been argued, in fact, that marriage alliances played a crucial role in the establishment of middle-class business at the turn of the eighteenth century, as enterprises gained both capital and expertise from cash dowries as well as from knowledgeable fathers, brothers, and cousins (Davidoff and Hall 1987, 221).

12. For Lévi-Strauss, the exchange of women is one of the most fundamental acts of exchange in primitive societies, serving to cement blood ties and thus alliances between men. The incest taboo elaborated by the French anthropologist in *The Elementary Structures of Kinship* (1969) prescribes one's mother, sister, or daughter be given to others in order to foster exogamy. It is a rule imposed upon the natural randomness of cosanguinity, in favor of the cultural fact of alliance. Like most anthropological thinking, Lévi-Strauss's theory collapses historical difference and assumes that only the primitive other has kinship relations governed by a set of identifiable rules.

13. Gilbert and Gubar experiment with another order of explanation, but theirs is no more successful in my estimation. On the contrary, their analysis reinforces the fact that the novel responds to the anthropological idiom, however much it deforms or erases the historical dimension of the family and the household. They interpret Catherine's marriage to Edgar as the inevitable result of her "fall into ladyhood," that is, her "seizure" by the Grange. Thus, in this analysis, the marriage is an aberration necessitated by patriarchal constraints on the female. "She cannot do otherwise than she does," Gilbert and Gubar write, she "must marry Edgar because there is no one else for her to marry and a lady must marry" (1979, 277). But of course there is someone else for her to marry, and that someone is Heathcliff. That she doesn't marry him is not simply a function of a plot cooked up in the author's warped imagination, but a symptom of a cultural logic that makes such a marriage impossible. There can be no other reason why the heroine would undertake a marriage so antithetical to her former passion for Heathcliff.

14. Such lack of differentiation took many forms in the early modern family. Shared bedrooms, for instance, as well as beds, were the norm in artisanal households prior to the nineteenth century. Thus a female servant might very well share a bed with a daughter of the household. At the same time, children of farm families often lodged with other families and worked as servants. It was these arrangements, carried over into industrial towns by the laboring classes, that middle-class social researchers interpreted as signs of disorder, illicit combination, even barbarism.

15. This aestheticizing moment of the female, with its underlying connections to eroticism and death, is a feature of numerous mid-nineteenth-century novels, including Mrs. Gaskell's *Mary Barton*, Dickens's *Hard Times*, and Brontë's *Jane Eyre*. The female in these instances dies out of "existence" and into static, aesthetic control. These written scenes bring to mind the tableaus of pale, wan females—all spirit and no flesh—painted in the style of Dante Gabriel Rossetti.

16. In novel-writing cultures, doubling and splitting often indicates the formation of a new individual or self. In *Jane Eyre*, *Mary Barton*, *Hard Times*, and other texts of the late 1840s and 1850's, the female characters undergo similar transformations.

17. Because they read the novel from a psychological perspective, Gilbert and Gubar attribute Catherine's death to anorexia nervosa. They see this malady, along with masochism and suicide, as "a complex of psychotic symptoms that is almost classically associated with female feelings of powerlessness and rage"

(1979, 285), to which they trace Catherine's distorted perception of her body in the mirror. Like Goetz's anthropological reading, this interpretation only reifies the female self that is just being produced at this moment, rather than describes the moment itself as such. Gilbert and Gubar base much of their analysis on the imagery of the sick and deviant female, that originates in the discourses of sexuality and self that were materialized, among other places, first in the nineteenth-century novel and later in psychology.

18. Or as Josiah Conder wrote to his fiancée at mid-century: "Tis where thou art, is home to me, / And home without thee cannot be" (Davidoff and Hall 1978, 178).

19. Brontë does not relinquish older historical figures of desire such as fusion, combination, materiality, and undifferentiation without a struggle. They continue to "haunt" the novel, not only in the form of the many "Catherines" who appear in the text, as outlined earlier, but in other figures that resist compartmentalization. Her grave on the edge of the churchyard, for instance, "where the wall is so low that the heath and bilberry plants have climbed over it from the moor and peat mould almost buries it" (1847, 205), refuses to be disciplined by the "simple headstone" and "plain grey block" at her feet.

20. The middle-class house and garden, as one would expect, benefitted from the appropriation of raw materials from colonized countries. Oak, indigenous to England, was replaced by the lighter mahogany imported from the colonies as the most favored wood for furniture making. Similarly, private and public English gardens bloomed with new and exotic varieties of plants and flowers brought from the empire and reproduced by plant breeding techniques (Davidoff and Hall 1987).

21. It is interesting to compare Bloom's assessment of the novel with that of Virginia Woolf. "There is no 'I' in *Wuthering Heights*," Woolf writes. "Emily was inspired by some more general conception. The impulse which urged her to create was not her own suffering or her own injuries. She looked out upon a world cleft into gigantic disorder and felt within her the power to unite it in a book" (1968, 101). Woolf figures text and author in terms of their openness to the world, while Bloom's trope is one of enclosure from the world.

22. Among the many studies that treat the novel as product of a damaged self are Leo Bersani, *A Future for Astyanax* (1969); Sandra M. Gilbert and Susan Gubar, *The Madwoman in the Attic* (1979); Margaret Homans, "Repression and Sublimation of Nature in *Wuthering Heights*" (1987); Kavanagh, *Emily Brontë* (1985); J. Hillis Miller, "*Wuthering Heights*: Repetition and the 'Uncanny'" (1987).

CHAPTER 5
PSYCHOLOGY: THE OTHER WOMAN AND THE OTHER WITHIN

1. Charles-Gaspard de la Rive described the most modern lunatic asylum of 1798, The Retreat at York, in the following terms. "This house is situated . . . in the midst of a fertile and smiling countryside," he wrote admiringly, "it is not at all the idea of a prison that it suggests, but rather that of a large farm; it is sur-

rounded by a great, walled garden. No bars, no grilles on the windows" (Foucault 1967, 242).

2. The Retreat at York opened its doors for business in 1793. That same year, Phillipe Pinel obtained permission from the Paris Commune to unchain the lunatics at Bicêtre and La Salpêtrière (Foucault 1967, Showalter 1985).

3. To be sure, such a major therapeutic revolution did not occur smoothly. In fact, the argument over moral therapy pitted two factions of the professional middle classes against each other. Throughout the first half-century, asylum managers and mad-doctors or "alienists" vied for bureaucratic and medical control of England's many asylums. Since moral treatment specifically refuted older medical "solutions" for insanity—such as bleeding and purges—it challenged the hegemony of the emergent medical profession over madness and madhouses. Many asylum doctors refused to abandon earlier physically coercive and invasive techniques, while they fought to extend their institutional and legal hegemony over asylums whenever possible (Scull 1979).

4. Klaus Doerner quotes from Hill's *A Concise History of the Entire Abolition of Mechanical Restraint and of the Non-Restraint System* (1857) in his *Madmen and the Bourgeoisie* (1981).

5. See Steedman, " 'The Mother Made Conscious' " (1985) for a description of the institutionalization of female authority in the English educational system. Steedman's documentation of "the feminine" "made official" in the nineteenth-century school supports my contention that forms of power modeled after female authority in the domestic sphere materialized not only in the asylum but in other institutions as well. In *Gender and History* (1986), Nicholson describes the same phenomenon occurring in America in the nineteenth century. Nineteenth-century American feminists described their participation in teaching or social work, according to Nicholson, as "bringing domesticity outward" (54).

6. Many have characterized the efforts of an earlier stage of feminism to right the sexual balance of history in this culinary manner.

7. Scull is even more explicit on the connections between moral management and capitalism in "Moral Treatment Reconsidered" (1981b). "Industrial capitalism," he writes,

> demands a reform of character on the part of every single workman, since their previous character did not fit the new industrial system. Entrepreneurs concerned to "make such machines of men as cannot err" soon discover that physical threat and economic coercion will not suffice: men have to be taught to internalize the new attitudes and responses, to discipline themselves. (113)

Scull's position resembles that of Doerner (1981), although Doerner also explores the constitutive role new definitions of madness played in the history of the middle class as a class. "Like paupers, the insane were not to be left solely to the mercy of nature," Doerner writes:

> Instead, society viewed itself increasingly as an autonomous sphere obligated to integrate those individuals as well, and as being in need of them as instruments of its dual expansionary drive. It needed the poor for its outward expansion—as workers in the economic

domain, and as soldiers in the colonial-military expansion. But it also needed the deranged for its internal expansion, for the establishment of an internal circulation essential to its self-understanding. (1981, 51)

8. I suggest that like the discourses of the human sciences, both colonialism and imperialism are semiotic practices of culture that mark boundaries by drawing maps to chart first outlying areas, then the interior; each "discovers" a geography innocent of indigenous historical features or erases those features in the course of exploration. Colonialist practices managed the "native," while imperialism furnished him or her with a new set of features suitable for specific ideological and practical ends. So too psychiatry would blot out all features of political person, place, and time in order to reconstitute the individual as a particular field of knowledge whose fate or "development" is motored by sexual desires. I am indebted to Lucia Folena and Leonard Tennenhouse for suggesting this set of relations to me.

9. Interestingly, both *Museums of Madness* and *The Female Malady* agree that such a shift in psychiatric care indeed occurred at mid-century, although Scull dates it to 1850, Showalter to 1860.

10. Donald Lowe explains in *History of Bourgeois Perception* (1982) that throughout the nineteenth century the "unconscious" gradually came to be defined as a realm within the individual. Importantly, this formulation won out over a competing definition of the unconscious as a realm of phenomena external to the individual. The term underwent etymological revision from the eighteenth to the nineteenth century, a shift Lowe associates with the corresponding change in semantic emphasis. "In the eighteenth century," Lowe writes, " 'unconscious' had meant not being conscious of, unaware; by the nineteenth century, 'unconscious' came to mean not realized or known as existing within oneself" (1982, 105). For a detailed history of the unconscious from a strictly traditional developmental viewpoint, see Henri F. Ellenberger, *The Discovery of the Unconscious* (1970). As the title suggests, Ellenberger's study assumes that the unconscious was "there" all along, just waiting to be discovered. I contend to the contrary that the unconscious is a discursive phenomenon produced in both fictive and psychological texts.

11. This scene, of course, is not an imaginary one. It comes from a famous lithograph of the French psychiatrist Charcot.

12. For those with strong stomachs, see Gustav Braun, "The Amputation of the Clitoris and Labia Minora" (1865).

13. See chapter 3 for a complete discussion of "Account of the Dissection of a Bushwoman."

14. It would be logical to expect Freud's psychoanalytic writing to occupy a special place here. My aim, however, is to precipitate out of this discussion the notions of psychoanalytic theory permeating our understanding of the modern self. The point is that the notions of female and male that are presupposed by contemporary feminist critics like Showalter have their origins here, and not simply in Freudian theory.

15. See Paul Robinson's *The Modernization of Sex* (1976) for an example of

this approach. Robinson opposes the "sexual modernism" of Ellis against a monolithic notion of "Victorianism," which he calls a "more or less unified nineteenth-century style in sexual theory" (2).

16. Havelock Ellis's work is generally understood as a landmark in modern sexology. He is held in high esteem especially "because of his key role in establishing sexology as a science and laying the foundations of modern sex research. In his own time he achieved world-wide recognition as the leading authority on sex, and his influence on the popular manuals of the 1920's and 1930's and even of the post war years was enormous" (Jackson 1987, 53).

17. Since Robinson's introduction is part of an "authorized" edition, I consider it to be a supplemental but highly meaningful component of the study itself.

18. In "The Fragmentation of Need: Women, Food and Marketing" (1987), Joan Dye Gussow names and analyzes a similar transference of knowledge and expertise from the domestic woman to the nutrition expert that occurred during the first thirty years of this century as the food industry expanded rapidly.

19. In *The Modernization of Sex* (1976), Robinson notes that Krafft-Ebing illustrated "major forms of sexual deviation," notably fetishism and bestiality, and the scatological perversions, urolagnia and coprolagnia, with "case histories that ranged from the ludicrous to the disgusting" (25).

20. Notice that Robinson uses the figure of inversion—the "world turned upside down," Bakhtin's trope for the carnivalesque—to describe the world of sex "revealed" in *Psychopathia Sexualis*. In "Hysteria and the End of Carnival: Festival and Bourgeois Neurosis" (1985), Allon White explores the suggestive relationship between carnivalesque imagery and the form and content of the unconscious. Although middle-class culture, White notes, suppressed the carnivalesque and its many manifestations in marketplace, fair, charivari, and tavern, he argues that it returns in the fantasies of middle-class individuals and comes bubbling out of the mouths of hysterics. As provocative as this thesis may be, it fails to historicize the figure of repression itself, which is granted transhistorical substantiality and authority. Instead of assuming that repression possesses universal significance, one might ask in what way remnants of the carnivalesque were appropriated to suit the needs of middle-class culture. By the nineteenth century, the carnivalesque indeed existed only in "remnants," since its appropriation by the official state culture had been well underway by the seventeenth century; Elizabeth I, to cite one instance, transformed traditional feast days where carnival reigned into state holidays. White implies, on the other hand, that carnival was dismantled all in a piece, rather than in a fragmented and scattered fashion. The "repressed" content he identifies in the hysteric's narrative may already be a piece of grotesque imagery sexualized by middle-class culture. After all, as one may recall from the work of the social researchers, features of the lower-class body and their bodily functions were consistently sexualized even as they were moralized. Perhaps it is this sexualized grotesque, by now associated with the working classes, that finds its way into or out of hysterics. Furthermore, White does not address how the "outside" (the grotesque material) becomes the "inside" (the hysterical imagery). I argue that such a transference occurs in and through writing.

In a later version of the same piece, White and coauthor Peter Stallybrass (1986) argue that four "processes" were involved in the breakup of carnival. While this theory represents a needed emendation to the earlier argument, the authors still rely on psychoanalytic categories to talk about an earlier moment in history. Thus "repression" and "sublimation" remain two fundamental "processes" and so transhistorical signifiers as well.

21. It is worthwhile to remember here that Freudian theory maintains that the unconscious may be accessed only by similar "gaps" in meaning such as slips of the tongue, jokes, and, above all, dreams.

22. Despite the exotic name, a pageist is simply one who delights in dressing and acting the part of a medieval page. What is intriguing is the sudden proliferation of forms of "deviant" sexual behavior ranging from the sublime to the ridiculous.

23. *The Manchurian Candidate*, a recently rereleased Cold War film, takes as its premise the fantastic yet plausible theme of the individual who conceals the enemy within, unbeknownst to all including himself. A soldier (Laurence Harvey) taken prisoner in the Korean War is brainwashed by sinister Russian and Chinese scientists from the "Pavlov Institute" in Moscow. There they employ brainwashing techniques to transform the good soldier into an assassin. He returns to the United States programmed to kill on command for "commies" plotting the seizure of power. When he is ultimately deprogrammed, perhaps by Frank Sinatra's bad acting, and the plot is thwarted, the soldier/assassin does not wait to be dispatched by the army or the police; he kills himself in what must be deemed the ultimate act of self-discipline. Of course, one could speculate endlessly and deliciously upon the timing of the film's rerelease, coming as it did in the last of the Reagan years.

24. The 1936 edition of the *Studies* begins with the less controversial, more "normal" phenomena of "modesty" and "sexual periodicity," while "sexual inversion" occupies a less prominent place at the end of the second volume. Thus when the editors corrected the order of the volumes to conform to Ellis's original intentions, they effectively destroyed an important piece of evidence, for it is in the original order of publication that one may trace the abnormal as it moves into the domain of the normal.

25. Apparently Ellis was not among those favored individuals either. Thanks to an abundance of biographical research scrutinizing Ellis's life with the same attention he gave to his patients' lives, we know that his wife carried on lesbian affairs while he indulged his passion for urolagnia. He derived sexual pleasure, in other words, from having women urinate on him (Kern 1975).

26. To Paul Robinson, for example, Ellis is one of the "pioneer sexual modernists" who oversaw a "major transformation in sexual theory" (1976, 2). Jeffrey Weeks considers Ellis a "major formulator" of "liberal sexual ideology" (1981, 152), while Alex Zwerdling comes to the same conclusion in *Virginia Woolf and the Real World* (1986, 167). Stephen Kern cites Ellis's enthusiastic endorsement of liberal causes, including sex education, contraception, and divorce, as proof of his modernity. Kern attributes Ellis's massive effort to catalogue

sexual practices to the need "to understand and explain his own struggle to achieve sexual gratification" (1975, 132). In so doing, Kern reifies two bourgeois myths of individuality: first, that the individual is motored purely by sexual factors, even in intellectual endeavors; second, that any such endeavor, like the discourse of psychology, is solely the product of individuals who think and work in splendid isolation from social or political determinants. Like many contemporary historians and sociologists, Weeks, Zwerdling, and Kern read history in terms of a myth of enlightenment that unfolds the figure of repression in narrative form. Foucault, among others, doubts whether there was indeed a "historical rupture" between the "age of repression" and the "critical analysis of repression." "Did the critical discourse that addresses itself to repression," he asks, "come to act as a roadblock to a power mechanism that had operated unchallenged up to that point, or was it not in fact part of the same historical network as the thing it denounces . . . by calling it repression?" (1978, 10).

27. It must be emphasized that psychological thinking about the nature of female desire, as well as about the psychological differences between the sexes, was not limited to the discipline of psychology per se. Numerous studies that we would now categorize as anthropological or sociological participated in the project that was responsible for attributing gendered characteristics to that internal arena, the product of almost a century of discourse and practice, that psychological thinking would ultimately dub the unconscious. Among them were J. McGrigor Allan, "On the Real Differences in the Minds of Men and Women" (1869); W. L. Distant, "The Mental Differences Between the Sexes" (1874); and Patrick Geddes and J. Arthur Thomson, *Evolution of Sex* (1899).

28. Extensive work has been done, for instance, on desire as a political formation in Renaissance England. See Tennenhouse, *Power on Display* (1987), for a discussion of the interrelationship between politics and sexuality in Elizabethan and Jacobean writing and cultural practice. Clearly, more work must be done on the intervening centuries to understand the nature and importance of nineteenth-century representations of the individual as a sexual being driven by instinct alone.

29. In *The Woman in the Body* (1987), Emily Martin finds the splitting of the body from the self to be the central image women use to talk about menstruation, pregnancy, childbirth, and menopause. Interestingly, "your self is separate from your body" finds its correlative in "your body needs to be controlled by your self," found in the language of the working- and middle-class white and black women Martin interviews. This confirms in the language of everyday life my supposition that the notion of the self enacts a powerful form of social control.

30. Much of the first part of the *Studies* is devoted to pinpointing the exact biological dimensions of sexuality. Sexual functions are first localized in reproductive functions, organs of generation, and general physiology. Only then are they extended to their psychical manifestations and functions. Ellis, and of course Freud, will jettison the biological in favor of the psychical model.

31. It should be noted that in this contractual model, the woman must desire the competitive male, much as the man must desire the female who can domesticate him.

32. Ellis calls this description of hysteria "rather fantastic" and dismisses it as "not a presentation of hysteria in the technical sense." Nevertheless, he admits that "it presents a state distinctly analogous" to the "hysterical convulsion" (1898, 1.1.230).

33. In the modern medical textbooks and popular images Emily Martin surveys, she finds that women are represented as "in some sinister sense out of control when they menstruate" (1987, 47), while women themselves use the vocabulary of control and its loss to describe their premenstrual selves (132).

34. In 1682 Thomas Sydenham issued his treatise on hysteria simply titled *Dissertation*, which followed closely on the heels of Thomas Willis's 1667 work on hysteria and anatomical neurology (Foucault 1967, Doerner 1981). These treatises sought to situate the mind in the individual body by using hysteria as the model for all nervous diseases. English studies described hysteria as an "excessive delicacy and sensibility of the nervous system—thus, falling ill became a moral failure prompting increasing attempts at self-observation and self-understanding" (Doerner 1981, 28). The bourgeois body, both male and female, was most susceptible to this debilitating malady; it was a testament to the unique sensitivity of the individual sufferer. By the eighteenth century, hysteria and the threat it posed both to the individual and the social body became the basis for an intense public debate around the notion of the self-regulated individual, "a self that comes into being and functions spontaneously rather than being imposed by external authority" (Doerner 1981, 28). One should note in this history of hysteria it was the female *body*, rather than the mind, that seventeenth- and eighteenth-century protopsychological writers considered most predisposed to hysterical weakness. Hysteria too was one of Freud's earliest preoccupations. He published *Studies in Hysteria* in 1895, three years before Ellis's *Studies in the Psychology of Sex*.

35. To support this claim, Ellis includes a long history of the use of the dildo in other cultures. This excursion into the past, similar to anthropological endeavors by Mayhew, McLennan, and Spencer, erases social, economic, and cultural specificity when it organizes the history of the other according to sexuality.

36. "We may have to recognize that on the side of the sexual emotions, as well as in general constitution, a condition may be traced among normal persons that is hysteroid in character, and serves as the healthy counterpart of a condition which in hysteria is morbid" (1898, 1.1.228).

37. The similarity of this etiology of hysteria and Freud's concerning the somatic symptoms in "conversion hysteria" in the case of Elizabeth von R. (1898) is striking.

38. The identical figure also appears in Charlotte Perkins Gilman's late nineteenth-century short story, "The Yellow Wallpaper."

39. Martin demonstrates how completely representations of the body, and the female body in particular, have been inscribed with features of the modern industrial state. Medical textbooks, for example, imagine cells as factories, while a recent issue of a popular news magazine likens the behavior of the AIDS virus to a factory manufacturing tiny armored tanks. Martin also notes that menstruation is represented in the medical and popular imagination as a "breakdown" in the

lining of the uterus, and menopause is regarded as a "breakdown of a system of authority" (42).

EPILOGUE
MODERNISM, PROFESSIONALISM, AND GENDER

1. Women are less involved in the production of science as a form of cultural activity, according to Evelyn Fox Keller, because of "a network of interactions between gender development, a belief system that equates objectivity with masculinity, and a set of cultural values that simultaneously (and conjointly) elevates what is defined as scientific and what is defined as masculine" (1985, 89).

2. See Woolf's 1925 essay, "Mr. Bennett and Mrs. Brown."

3. This group, according to Jameson, includes Anglo-American and Russian modernists, Theodor Adorno, and the *Tel Quel* group (1979, 13).

4. William Bennett was the secretary of education under Ronald Reagan. In 1989 he was enlisted in the war on drugs to become "drug Czar" in the Bush administration. Allan Bloom, the self-appointed arbiter of "good" taste and "good" education, is author of *The Closing of the American Mind* (1987).

5. Modernist authors revise their names, as well as their writing, with considerable stylistic flair: Hilda Doolittle is transformed into "H.D."; American Pauline Tarn becomes French poet "Renee Viviane"; Cicely Fairfield changes into "Rebecca West"; and Karen Blixen becomes "Isak Dinesen" (Gilbert and Gubar 1988, 242). Gilbert and Gubar interpret the pseudonym, however, as the female's entry into language and authority previously denied them; accordingly it functioned "as a name of power, the mark of private christening into a second self, a rebirth into linguistic primacy" (242). The notion of the female author as a disembodied imaginative and emotive being, as I have argued, is a discursive and historical fiction traceable at least to the mid-nineteenth century. Since Gilbert and Gubar interpret the pseudonym as a sign of the female author's reentry into a world from which she was never really absent, their analysis is a beautiful example of this notion translated into literary critical logic. The authorial persona, I suggest instead, becomes an extension of the personal text at this moment in history. Even if male authors did not change their names with such alacrity, many lived equally "pseudonymous" lives in avante-garde intellectual circles such as Bloomsbury, where both men and women established their artistic credentials by flagrantly violating social, and especially sexual, codes of middle-class conduct.

REFERENCES

Abrams, Philip. 1968. *The Origins of British Sociology 1834–1914*. Chicago: University of Chicago Press.

Allan, J. McGrigor. 1869. "On the Real Differences in the Minds of Men and Women." *Journal of the Anthropological Society* 7 (no. 28): cxcv–ccxix.

Allott, Miriam, ed. 1970. *Emily Brontë*—Wuthering Heights, *A Casebook*. London: Macmillan.

Althusser, Louis, and Etienne Balibar. 1970. *Reading Capital*. Trans. Ben Brewster. London: Verso Books.

Armstrong, Nancy. 1988. "Hysteria as History, 1857–1885." Unpublished paper.

———. 1987a. *Desire in Domestic Fiction: A Political History of the Novel*. Oxford: Oxford University Press.

——— 1987b. "The Politics of Domesticating Culture." Unpublished paper.

——— 1986. "Literature as Women's History: A Necessary Transgression of Genres." *Genre* 19 (no. 4): 347–69.

———. 1983. "A Language of One's Own: Communication-Modeling Systems in *Mrs. Dalloway*." *Language and Style* 16: 343–60.

———, and Leonard Tennenhouse. "The Imaginary Puritan: Literature and the Origins of Personal Life." Unpublished manuscript.

———, and Leonard Tennenhouse, eds. 1988. *The Violence of Representation: Literature and the History of Violence*. London: Methuen.

Arnold, Matthew. 1869. *Culture and Anarchy*. 1971. New York: Bobbs Merrill.

Aronowitz, Stanley. 1988. "Postmodernism and Politics." *Social Text* 6 (no. 3): 99–115.

Asad, Talal, ed. 1973. *Anthropology and the Colonial Encounter*. New York: Humanities Press.

Bakhtin, Mikhail M. 1984. *Rabelais and His World*. Trans. Helene Iswolsky. Bloomington: University of Indiana Press.

———. 1981. *The Dialogic Imagination*. Ed. and trans. Michael Holquist and Caryl Emerson. Austin: University of Texas Press.

Barker, Francis, et al., eds. 1986. *Literature, Politics, Theory—Papers from the Essex Conference 1976–84*. London: Methuen.

Barker, Francis, et al., eds. 1985. *Europe and Its Others*. Proceedings of the Essex Conference on the Sociology of Literature. Colchester: University of Essex.

Barker, Francis, et al., eds. 1981. *1642: Literature and Power in the Seventeenth Century*. London: University of Essex.

Barker, Simon. 1986. "Images of the Sixteenth and Seventeenth Centuries as a History of the Present." In Barker et al., eds. (1986)

Barthes, Roland, 1972. *Mythologies*. Trans. Annette Lavers. New York: Hill and Wang.

Bateson, Gregory. 1972. *Steps to an Ecology of Mind: Collected Essays in An-*

thropology, Psychiatry, Evolution, and Epistomology. New York: Ballantine Books.

Batsleer, Janet, et al. 1985. *Rewriting English: Cultural Politics of Gender and Class.* London: Methuen.

Benhabib, Seyla, and Drucilla Cornell, eds. 1987. *Feminism as Critique: On the Politics of Gender.* Minneapolis: University of Minnesota Press.

Bersani, Leo. 1969. *A Future for Astyanax: Character and Desire in Literature.* Boston: Little, Brown and Co.

Bhabha, Homi K. 1986. "The Other Question: Difference, Discrimination and the Discourse of Colonialism." In Barker et al., eds. (1986).

Bloom, Allan. 1987. *The Closing of the American Mind.* New York: Simon and Schuster.

Bloom, Harold, ed. 1987a. *The Brontës.* New York: Chelsea House.

———. 1987b. "Introduction." In Bloom (1987a).

Boon, James A. 1982. *Other Tribes, Other Scribes: Symbolic Anthropology in the Comparative Study of Cultures, Histories, Religions, and Texts.* Cambridge: Cambridge University Press.

Bowersock, G. W. 1988. "Palestine: Ancient History and Modern Politics." In Hitchens and Said, eds. (1988).

Brantlinger, Patrick. 1985. "Victorians and Africans: The Genealogy of the Myth of the Dark Continent." *Critical Inquiry* 12 (no. 1): 166–203.

Braun, Gustav. 1865. "The Amputation of the Clitoris and Labia Minora: A Contribution to the Treatment of Vaginismus." Trans. Jeffrey Masson. In Masson (1986).

Briggs, Asa. 1973. "The Human Aggregate." In Dyos and Wolff, eds. (1973).

Brontë, Emily. 1847. *Wuthering Heights.* 1965. New York: Penguin Books.

Brown, Paul. 1985. " 'This thing of darkness I acknowledge mine': *The Tempest* and the Discourse of Colonialism." In Dollimore and Sinfield, eds. (1985).

Burrow, J. W. 1966. *Evolution and Society: A Study in Victorian Social Theory.* Cambridge: Cambridge University Press.

Bynum, William F., Jr. 1981. "Rationales for Therapy in British Psychiatry, 1780–1835." In Scull, ed. (1981a).

Caplan, Pat, ed. 1987. *The Cultural Construction of Sexuality.* London: Tavistock Publications.

Caulfield, Mina Davis. 1974. "Culture and Imperialism: Proposing a New Dialectic." In Hymes, ed. (1974a).

Chadwick, Edwin. 1842. *The Sanitary Condition of the Labouring Population of Great Britain.* 1965. Edinburgh: University Press.

Chitham, Edward. 1987. *A Life of Emily Brontë.* Oxford: Basil Blackwell.

Clifford, James. 1986. "Introduction: Partial Truths." In Clifford and Marcus, eds. (1986).

———. and George E. Marcus, eds. 1986. *Writing Culture: The Poetics and Politics of Ethnography.* Berkeley and Los Angeles: University of California Press.

Coetzee, John M. 1985. "Anthropology and the Hottentots." *Semiotica* 54 (nos. 1, 2): 87–95.

Comaroff, Jean. 1985. *Body of Power, Spirit of Resistance*. Chicago: University of Chicago Press.

Conway, Jill. 1972. "Stereotypes of Femininity in a Theory of Sexual Evolution." In Vicinus, ed. (1972).

Corrigan, Philip, and Derek Sayer. 1985. *The Great Arch: English State Formation as Cultural Revolution*. Oxford: Basil Blackwell.

Coward, Rosalind. 1983. *Patriarchal Precedents—Sexuality and Social Relations*. London: Routledge and Kegan Paul.

Cullen, Michael J. 1975. *The Statistical Movement in Early Victorian Britain—The Foundations of Empirical Research*. New York: Barnes and Noble.

Curtin, Philip D. 1964. *The Image of Africa: British Ideas and Action 1780–1850*. Madison: University of Wisconsin Press.

Dalla Costa, Mariarosa, and Selma James. 1972. *The Power of Women and the Subversion of the Community*. Bristol: Falling Wall Press.

Darwin, Charles. 1871. *The Descent of Man, and Natural Selection in Relation to Sex*. Vol. 2. New York: Appleton and Co.

Davidoff, Leonore, and Catherine Hall. 1987. *Family Fortunes: Men and Women of the English Middle Class 1780–1850*. Chicago: University of Chicago Press.

Davis, Lennard J. 1983. *Factual Fictions: The Origins of the English Novel*. New York: Columbia University Press.

de Certeau, Michel. 1986a. *The Practice of Everyday Life*. Berkeley and Los Angeles: University of California Press.

———. 1986b. *Hetereologies—Discourse on the Other*. Trans. Brian Massumi. Minneapolis: University of Minnesota Press.

de Lauretis, Teresa. 1985. "The Violence of Rhetoric: Considerations on Representation and Gender." *Semiotica* 54 (no. 1/2): 11–31.

Delamont, Sara, and Lorna Duffin, eds. 1976. *The Nineteenth-Century Woman—Her Cultural and Physical World*. London: Croom Helm.

Distant, W. L. 1874. "The Mental Differences Between the Sexes." *Journal of the Anthropological Institute* 4: 79–87.

Doerner, Klaus. 1981. *Madmen and the Bourgeoisie: A Social History of Insanity*. Trans. Joachim Neugroschel and Jean Steinberg. Oxford: Basil Blackwell.

Dollimore, Jonathan, and Alan Sinfield, eds. 1985. *Political Shakespeare: New Essays in Cultural Materialism*. Ithaca, N.Y.: Cornell University Press.

Donzelot, Jacques. 1979. *The Policing of Families*. Trans. Robert Hurley. New York: Pantheon Books.

Douglas, Mary. 1966. *Purity and Danger*. London: Routledge and Kegan Paul.

Du Bois, Page. 1988. *Sowing the Body: Psychoanalysis and Ancient Representations of Women*. Chicago: University of Chicago Press.

Duffin, Lorna. 1978. "Prisoners of Progress: Women and Evolution." In Delamont and Duffin, eds. (1976).

Dyos, H. J., and D. A. Reeder. 1973. "Slums and Suburbs." In Dyos and Wolff, eds. (1973).

———, and Michael Wolff, eds. 1973. *The Victorian City: Images and Realities*, vol. 1. London: Routledge and Kegan Paul.

Eden, Frederic Morton. 1797. *The State of the Poor.* 2 vols. 1965. New York: Augustus M. Kelley.

Ehrenreich, Barbara. 1989. "The Silenced Majority." *Zeta Magazine* 2 (no. 9): 22–23.

Eisenstein, Zillah, ed. 1979. *Capitalist Patriarchy and the Case for Socialist Feminism.* New York: Monthly Review Press.

Elesh, David. 1972. "The Manchester Statistical Society: A Case Study of Discontinuity in the History of Empirical Research." In Oberschall, ed. (1972a).

Ellenberger, Henri F. 1970. *The Discovery of the Unconscious.* New York: Basic Books.

Ellis, Havelock. 1898. *Studies in the Psychology of Sex.* Vol. 1. 1936. New York: Random House.

Engels, Frederick. 1845. *The Condition of the Working-Class in England in 1844.* 1952. London: George Allen and Unwin Ltd.

Fabian, Johannes. 1983. *Time and the Other: How Anthropology Makes Its Object.* New York: Columbia University Press.

Fee, Elizabeth. 1976. "The Sexual Politics of Victorian Social Anthropology." In Hartman and Banner, eds. (1976).

Figlio, Karl. 1978. "Chlorosis and Chronic Disease in Nineteenth-Century Britain: the Social Constitution of Somatic Illness in a Capitalist Society." *Social History* 3 (no. 2): 167–97.

Flechsig, Paul. 1884. "On the Gynecological Treatment of Hysteria." 1986. Trans. Jeffrey Masson. In Masson (1986).

Flower, W. H., and James Murie. 1867. "Account of the Dissection of a Bushwoman." *Journal of Anatomy and Physiology* 1: 189–208.

Foucault, Michel. 1980. *The History of Sexuality.* Vol. 1: *An Introduction.* Trans. Robert Hurley. New York: Random House.

———. 1979. *Discipline and Punish: The Birth of the Prison.* Trans. Alan Sheridan. New York: Vintage Books.

———. 1972. *The Archealogy of Knowledge.* Trans. Alan Sheridan. New York: Harper and Row.

———. 1967. *Madness and Civilization: A History of Insanity in the Age of Reason.* Trans. Richard Howard. New York: Random House.

Freud, Sigmund. 1930. *Civilization and Its Discontents.* 1961. New York: W. W. Norton.

Gallagher, Catherine. 1986. "The Body Versus the Social Body in the Works of Thomas Malthus and Henry Mayhew." *Representations* 14 (Spring): 83–106.

Gaskell, Peter. 1836. *Artisans and Machinery: The Moral and Physical Condition of the Manufacturing Population.* 1968. London: Frank Cass.

Gavin, Hector. 1851. *The Habitations of the Industrial Classes.* 1985. New York: Garland.

Geddes, Patrick, and J. Arthur Thomson. 1890. *The Evolution of Sex.* New York: Scribner and Welford.

Gilbert, Sandra M., and Susan Gubar. 1989. *No Man's Land: The Place of the Woman Writer in the Twentieth Century.* Vol. 2. New Haven, Conn.: Yale University Press.

———. 1988. *No Man's Land: The Place of the Woman Writer in the Twentieth Century*. Vol. 1. New Haven, Conn.: Yale University Press.

———. 1979. *The Madwoman in the Attic: The Woman Writer and the Nineteenth-Century Literary Imagination*. New Haven, Conn.: Yale University Press.

Gilman, Sander L. 1985a. "Black Bodies, White Bodies: Towards an Icongraphy of Female Sexuality in Late Nineteenth-Century Art, Medicine and Literature." *Critical Inquiry* 12: 204–42.

———. 1985b. *Difference and Pathology: Stereotypes of Sexuality, Race, and Madness*. Ithaca, N.Y.: Cornell University Press.

Goetz, William. 1982. "Genealogy and Incest in *Wuthering Heights*." *Studies in the Novel* 14: 359–76.

Goldman, Lawrence. 1987. "A Peculiarity of the English? The Social Science Association and the Absence of Sociology in Nineteenth Century Britain." *Past and Present* 114: 133–71.

Goonatilake, Susantha. 1984. *Aborted Discovery: Science and Creativity in the Third World*. London: Zed Books.

Gough, Kathleen. 1968. "Anthropology and Imperialism." *Monthly Review* 19: 12–27.

Gould, Stephen Jay. 1982. "The Hottentot Venus." *Natural History* 91: 20–27.

———. 1981. *The Mismeasure of Man*. New York: W. W. Norton.

Gouldner, Alvin W. 1979. *The Future of Intellectuals and the Rise of the New Class*. New York: Continuum.

Gramsci, Antonio. 1957. *The Modern Prince and Other Writings*. New York: International Publishers.

Greene, Gayle, and Coppelia Kahn, eds. 1985. *Making a Difference: Feminist Literary Criticism*. London: Methuen.

Gussow, Joan Dye. 1987. "The Fragmentation of Need: Women, Food and Marketing." *Heresies* 21: 39–43.

Hartman, Mary S., and Lois Banner, eds. 1976. *Clio's Consciousness Raised: New Perspectives on the History of Women*. New York: Octagon Books.

Hartmann, Heidi. 1981. "The Unhappy Marriage of Marxism and Feminism: Toward a More Progressive Union." In Sargent, ed. (1981).

Herbert, Christopher. 1988. "Rat Worship and Taboo in Mayhew's London." *Representations* 23: 1–24.

Himmelfarb, Gertrude. 1985. *The Idea of Poverty: England in the Early Industrial Age*. New York: Random House.

———. 1973. "The Culture of Poverty." In Dyos and Wolff, eds. (1973).

Hitchens, Christopher, and Edward Said, eds. 1988. *Blaming the Victims: Spurious Scholarship and the Palestinian Question*. London: Verso Books.

Hodgen, Margaret T. 1964. *Early Anthropology in the Sixteenth and Seventeenth Centuries*. Philadelphia: University of Pennsylvania Press.

Homans, Margaret. 1987. "Repression and Sublimation: Nature in *Wuthering Heights*." In Bloom, ed. (1987).

Hulme, Peter. 1981. "Hurricane in the Caribees: The Constitution of the Discourse of English Colonialism." In Barker et al., eds. (1981).

Hymes, Dell. ed. 1974a. *Reinventing Anthropology*. New York: Random House.

———. 1974b. "The Use of Anthropology." In Hymes, ed. (1974a).

Jackson, Margaret. 1987. " 'Facts of life' or the Eroticization of Women's Oppression? Sexology and the Social Construction of Heterosexuality." In Caplan, ed. (1987).

Jameson, Fredric. 1984. "Postmodernism, or the Cultural Logic of Late Capitalism." *New Left Review* 146: 53–92.

———. 1981. *The Political Unconscious: Narrative as a Socially Symbolic Act*. Ithaca, N.Y.: Cornell University Press.

———. 1979. *Fables of Aggression—Wyndham Lewis, the Modernist as Fascist*. Berkeley and Los Angeles: University of California Press.

Jeffreys, Sheila. 1985. *The Spinster and Her Enemies: Feminism and Sexuality 1880–1930*. Boston: Pandora.

Jones, Gareth Stedman. 1984. *Outcast London: A Study in the Relationship between Classes in Victorian Society*. 2d ed. New York: Pantheon Books.

JSSL. 1839. (*Journal of the Statistical Society of London*) Vol. 1. London: Charles Knight.

Kanner, S. Barbara. 1972. "The Women of England in a Century of Social Change, 1815–1914: A Select Bibliography." In Vicinus, ed. (1972).

Kaplan, Cora. 1986. *Sea Changes: Culture and Feminism*. London: Verso Books.

———. 1985. "Pandora's Box: Subjectivity, Class and Sexuality in Socialist Feminist Criticism." In Greene and Kahn, eds. (1985).

Kavanagh, James H. 1985. *Emily Brontë*. Oxford: Basil Blackwell.

Kay Shuttleworth, James. 1832. *The Moral and Physical Condition of the Working Classes Employed in the Cotton Manufacture in Manchester*. 1969. Manchester: E. J. Morton.

Keller, Evelyn Fox. 1985. *Reflections on Gender and Science*. New Haven, Conn.: Yale University Press.

Kent, Raymond A. 1981. *A History of British Sociology*. London: Gower Publishing Co.

Kern, Stephen. 1975. *Anatomy and Destiny: A Cultural History of the Human Body*. New York: Bobbs-Merrill Co.

Krafft-Ebing, Richard von. 1886. *Psychopathia Sexualis*. 1939. New York: Pioneer Publications.

Kuhn, Thomas S. 1962. *The Structure of Scientific Revolutions*. Chicago: University of Chicago Press.

LaClau, Ernesto, and Chantal Mouffe. 1985. *Hegemony and Socialist Strategy—Towards a Radical Democratic Politics*. Trans. Winston Moore and Paul Commack. London: Verso Books.

Lears, T. J. Jackson. 1985. "The Concept of Cultural Hegemony: Problems and Possibilities." *American Historical Review* 90 (no. 3): 567–93.

Lévi-Strauss, Claude. 1969. *The Elementary Structures of Kinship*. Trans. James Harle Bell et al. Boston: Beacon Press.

Levidow, Les, ed. 1986. *Radical Science Essays*. London: Free Association Books.

Lombroso, Caesar, and William Ferrero. 1889. *La Donna Deliquente.* 1923. Torino: Fratelli Bocca.

———. 1895. *The Female Offender.* London: T. Fisher Unwin.

Lowe, Donald. 1982. *History of Bourgeois Perception.* Chicago: University of Chicago Press.

Lubbock, John. 1870. *The Origin of Civilisation and the Primitive Condition of Man.* London: Longmans.

Lutz, Catherine. 1988. *Unnatural Emotions: Everyday Sentiments on a Micronesian Atoll and Their Challenge to Western Theory.* Chicago: University of Chicago Press.

Maine, Henry. 1861. *Ancient Law—Its Connection with the Early History of Society, and Its Relation to Modern Ideas.* London: John Murray.

Martin, Emily. 1987. *The Woman in the Body: A Cultural Analysis of Reproduction.* Boston: Beacon Press.

Marx, Karl. 1887. *Capital.* Vol. 1. Ed. Frederick Engels. 1967. New York: International Publishers.

———. 1845–46. *The German Ideology.* In *The Marx-Engels Reader.* Ed. Robert C. Tucker. 1978. New York: W. W. Norton and Co.

Masson, Jeffrey, ed. 1986. *Dark Science: Women, Sexuality and Psychiatry in the Nineteenth Century.* New York: Farrar, Straus and Giroux.

Mayhew, Henry. 1861. *London Labour and the London Poor.* Vol. 4. 1967. New York: Augustus Kelley.

McKeon, Michael. 1987. *The Origins of the English Novel 1600–1740.* Baltimore, Md.: Johns Hopkins University Press.

McLennan, John. 1865. *Primitive Marriage.* 1970. Ed. Peter Riviere. Chicago: University of Chicago Press.

Medick, Hans. 1976. "The Proto-Industrial Family Economy: The Structural Function of Household and Family during the Transition from Peasant Society to Industrial Capitalism." *Social History* 3 (October): 291–316.

Miller, J. Hillis. 1987. "*Wuthering Heights*: Repetition and the 'Uncanny'." In Bloom, ed. (1987a).

———. 1963. *The Disappearance of God.* Cambridge, Mass.: Harvard University Press.

Milton, John. 1667. *Paradise Lost and Paradise Regained.* 1968. Ed. Christopher Ricks. New York: Signet.

Miyoshi, Masao. 1988. "Against the Native Grain: The Japanese Novel and the 'Postmodern' West." *South Atlantic Quarterly* 3:525–50.

———. 1969. *The Divided Self: A Perspective on the Literature of the Victorians.* New York: New York University Press.

Modleski, Tania. 1982. *Loving with a Vengeance: Mass-Produced Fantasies for Women.* New York: Methuen.

Morgan, Lewis Henry. 1877. *Ancient Society.* 1964. Cambridge, Mass.: Harvard University Press.

Mort, Frank. 1988. *Dangerous Sexualities: Medico-Moral Politics in England Since 1830.* New York: Routledge, Kegan, Paul.

Newton, Judith. 1984. "Making and Remaking History: Another Look at 'Patriarchy'." *Tulsa Studies in Women's Literature* 3 (Spring/Fall): 125–41.

Nicholson, Linda. 1987. "Feminism and Marx: Integrating Kinship with the Economic." In Benhabib and Cornell, eds. (1987).

———. 1986. *Gender and History: The Limits of Social Theory in the Age of the Family.* New York: Columbia University Press.

Oberschall, Anthony, ed. 1972a. *The Establishment of Empirical Sociology: Studies in Continuity, Discontinuity, and Institutionalization.* New York: Harper and Row.

———. 1972b. "Introduction: The Sociological Study of the History of Social Research." In Oberschall, ed. (1972a).

Orgel, Stephen. 1985. "Caliban and Carthage, Dido and Virginia." Paper delivered at the "Drama, Theatre, and Society in Renaissance England" conference at the University of California, San Diego.

Patton, Cindy. 1985. *Sex and Germs: The Politics of AIDS.* Boston: South End Press.

Penniman, T. K. 1935. *A Hundred Years of Anthropology.* London: Duckworth.

Perkin, Harold. 1989. *The Rise of Professional Society: England since 1880.* London: Routledge.

———. 1981a. *The Structured Crowd: Essays in English Social History.* Sussex: Harvester Press.

———. 1981b. " 'The Condescension of Posterity': Middle-Class Intellectuals and the History of the Working Class." In Perkin (1981a).

———. 1969. *Origins of Modern English Society: 1780–1880.* Boston: Routledge and Kegan Paul.

Petchesky, Rosalind. 1979. "Dissolving the Hyphen: A Report on Marxist-Feminist Groups 1–5." In Eisenstein, ed. (1979).

Poovey, Mary. 1988. *Uneven Developments: The Ideological Work of Gender in Mid-Victorian England.* Chicago: University of Chicago Press.

———. 1984. *The Proper Lady and the Woman Writer: Ideology as Style in the Works of Mary Wollstoncraft, Mary Shelley, and Jane Austen.* Chicago: University of Chicago Press.

Rabinow, Paul. 1986. "Representations Are Social Facts: Modernity and Post-Modernity in Anthropology." In Clifford and Marcus, eds. (1986).

Radway, Janice. 1984. *Reading the Romance: Women, Patriarchy, and Popular Literature.* Chapel Hill: University of North Carolina Press.

Rainger, Ronald. 1978. "Race, Politics, and Science: The Anthropological Society of London in the 1860's." *Victorian Studies* 22 (no. 1): 51–70.

Reed, Adolph, Jr. 1988. "The Liberal Technocrat." *Nation* 246 (no. 5) 167–70.

Robinson, Paul. 1976. *The Modernization of Sex.* New York: Harper and Row.

Rose, Sonya O. 1986. " 'Gender at Work': Sex, Class and Industrial Capitalism." *History Workshop* 20 (Spring): 113–31.

Rowbotham, Sheila, and Jeffrey Weeks, eds. 1977. *Socialism and the New Life.* London: Pluto Press.

Rueschemeyer, Dietrich. 1986. *Power and the Division of Labour.* Palo Alto, Calif.: Stanford University Press.

Said, Edward. 1985. "Orientalism Reconsidered." *Cultural Critique* 1 (Fall): 89–107.

———. 1983. *The World, the Text, and the Critic.* Cambridge, Mass.: Harvard University Press.

———. 1979. *Orientalism.* New York: Random House.

Sargent, Lydia. ed. 1981. *Women and Revolution: A Discussion of the Unhappy Marriage of Marxism and Feminism.* Boston: South End Press.

Schulte-Sasse, Jochen. 1988. "Can the Disempowered Read Mass-Produced Narratives in their Own Voice?" *Cultural Critique* 10: 171–99.

Scott, Joan Wallach. 1988a. *Gender and the Politics of History.* New York: Columbia University Press.

———. 1988b. "Women in the Making of the English Working Class." In Scott (1988a).

———. 1985. "Gender: A Useful Category of Historical Analysis." *American Historical Review* 91: 1053–75.

Scull, Andrew. ed. 1981a. *Madhouses, Mad-doctors and Madmen: The Social History of Psychiatry in the Victorian Era.* Philadelphia: University of Pennsylvania Press.

———. 1981b. "Moral Treatment Reconsidered: Some Sociological Comments on an Episode in the History of British Psychiatry." In Scull, ed. (1981a).

———. 1979. *Museums of Madness: The Social Organization of Insanity in Nineteenth-Century England.* London: Penguin Books.

Showalter, Elaine. 1985. *The Female Malady: Women, Madness, and English Culture, 1830–1980.* New York: Penguin Books.

———. 1981. "Victorian Women and Insanity." In Scull, ed. (1981a).

———. 1977. *A Literature of Their Own: British Women Novelists from Brontë to Lessing.* Princeton, N.J.: Princeton University Press.

Smail, John. 1987. "New Languages for Labour and Capital: The Transformation of Discourse in the Early Years of the Industrial Revolution." *Social History* 12 (no. 1): 49–72.

Spencer, Herbert. 1898. *Principles of Sociology.* Vol. 1, 1876–96. New York: D. Appleton.

Stalleybrass, Peter, and Allon White. 1986. *The Politics and Poetics of Transgression.* London: Methuen.

Stauder, Jack. 1986. "The 'Relevance' of Anthropology to Colonialism and Imperialism." In Levidow, ed. (1986).

Steedman, Caroline. 1985. " 'The Mother Made Conscious': The Historical Development of a Primary School Pedagogy." *History Workshop* 20 (Autumn): 149–63.

Steichen, Edward, and Carl Sandburg. 1955. *The Family of Man.* New York: The Museum of Modern Art.

Stocking, George W., Jr. 1987. *Victorian Anthropology.* New York: Macmillan.

———. 1968. *Race, Culture and Evolution: Essays in the History of Anthropology.* New York: Macmillan.

Stone, Lawrence. 1979. *The Family, Sex and Marriage in England 1500–1800.* Abridged edition. New York: Random House.

———. 1965. *The Crisis of the Aristocracy 1558–1641*. Oxford: Oxford University Press.

Street, Brian. 1975. *The Savage in Literature—Representations of 'Primitive' Society in English Fiction 1858–1920*. London: Routledge and Kegan Paul.

Taylor, W. Cooke. 1841. *Notes of a Tour in the Manufacturing Districts of Lancashire*. 1968. London: Frank Cass and Co.

Tennenhouse, Leonard. 1986. *Power on Display: The Politics of Shakespeare's Genres*. London: Methuen.

Thompson, E. P. 1978. "Eighteenth-century English Society: Class Struggle without Class?" *Social History* 3 (no. 2): 133–65.

———. 1971. "The Moral Economy of the English Crowd in the Eighteenth Century." *Past and Present* 50: 76–131.

———. 1967. "Time, Work-Discipline, and Industrial Capitalism." *Past and Present* 38: 56–97.

———. 1966. *The Making of the English Working Class*. New York: Vintage Books.

Trumbach, Randolph. 1978. *The Rise of the Egalitarian Family*. New York: Academic Press.

Tuke, Samuel. 1813. *Description of The Retreat*. 1964. London: Dawsons.

Turner, William. 1878. "Notes on the Dissection of a Negro." *Journal of Anatomy and Physiology* 13: 382–86.

Tylor, Edward Burnett. 1896a. *Anthropology*. New York: D. Appleton.

———. 1896b. "The Matriarchal Family System." *Nineteenth Century*. (July): 29–47.

———. 1874. *Primitive Culture—Researches into the Development of Mythology, Philosophy, Religion, Language, Art and Custom*. Vols. 1 and 2. Boston: Estes and Lauriat.

Vicinus, Martha, ed. 1972. *Suffer and Be Still: Women in the Victorian Age*. Bloomington: University of Indiana Press.

Vogler, Thomas, ed. 1968. *Twentieth-Century Interpretations of "Wuthering Heights"*. Englewood Cliffs, N.J.: Prentice Hall.

Walkowitz, Judith R. 1988. "Science and the Seance: Transgressions of Gender and Genre in Late Victorian England." *Representations* 22: 3–29.

———. 1986. "Science, Feminism and Romance: The Men and Women's Club 1885–1889." *History Workshop* 21: 37–59.

———. 1980. *Prostitution and Victorian Society: Women, Class and the State*. Cambridge: Cambridge University Press.

Weeks, Jeffrey. 1981. *Sex, Politics and Society: The Regulation of Sexuality Since 1800*. London: Longmans.

———. 1977. "Havelock Ellis and the Politics of Sex Reform." In Rowbotham and Weeks, eds. (1977).

White, Allon. 1985. "Hysteria and the End of Carnival: Festivity and Bourgeois Neurosis." *Semiotica* 54: 97–111.

Wilden, Anthony. 1972. *System and Structure: Essays in Communication and Exchange*. London: Tavistock.

Williams, Raymond. 1976. *Keywords*. New York: Oxford University Press.

———. 1961. *The Long Revolution*. London: Chatto and Windus.

Willis, William S., Jr. 1974. "Skeletons in the Anthropological Closet." In Hymes, ed. (1974a).

Wohl, Anthony S. 1973. "Unfit for Human Habitation." In Dyos and Wolff, eds. (1973).

Woolf, Virginia. 1925. "Jane Eyre and *Wuthering Heights*." In Vogler, ed. (1968).

Yeo, Eileen, and Stephen Yeo, eds. 1981a. *Popular Culture and Class Conflict 1590–1914 : Explorations in the History of Labor and Leisure*. New York: Humanities Press.

———. 1981b. "Ways of Seeing: Control and Leisure Versus Class and Struggle." In Yeo and Yeo, eds. (1981a).

Yeo, Eileen, and E. P. Thompson. 1971. *The Unknown Mayhew*. New York: Pantheon.

Zaretsky, Eli. 1976. *Capitalism, The Family and Personal Life*. New York: Harper and Row.

Zwerdling, Alex. 1986. *Virginia Woolf and the Real World*. Berkeley and Los Angeles: University of California Press.

INDEX